Western Esotericism
and Rituals of Initiation

SUNY series in Western Esoteric Traditions
David Appelbaum, editor

Western Esotericism
and Rituals of Initiation

Henrik Bogdan

STATE UNIVERSITY OF NEW YORK PRESS

Published by $4|06$ MH
State University of New York Press, Albany

© 2007 State University of New York

For information, address State University of New York Press,
194 Washington Avenue, Suite 305, Albany, NY 12210-2384

Production by Diane Ganeles
Marketing by Fran Keneston

Library of Congress Cataloging-in-Publication Data

Bogdan, Henrik.
   Western esotericism and rituals of initiation / Henrik Bogdan.
       p. cm. — (SUNY series in Western esoteric traditions)
   Includes bibliographical references and index.
   ISBN-13: 978-0-7914-7069-5 (hardcover : alk. paper)
   1. Occultism.   2. Initiation rites.   3. Freemasonry.   I. Title.

BF1411.B64 2007
130—dc22   2006020829

10 9 8 7 6 5 4 3 2 1

To Maria

Contents

Tables

Acknowledgments

It has become apparent to me, more than once, that the process of writing a book resembles a ritual of initiation. The years of writing this book have been characterized by a state of constant liminality, and sometimes it has even felt as if I were undergoing some kind of mystical ordeal. The officiating officers of this great initiation, however, were not any mysterious adepts but friends and colleagues. I feel privileged to express my gratitude to a number of persons who have helped me, in different ways, in completing this book.

My greatest debt and deepest thanks are owed to J. A. M. Snoek (University of Heidelberg) without whose encouraging help this work would have suffered severely. I am deeply grateful to Wouter J. Hanegraaff (University of Amsterdam) for sharing his unpublished articles and for making it possible for me to spend a semester at the department of the history of hermetic philosophy and related currents, University of Amsterdam.

I also wish to acknowledge with thanks Mikael Rothstein (University of Copenhagen) who read a draft version of the book and offered his criticism at a seminar arranged for the occasion by the department of religious studies, Göteborg University. I owe an immense debt to my friend and colleague Martin P. Starr for offering comments and providing information, as well as sharing his draft version of *The Unknown God: W. T. Smith and the Thelemites* (published in 2003).

Thanks are also due to Antoine Faivre (Sorbonne University) who kindly allowed me to visit him and discuss my book. Likewise, I wish to express my gratitude to R. A. Gilbert for a most memorable one-day visit in Bristol where I had the opportunity to discuss my work.

To my colleagues from Göteborg University thanks are especially due to my dear friend Jonathan Peste who not only offered valuable criticism to my text, but also showed an unfailing support throughout these years; I should also like to record my appreciation to the members of the Higher Seminar at the department of religious studies.

More often than not, the most rewarding insights are not made while sitting at the desk hard at work, but in the conversion with fellow scholars. I have had the opportunity to discuss matters pertaining to Western esotericism with a number of persons, and I would like to mention with gratitude my two colleagues from the time in Amsterdam Olav Hammer and Jean-Pierre Brach. Many thanks are due to Mathew Scanlan who shared information on masonic terminology and the early history of Freemasonry. Mention of gratitude should also be made to Kenneth Grant for kindly answering my letters concerning Aleister Crowley and Gerald Gardner.

In addition, I wish to express my gratitude to the Swedish Foundation for International Cooperation in Research and Higher Education (STINT) for awarding me a grant that enabled me to spend six months at the department of the history of hermetic and related currents, University of Amsterdam; to Frimureriska Forskningsgruppen i Göteborg where I presented a short part of my thesis at an initial stage: and to the ARIES Netherlands, where I presented a part of my work at a lecture. I also offer my sincere thanks to S. Brent Morris, editor of *Heredom*, Transactions of the Scottish Rite Research Society, for kindly supplying me with articles that were of use to me.

The staffs of many libraries have been generous and helpful, and I would in particular like to mention those of Göteborgs Universitetsbibliotek; the British Library; the Warburg Institute, University of London; the Library of the United Grand Lodge of England; the Library of the University of Amsterdam; the Bibliotheca Philosophica Hermetica, Amsterdam; and the Archives and Library of the Grand East of the Netherlands, the Hague.

Last but not least, thanks are due to my parents, George and Kerstin Bogdan, to my brother Frederic, and to my fiancée and companion through life, Maria Lindberg. This work is dedicated to her.

Introduction

Historians of religions and anthropologists have written extensively on the subject of rituals of initiation. The primary object of their research, however, has been focused on non-Western rituals to such an extent that, with a few notable exceptions, there hardly are any scholarly works dealing in depth with Western rituals of initiation. There are a number of reasons for this situation, but chief among them is the connection of Western initiatory societies with Western esotericism—and the latter only recently received a long overdue scholarly attention. As will presently be discussed, scholars such as Antoine Faivre and Wouter J. Hanegraaff have demonstrated how Western esotericism has developed from a subject deemed unworthy of scholarly interest, to a fruitful and challenging field of research that has received wide academic recognition.

The purpose of this study is twofold; first, on a more general level, I wish to present the development of the phenomenon of, what I call, "masonic rituals of initiation" from an historical perspective. By masonic rituals of initiation I do not merely mean rituals of initiation of Freemasonry, but also rituals deriving from Freemasonry, which have certain structural components in common with the former. Second, I will analyze the relationship between masonic rituals of initiation and Western esotericism, and thus analyze how esotericism is transmitted through, what I call, "Western esoteric rituals of initiation." In this connection I will address two basic questions: How is Western esotericism transmitted through the Western esoteric rituals of initiation? And: What "types" of esotericism are transmitted? The study thus consequently covers two fields of research, rituals of initiation and Western esotericism.

My methodological approach is historical and contextual, which in practice means that the rituals that are analyzed are placed in their historical context. Furthermore, I have restricted myself to written ritual texts only in my analysis. In other words, I make no claims to have availed myself of any in-depth or quantitative interviews, nor any participant observations. Valuable as such methods undeniably are, I have chosen to limit myself in this capacity. However, over the years of writing this book, I have had ample opportunities to meet and discuss the practical aspects of rituals of initiation with modern practitioners of Western esoteric rituals of initiation, and to a lesser extent personally experienced various forms of rituals of initiation, both as an initiate and in the capacity of an officiating officer. These contacts and experiences have been important for my understanding of the texts I have chosen to analyze, but I have deliberately chosen not to include these aspects in this study. My methodological approach to Western esotericism can be described, in the words of Hanegraaff, as a generalist in the study of Western esotericism; that is, my approach to the subject is from a broader perspective, concretized by basic research paradigms. The latter consist of the paradigms proposed by Faivre and Hanegraaff, which for the sake of simplicity can be called esotericism as "a form of thought" (Faivre) and esotericism as *gnosis* (Hanegraaff). The ritual texts that are analyzed have been chosen because they are representative of different historical periods, and thus reflect major trends in the development of Western esoteric rituals of initiation. I have limited myself strictly to published ritual texts in the analysis, and as far as possible tried to avail myself of more than one published version in order to discuss variant readings. In certain cases I have used manuscript versions of the rituals in order to check the accuracy of the printed versions.

It should be stressed that, from a methodological perspective, this thesis is not concerned with what masonic rites of initiation might "do" with the initiate, nor what the implications of this type of rite might be. This work is concerned with the relationship of Western esotericism and masonic ritual texts.

Chapters 1 and 2 are devoted to the previous research of Western esotericism and rituals of initiation. Chapter 3 is an outlined historical background of Western esotericism offered as an introduction to readers unfamiliar with the history of Western esotericism. It stretches from the Renaissance to the publication of the so-called Rosicrucian manifestos at the beginning of the seventeenth century. Although there probably never existed a secret Rosicrucian fraternity at this period, the idea of secret or closed societies that were considered to be guardians of an esoteric doctrine, was firmly imbedded in Western culture as a result of the publication of, and the subsequent debate on, these manifestos. Chapter 4 is devoted to an analysis of the Craft rituals of Freemasonry— the blueprints, as it were, of all later masonic rituals of initiation. It covers the period from 1697 to 1730, during which the masonic system of initiation developed from a system of two degrees to a three-degree system. Chapter 5 deals with so-called high or additional degrees of

Freemasonry, exemplified through an analysis of the ritual of True Mason, or Académie des Vrais Maçons, of the *Rite Ecossais philosophique.* In chapter 6 the most influential of all nineteenth-century occultist initiatory societies, *The Hermetic Order of the Golden Dawn,* is discussed, and its Neophyte ritual is analyzed. Finally, chapter 8 is devoted to the first Western esoteric initiatory New Religious Movement in the true sense of the word, Gerald Gardner's witchcraft movement of the 1950s.

Chapter 1

Western Esotericism

Introduction

The academic study of Western esotericism has in recent years developed into an important field of research. Scholars such as Antoine Faivre and Wouter J. Hanegraaff have contributed in placing Western esotericism firmly on the agenda of modern scholarship.[1] The impact and recognition of this new field of research is shown by conferences and organizations being formed on the subject;[2] academic journals and book series with a focus on esotericism are established;[3] and academic chairs devoted to esotericism have been created.[4]

The area covered by the term Western esotericism is vast, and it includes such apparently diverse phenomena as Renaissance hermeticism, nineteenth- and twentieth-century occultism, and New Age *inter alia*. Somewhat crudely, esotericism can be described as a Western form of spirituality that stresses the importance of the individual effort to gain spiritual knowledge, or *gnosis*, whereby man is confronted with the divine aspect of existence. Furthermore, there usually is a strong holistic trait in esotericism where the godhead is considered manifest in the natural world—a world interconnected by so-called correspondences. Man is seen as a microcosm of the macrocosm, the divine universe. Through increased knowledge of the individual self, it is often regarded as possible to achieve corresponding knowledge about nature, and thereby about God. However, the interpretation of what gnosis "actually is," or what the correspondences "actually are," differs considerably in the history of Western esotericism.

These ideas can be found already in antiquity, especially in gnosticism and hermetism, but it was not until the Renaissance that Western

5

esotericism, as understood by the majority of scholars today, emerged. At this particular point in history, there occurred a period of intensified syncretism in which a number of diverse traditions intermingled: traditions such as Neoplatonism, mysticism, Jewish Kabbalah, medieval ritual magic, and hermetism/hermeticism were seen as compatible, and a "new" form of thought gradually appeared—Western esotericism.

From the Renaissance onward esotericism can be seen as an underlying form of thought that can be traced in a number of currents or traditions. In the present work it will be analyzed how this form of thought entered the world of initiatory societies, and more specifically how esotericism was transmitted through masonic rituals of initiation. It should, however, be emphasized at the outset that Western esotericism, in the present context, is not to be understood as a tradition in itself, but rather as a scholarly construct. This construct is aimed at providing an understanding of diverse currents, which, although they have certain aspects in common, more often than not differ significantly in form and content. It should furthermore be stressed that Western esotericism is not to be interpreted as dealing with a separate phenomenon as such, but as a number of phenomena that have been more or less integrated with various trends of Western culture. It is thus a highly complex field of research that constitutes the academic discipline of Western esotericism.

The Delimitation of a Field of Research

Western esotericism, as an academic discipline, is of a relatively recent date. Prior to the appearance of the works of Frances Yates in the 1960s the study of Western esotericism had been confined to works dealing with only specific aspects of esotericism, often without any attempt at placing these aspects in a larger context.[5] In fact, the academic community at large often viewed areas of research connected to Western esotericism with suspicion, or even contempt. There are a number of reasons for this negative attitude toward study of Western esotericism. Hanegraaff stresses the fact that esotericism "emerged as a syncretistic type of religiosity in a Christian context, and its representatives were Christians until far into the eighteenth century,"[6] and this is probably one of the reasons why the study of Western esotericism was reserved to theologians. By tradition, historians of religion have to a large extent left the research into Christian currents to theologians, and they, in their turn, have often viewed esoteric currents as heresies.

Another reason for the negative attitude can be traced in the particular form of knowledge at which esotericists have aimed. Western culture is sometimes, somewhat simplistically, viewed as resting on two pillars: Greek rationality and Christian faith. The knowledge strived for by the esotericists is, however, "characterised by a resistance to the dominance of either pure rationality or doctrinal faith."[7] According to van den Broek and Hanegraaff, the knowledge of the esotericists is of a revelatory and experiential nature:

> The adherents of this tradition emphasized the importance of inner enlightenment or gnosis: a revelatory experience that mostly entailed an encounter with one's true self as well with the ground of being, God.[8]

Western esotericism can thus be viewed as a third pillar of Western culture, a form of thought that took a middle position between doctrinal faith and rationality. To the adherents of doctrinal faith, however, this type of knowledge or gnosis smacked of heresy, while the promoters of rationality accused it of irrationality and metaphysical reasoning. It should, however, be stressed that these three forms of knowledge were not watertight compartments, but on the contrary highly complex and inter-connected currents. For instance, esotericism played a significant part in the development of modern science, with many scientists being esotericists at the same time.[9] In other words, different strategies of attaining knowledge did not necessarily exclude one another. This would later change and lead to a forceful denunciation of, and distancing from, esotericism by the promoters of modern natural sciences.

The study of Western esotericism can be approached from a number of perspectives, and Hanegraaff has distinguished authors on esotericism into five groups:

(1) perennialists or traditionalists
(2) religionists
(3) historians of science and philosophy
(4) specialists on specific currents
(5) generalists in the study of Western esotericism[10]

The first group, perennialists or traditionalists, sees the established world religions as outer manifestations of an inner, common, "esoteric" tradition based on specific metaphysical doctrines. According to Hanegraaff, this group parallels dogmatic theology and can thus be seen as an explicit religious pursuit, rather than an academic approach to the study of Western esotericism.[11] Furthermore, traditionalists are essentially anti-modern and reject the values of modern society. Nevertheless, the academic merits of scholars influenced by perennialism, such as Mircea

Eliade, should not be underestimated. Their approach to the study of religions in general is comparative, and this is reflected in their understanding of esotericism, which is seen as a universal phenomenon.

The religionists, on the other hand, are more implicit in their dogmatic approach to the study of esotericism.[12] This approach is typified by the cultic milieu of *Eranos* meetings from 1933 onward.[13] Many of the scholars associated with the *Eranos*, such as Mircea Eliade (1907–1986) and Joseph Campbell (1904–1987), were driven by the conviction that modern man needs religious symbols and myths, and the nondenominational spirituality that evolved in connection with the *Eranos* meetings was well adapted to the beliefs and principles of the counterculture of the 1960s. Ideas originating from the *Eranos* group were well received in the New Age movement and in popular culture. For instance, the enormously successful Star Wars movies were to a large extent influenced by the writings of Joseph Campbell.[14]

The third group, historians of science and philosophy, generally maintained a negative attitude toward esotericism up until the appearance of the works of Frances Yates. Esoteric beliefs and practices were often considered to embody unreason and unscientific reasoning, and were thus held to be in opposition to the positivistic ideals of natural science. Yates, on the contrary, argued that the hermetic tradition (understood as esotericism) was not only congenial to modern science, but the causal factor in the emergence of modern science. This drastic reinterpretation of the emergence of modern science has been criticized, but Yates' theories have nonetheless been instrumental in changing the attitude of historians of science and philosophy toward esotericism. Today, the categorical stance against everything connected to esotericism is not as prevalent as it used to be among this category of scholars. Instead, esotericism is often seen as an important factor in the understanding of early modern science.

The specialists of particular currents and personalities of esotericism form a large category of scholars. The prime characteristic of this type of scholar, from a methodological point of view, is that the subject of their research is not placed in a larger context, but rather studied as an independent phenomenon.

Finally, the generalists in the study of Western esotericism approach the subject of their research from a broader perspective, concretized by a basic research paradigm. In the following discussion of research paradigms formulated specifically for the study of Western esotericism in a general sense, I will limit myself to the ones proposed by Yates, Faivre, and Hanegraaff.

The Research Paradigms of Western Esotericism

Before discussing the research paradigms of Yates, Faivre, and Hanegraaff, mention should be made of an often-overlooked early generalist approach to the study of Western esotericism. The amateur scholar Arthur Edward Waite (1857–1942) wrote extensively on various aspects of Western esotericism, such as alchemy, Rosicrucianism, ceremonial magic, occultism, and Freemasonry, and actually saw these different aspects as part of a larger whole, which he termed *The Secret Tradition*. While lacking a research paradigm, and not offering a clear definition of *The Secret Tradition*, it is clear that to Waite the prime object of this tradition is a mystical union with Christ. Waite's "scholarly" approach to Western esotericism was, to a certain extent, a mixture of a traditionalist, religionist, and generalist approach. Notwithstanding the fact that Waite's research to a large extent today is outdated, he was often cited as an authority on Western esotericism by scholars, such as Yates, working in this field.[15]

Dame Frances Yates (1899–1981), historian and art historian of the Renaissance, was the first scholar to study Renaissance esotericism and Rosicrucianism as a coherent cultural phenomenon. By the early 1940s Yates was employed by the Warburg Institute, today part of the University of London, where she concentrated her research on the artistic and literary efforts of the French academies of the sixteenth century. At the end of the 1940s she began to concentrate her research on the hermeticism of the Renaissance. Her research resulted in *Giordano Bruno and the Hermetic Tradition* (1964), and it was further expanded into *The Art of Memory* (1967), *The Rosicrucian Enlightenment* (1972), and *The Occult Philosophy in the Elizabethan Age* (1979). Yates challenged the established history of the Renaissance and showed the importance of, what she called, "the Hermetic Tradition" to influential Renaissance thinkers such as Marsilio Ficino, Pico della Mirandola, and Giordano Bruno. She argued that the Hermetic Tradition is crucial to the understanding of the Renaissance and the development of modern science. Yates set out to rediscover what she perceived to be an ignored part of our cultural heritage, and thereby to rewrite history. The main thesis of Yates research has been summarized by Hanegraaff as the "Yates Paradigm":

This "Yates Paradigm," which has remained dominant through the 1970s and only gradually began to wane during the 1980s, has two main characteristics. First, "the Hermetic Tradition" (and by implication, Western esotericism generally) is presented as a quasi-autonomous counter-tradition pitted against the mainstream traditions of Christianity and rationality. Second, the presentation of this Hermetic Tradition is inextricably linked to modernist narratives of progress by means of science. Yates' grand narrative was based upon an exciting paradox: she claimed that the "great forward movement" of the scientific revolution, from which the modern world has emerged, was crucially indebted not to rational traditions but—of all things—to the hermetic magic epitomized by figures such as Giordano Bruno. In other words: precisely this forgotten hermetic counterculture of the West, long decried as merely superstitious and reactionary, has supposedly been the true motor of progress.[16]

The two main components of the "Yates Paradigm" have today been refuted.[17] The very notion of a Hermetic Tradition, in the sense of an autonomous and demarcated single tradition, has been abandoned by modern scholars in favor of a number of traditions, loosely connected. Yates' arguments for a single tradition were simplistic and did not take into account the highly complex nature of cultural phenomena. Further, the idea that the Hermetic Tradition was the impetus of the emergence of modern science has been discarded, and it is today assumed that Western esotericism was merely one among a number of factors that contributed to the emergence of modern science—not the only one.

In 1992 Antoine Faivre proposed a definition of Western esotericism as a "form of thought," which consists of four intrinsic and two secondary constituting components.[18] Faivre's definition has had a large impact on the academic community, and it has become the standard definition in works dealing with Western esotericism. According to Faivre, the historical scope of Western esotericism covers the period from the Renaissance at the end of the fifteenth century to modern movements of today. Geographically, the field is restricted to the Western cultural hemisphere, and there are thus no claims to study a so-called "universal esotericism."[19] The four constituting components are: (1) *The idea of correspondence*; (2) *Living nature*; (3) *Imagination and mediations*; (4) *The experience of transmutation*; and the secondary (5) *The practice of the concordance*; (6) *Transmission*.[20] This form of thought, expressed in different ways, can be found in a number of traditions from the Renaissance and onward: hermeticism, Christian Kabbalah, Rosicrucianism, spiritual alchemy, astrology, magic, theosophy, occultism, etc. Different as all these traditions most certainly are, they share Western esotericism as their common basic form of thought around which their individual traits and characteristics are centered. It is this common aspect that gives them a shared *air de famille*.[21]

(1) *Correspondences.* There are symbolic and concrete correspondences between all the visible and invisible parts of the universe. Man corresponds as a microcosm to the universe (macrocosm). The idea of correspondences is vital to the three "royal arts" of Western esotericism; that is, magic, alchemy, and astrology. There are primarily two kinds of correspondences. First, "those that exist in nature, seen and unseen."[22] For instance, the seven planets correspond to the seven metals, and the seven metals correspond to specific parts of the human body. The human *spiritus* corresponds to the *spiritus mundi,* and so on. Second, "correspondences between Nature (the cosmos) or even history and revealed texts."[23] Scriptures, such as the Bible, are considered to be in harmony with nature, and through careful study of one, greater knowledge is reached about the other. This type of correspondence is particularly important to the Kabbalah.

(2) *Living Nature.* The entire universe is "complex, plural, hierarchical." It is alive and traversed by a network of sympathies or antipathies that link the things of nature. The knowledge of this network (usually described as mystical links) enables the magician to manipulate it, and thereby causes results in the natural world according to his will. The manipulation of this network of mystical links, is in fact the core of Renaissance magic, or *magia.*

(3) *Imagination and Mediations.* The esotericist regards the imaginative faculty of man to be of great importance. That which is being revealed to his "inner eyes," or creative imagination, is the material (i.e., invisible part of the Universe) that interests him. Connected to the imagination or *vis imaginativa* is the use of rituals, symbolic images, mandalas, and intermediary spirits. As Couliano has pointed out, magic works primarily through the imagination.[24]

(4) *Experience of Transmutation.* Transmutation is a term borrowed from alchemy, which signifies the passage from one plane to another, the modification of a subject in its very nature. Just as the alchemists aimed at turning lead into gold through a process that included the stages of *nigredo, albedo,* and *rubedo* (sometimes even *citrinitas*), this process could be viewed as a spiritual one. For the present study, the experience of transmutation is of great importance, since the idea of initiation is partly connected to it. The initiate is often viewed as going through a process of transmutation as he passes through the various rites of initiation.

(5) *The Praxis of the Concordance.* From the end of the fifteenth century and during the sixteenth century an idea of acquiring "a gnosis embracing diverse traditions and melding them in a single crucible" existed. This is exactly how Western esotericism got its form during the Renaissance. By taking ideas from Neoplatonism, pythagorism,

hermeticism, Christian Mysticism, and kabbalah the esoteric form of thought was formed. Faivre describes the practice of the concordance as "a consistent tendency to try to establish common denominators between two different traditions or even more, among all traditions, in the hope of obtaining an illumination, a gnosis, of superior quality."[25] Connected to this is the popular idea of the *philosophia perennis,* which claimed that a tradition of mystical knowledge had been handed down from Hermes Trismegistus through Moses, Zarathustra, Plato, and many others.

(6) *Transmission.* The esoteric knowledge must be transmitted from master to disciple according to set rules. The knowledge that is transmitted cannot be questioned, and it is seen as part of a tradition that must be respected and regarded as an "organic and integral ensemble." The importance of this idea for initiation is clear: there must be someone who initiates the disciple—he cannot initiate himself. This last criterion is of vital importance for the masonic initiatory societies.

According to Hanegraaff, Faivre's definition of Western esotericism is problematic as foundation for a disciplinary paradigm. While Hanegraaff does not deny the "heuristic value" of Faivre's paradigm, "as based upon a scholarly construct," he questions the validity of the definition for post-sixteenth and particularly post-eighteenth-century esoteric currents. Hanegraaff argues that Faivre's definition is based on the esotericism of the Renaissance, and that it does not take into account that esotericism changes through history.

> The problem becomes all the more pressing if one applies the definition to post-eighteenth century "occultist" currents. Precisely Faivre's first—and arguably central—intrinsic characteristic, the worldview of correspondences, was severely compromised, to say the least, under the impact of a "mechanical" and positivist worldview based on instrumental causality. Obviously this is not to deny that doctrines of "correspondences" may be encountered in various nineteenth- and twentieth-century forms of esotericism. The point is that the disenchantment of the world may cause the meaning of "correspondences" to get thoroughly reinterpreted; one might even go as far as suggesting that at least some nineteenth- and twentieth-century "esoteric" currents reflect a (neo)positivist "form of thought" adorned with some of the trappings of pre-Enlightenment esotericism, rather than the reverse. In sum, it seems that Faivre's paradigm runs the risk of ignoring or minimizing the creative innovations and transformations of Western esotericism under the impact of secularization, in favour of a "grand continuity" on phenomenological foundations.[26]

Hanegraaff's criticism implies that Faivre's definition of esotericism as a "form of thought" is static, and that esotericism instead should be studied as something complex and changeable. It should, however, be noted that Hanegraaff does not seem to contest Faivre's constituting components as such, but instead focuses on the interpretation of their meaning. According to Hanegraaff, the meaning of the basic components of esotericism changes due to "disenchantment of the world" and the secularization of esotericism.

In order to understand the finer points of Hanegraaff's criticism it is necessary to be familiar with his idea of how occultist forms of esotericism of the nineteenth and twentieth century differ from traditional, or Renaissance, esotericism. First, the understanding of what the "correspondences" actually consist of changed dramatically due to the impact of scientific materialism and nineteenth-century positivism. The mechanical and "disenchanted" worldviews stood in sharp contrast to the enchanted worldview of the Renaissance, in which the divine power permeated the micro- and macrocosmic worlds through the noncausal correspondences.

> Accordingly, occultism is characterized by hybrid mixtures of traditional esoteric and modern scientistic-materialist worldviews: while originally the religious belief in a universe brought forth by a personal God was axiomatic for esotericism, eventually this belief succumbed partly or completely to popular scientific visions of a universe answering to impersonal laws of causality.[27]

Second, Hanegraaff stresses the fact that Western esotericism emerged as a "syncretistic type of religiosity in a Christian context, and its representatives were Christian until far into the eighteenth century." The dominance of traditional Christianity on esotericism decreased in favor of an influx of eastern religiosity, particularly Hinduism and Buddhism. According to the first nonintrinsic component of Faivre's definition of esotericism, the *Praxis of the Concordance,* the esotericists often saw the various established religions as different branches of one and the same tree. This view is especially apparent in nineteenth- and twentieth-century occultist movements. The eastern religiosity that came to influence Western esotericism was, however, a Westernized form, as it was in particular through theosophical literature that the general public encountered it. The interest of the theosophical leaders, Helena Petrovna Blavatsky (1831–1891) and Henry Steel Olcott (1832–1907), in Buddhism drove them to visit Ceylon in 1880. This visit can, to a certain extent, be considered as the commencement of the so-called Buddhist revival that would spread across Asia around the turn of the twentieth century. During his visit to Ceylon, Olcott founded the Buddhist Theosophical Society "with the aim of preserving the heritage of Buddhism and spreading Buddhist education by setting up Buddhist schools."[28] It is noteworthy that many of the early westerners who converted to Buddhism came from occultist milieus. For instance, the first European to enter the *sangha* and become an ordained monk was the Englishman Allan Bennett (1872–1923), who took Ananda Metteyya as his ecclesiastical name. Allan Bennett had been an active member of the *Hermetic Order of the Golden Dawn*, and it is often assumed that he was the adopted son of MacGregor Mathers (1854–1918), the chief of the order from around 1895 to its collapse in 1900. Prior to his departure for the east, Bennett lived with the occultist Aleister Crowley (1875–1947) and trained him in ritual magic.[29]

The most significant impact of Hinduism on Western esotericism can be attributed to the endeavors of Swami Vivekananda (1863–1902). In 1893 Vivekananda attended the World Parliament of Religions and his contribution is of paramount importance for the interpretation of Hinduism as a modern teaching of wisdom. Vivekananda preached a form of neovedanta, which was congenial to the sentiments of the occultist currents. According to Vivekananda, his teachings were of a universal nature and not limited to the sects of individual religions.[30]

Third, the impact of the new theories of evolution, and in particular the philosophical models originating in German Idealism and romanticism, became connected to a universal process of spiritual progress. The idea of a universal spiritual progress became, according to Hanegraaff, fundamental to almost all forms of occultism. This is especially true for New Age, of which one feature is the belief that mankind is about to enter a new age, astrologically termed the Age of Aquarius, characterized by a higher spiritual development. This spiritual development is often considered to be connected to a monistic form of thought, as opposed to the supposed dualism of the previous age, the Age of Pisces.[31]

Fourth, the influence of psychology, and in particular the influence of Carl Gustav Jung (1875–1961). Jung's theory of the anima and animus, the importance attributed to the unconscious, the process of individuation, and the universally applicable archetypes have all become standard features of contemporary esotericism. Psychological terminology is often used to explain religious concepts to such an extent that it is valid to speak of a "psychologisation" of the occult.[32]

Finally, the fifth aspect, which Hanegraaff mentions, in which the occultist movements differ from earlier forms of esotericism, is the impact of capitalist market economy on the domain of spirituality. This aspect is especially prevalent in the New Age movement.[33]

Hanegraaff's dissatisfaction with Faivre's definition of Western esotericism as a form of thought is to be contrasted with his own proposition for a new research paradigm. According to Hanegraaff, Western esotericism should not be studied as an essentially static worldview, but as something that is continually transformed and that adapts to new circumstances. His theoretical definition of Western esotericism is based on the previously mentioned three different ways of achieving knowledge: doctrinal faith, rationality, and the "middle way," which is characterized by knowledge, or *gnosis*, of a revelatory nature:

> It is indeed hard to deny that an emphasis on *gnosis*, rather than on rationality or the reliance on religious authority, is quite typical of the currents and personalities usually considered as falling under the heading of "Western esotericism"; and one may add that a marked preference for mythical and symbolic rather than logical and discursive language follows naturally from these premises. *The great risk of such a definition consists in the frequent tendency to misunderstand its ideal-typical and heuristic nature, and use it in a reductionist fashion.*[34] [My emphasis.]

Hanegraaff's theoretical definition of Western esotericism as a strategy of knowledge does not, however, only run the risk of being used in a reductionist fashion, but it also runs the risk of being used in such a wide manner that it becomes all-inclusive—and consequently useless as an alternative to Faivre's definition. The nature of the gnosis strived for by the esotericists needs to be further analyzed. The already-quoted definition of gnosis as "a revelatory experience that mostly entailed an encounter with one's true self as well with the ground of being, God" is a good starting point for a theoretical stance, but it needs to be further elaborated in order to be used in a satisfactory way. For instance, is gnosis to be seen as a way of salvation (not forgetting that esotericism is seen as a form of Christian spirituality)? In what way does gnosis differ from the aim of the mystic—or indeed, is there a difference at all? Questions such as these need to be addressed before Hanegraaff's proposal for a new definition of esotericism can be used with any greater result.[35]

At present, Hanegraaff's definition does not exclude the use of Faivre's definition of esotericism. On the contrary, the two definitions can be used as two parallel ways of approaching esoteric discourses. Faivre's constituting components do not necessarily have the same import in the nineteenth century as they had in the Renaissance, but this does not mean that they are not applicable to esoteric currents after the Renaissance.

Finally, a word or two needs to be said concerning Hanegraaff's valuable contribution to the understanding of the development of esotericism under the impact of secularization and modernity. It is, in my opinion, undeniable that the five above-mentioned changes can be traced in nineteenth- and twentieth-century esotericism, but I would also like to mention the importance of yet two other significant new aspects of occultist currents. First, the importance attached to personal religious experiences. The pragmatic nature of occultism is evident already in the writings of Éliphas Lévi (pseudonym of Alphonse Louis Constant, 1810–1875), often considered to be the chief instigator of nineteenth-century occultism. This pragmatism was often directed toward the achievement of various "altered states of consciousness," for example, by the invocations and evocations of higher beings, angels, or gods. The religious/mystical experiences strived for were often very specific in nature: for instance, in the A∴A∴, an order founded by Aleister Crowley in 1907, the adepts were expected to reach a state that was called "the Knowledge of and Conversation with the Holy Guardian Angel," which can be described as a union of the conscious mind with the unconsciousness. The terminology was taken from a medieval manuscript at the Bibliothèque de l'Arsenal that MacGregor Mathers had translated and published as *The Book of the Sacred Magic of Abra-Melin the Mage* (1898). Other examples of the importance placed on religious experiences are the popularity of works on yoga among adherents of occultism, and the use of sex in magical rituals. The experiential aspect of occultist currents has continued to be an important feature of nineteenth- and twentieth-century occultism, but it is also a significant part of the New Age movement.

The second new important aspect of nineteenth- and twentieth-century occultist currents is the importance placed on the personal will of the esotericist. The will is not only seen as a fundamental tool in magical rituals, it is often seen as a divine or supernatural aspect of man. This latter view is not as prevalent in the writings of early French occultists, such as Eliphas Lévi, as compared to later British occultists. But the will is nonetheless important to Lévi as the prerequisite to attain "magical power":

> Two things, as we have already said, are necessary for the acquisition of magical power—the emancipation of the will from all servitude, and its instruction in the art of domination.[36]

The later occultist view of the will as something divine was to a large extent influenced by modern philosophers, most notably Friedrich Nietzsche (1844–1900). Although, for instance, Helena Petrovna Blavatsky and the founders of the *Hermetic Order of the Golden Dawn* attributed great importance to the will,[37] it is with Aleister Crowley that the religious nature of the will reaches its climax. The new religious movement that Crowley founded in the first decade of the twentieth century, *Thelema* (Greek for will), has as its basic tenet that all men and women have a "purpose" with their lives—a "True Will." With the help of "Magick" and "Mysticism," which were seen by Crowley as the two roads of attainment, the adherents of *Thelema* aim to find out what their True Will is. Crowley summarized the formula of the law of *Thelema* thus:

> The formula of this law is: Do what thou wilt. Its moral aspect is simple enough in theory: Do what thou wilt does not mean Do as you please, although it implies this degree of emancipation, that it is no longer possible to say *à priori* that a given action is "wrong." Each man has the right—and an absolute right—to accomplish his True Will.[38]

These two additional features (i.e., the importance attached to personal religious experiences and the emphasis of the will), in occultist currents are important in many contemporary forms of esotericism, such as Wicca, ritual magic and certain forms of Satanism.

Western Esotericism in Theory and Practice

Faivre's methodological paradigm of Western esotericism as a "form of thought" is an abstract construct aimed at capturing the essence of a wide variety of phenomena. To be sure, the criteria required of a material in order for it to be classed as esoteric are simple enough. If the constituting components of Western esotericism, and preferably the secondary ones as well, are present in a material, then it is regarded as esoteric. If one, or more, of the constituting components are not to be found, then the material is consequently not regarded as esoteric. The esoteric discourses are characterized by a highly symbolic language, often accompanied by images and emblems through which esotericism is expressed:

> The best way to locate any of these six components in a discourse, a work, a ritual, etc., is not to look for doctrinal tenets, but to try to find evidence of their presence in concrete manifestations like images, symbols, styles, etc.[39]

The complexity of symbols and images found in the esoteric material requires that the scholars who endeavor to trace esotericism have a thorough knowledge of the esoteric currents and their particular symbolism. In theory, Faivre's methodology of Western esotericism is a simple, yet precise, tool where the scholar can identify the form of thought in question. In practice, however, I would argue that the identification of the esoteric form of thought is not always as simple as one might expect. In fact, the scholar is confronted on numerous occasions with material that apparently belongs to the corpus of specific esoteric currents or traditions, such as alchemy, but in which it is impossible to detect some, or all, of the constituting components. Furthermore, as Faivre points out, a material is never exclusively esoteric—it is the question, based on a particular methodological approach, posed to the material that to a large extent direct the subsequent answers.[40] That is, depending on what aspects one chooses to address in a material, different answers will be found. For instance, *The Chemical Wedding of Christian Rosenkreutz* can be described as, for example, Rosicrucian, alchemical, mystical, Christian, hermetic, or simply as a joke—depending on what questions we pose to the text. This fact presents us with a number of problems. For instance, can a Rosicrucian text be *nonesoteric*? Can a text in which it is impossible to detect the constituting components of the esoteric form of thought still be classified as esoteric? What follows is an attempt to classify four different types of texts related to Western esotericism.

(1) *Texts belonging to one (or more) esoteric current(s), in which the constituting components of the esoteric "form of thought" are explicitly present*:
This category is that which we normally term esoteric; that is, texts in which the constituting components of Western esotericism are clearly present. Thus, esoteric currents such as Christian Kabbalah, paracelsism, Rosicrucianism, theosophy, alchemy, astrology, magic (Magia), occultism and perennialism all have the common feature that they are permeated with the esoteric "form of thought," expressed through the constituting components. The esoteric form of thought is to a large extent explicitly present in these currents; that is, the constituting components of Western esotericism are detectable—and thereby these currents answer to the required criteria of designing them as esoteric. Important to note is that the esoteric form of thought is a fundamental aspect of these currents, and that their individual traits and developments are in accordance with Western esotericism.

(2) *Texts belonging to one (or more) esoteric current(s), in which the constituting components of esoteric form of thought are implicitly present*:
In the majority of the discourses related to the esoteric traditions discussed above, Faivre's constituting components of Western esotericism are easily detectable. However, there are a certain amount of texts that

belong to one, or more, of the esoteric traditions, in which it is not possible to trace the constituting components of the esoteric form of thought. That is, it is not possible to trace any explicit references to the components, but the context and subject of the texts are nonetheless pointing toward the components in an implicit manner. Indeed, even nonesoteric texts can be interpreted as esoteric, depending on the circumstances in which they appear, and how they are used.[41] Western esotericism is, according to Faivre, a form of thought, a certain manner through which the esotericist interprets phenomena. As esoteric materials are composed by esotericists, and more often than not, for other fellow-esotericists, it is important to take into account the possibility that the constituting components of Western esotericism were not always expressed explicitly as they already played such an integrated part of the authors' and readers' shared worldview. It is more than likely that the fundamental components often were taken for granted, and there was consequently no need to express them.[42] However, by a thorough study of the text it is possible to trace them implicitly. For instance, an alchemical recipe might not explicitly refer to the correspondences between the seven metals and the seven planets, but an alchemist would nonetheless immediately see the connection, and further, he or she would relate the correspondences to man, as man is the microcosm of macrocosm.[43] This is admittedly an oversimplified example, but it serves to illustrate that since the constituting components of Western esotericism are such fundamental features, they must be taken into account even though they are not explicitly present. It is the context that determines whether or not esotericism can be considered to be implicitly present, and not the mere fact that it belongs to an esoteric tradition.[44]

(3) *Texts belonging to one (or more) esoteric current(s), in which the esoteric form of thought is not present*:
There are, however, instances when a text clearly belongs to a certain esoteric current, but in which the esoteric form of thought is not present. At first appearance this statement might seem as a contradiction. However, a text that is clearly part of an esoteric tradition, such as Rosicrucianism, can be dealing with subjects that are not dependent on the esoteric form of thought.[45] In other words, a text can be Rosicrucian, but that does not necessarily make it esoteric. A text can only be termed esoteric when the constituting components are present in it, in an explicit or implicit manner (vide supra). A text dealing with organizational questions, such as *The Laws of the Fraternity of the Rosie Cross* (in which the esoteric form of thought is not explicitly present), is not dependent on the esoteric form of thought, and it is therefore possible to rule out

the presence of esotericism in an implicit manner. The criteria for as-
signing a text as esoteric should not be based on the mere account of
it belonging to one or more of the esoteric currents, but to whether
or not the constituting components can be ascertained in an explicit or
implicit manner in it.

(4) *Migration of esoteric ideas into nonesoteric materials*:
It is common enough to find symbols, ideas, or techniques that
traditionally are connected to a certain esoteric tradition in nonesoteric
materials. For instance, references to magic or alchemy can frequently
be found in modern literature, such as the Fantasy genre, in which the
esoteric form of thought is not present.[46] Magic, for example, can have
either a seminal or nominal presence in the material, but that does not
make it esoteric, as we understand the term. Another example can be
found in the New Age movement in which the eclectic attitude is apparent. A person might use techniques that traditionally are connected to
the esoteric traditions, such as Tarot, in a purely divinatory or meditational
manner without taking into account the underlying esoteric form of
thought. Such practice cannot be termed esoteric, as it is an example of
a nonesoteric usage of a traditionally esoteric technique. These two
examples illustrate two different ways in which esoteric ideas can mi-
grate into nonesoteric areas.

All classifications are reductions, and ultimately simplifications, of
complex data, and the above classification is no exception. Furthermore,
theoretical classifications tend to become awkward instruments when
practically applied. It is nonetheless important to stress the different
aspects of esotericism in order to understand its various modes of manifestation. It should be stressed that the notion of *implicit esotericism*
should be used with caution and only when there are valid reasons for
applying the term. A liberal usage of the term might render it too inclusive and thus distancing it from the definition of Western esotericism as
understood by Faivre. Used with proper reserve it will, however, serve
the scholar with a means to draw attention to a hitherto largely ignored
aspect of Western esotericism.

Western Esoteric Currents

Criticism to Frances Yates's theory of a so-called Hermetic Tradition
shows that there is no such thing as a homogenous hermetic tradition,
but rather a number of complex and intertwining hermetic traditions or
currents.[47] In a similar manner it is necessary to be cautious toward the

notion of a single esoteric tradition. As already stated, Western esotericism, as a form of thought, is an abstract construction that only exists as a methodology. There is no such thing as an esoteric tradition *per se*, in which the esoteric form of thought can be traced historically. What we can study, however, are the various currents through which the esoteric form of thought manifests itself. The components of esotericism are traceable through a number of historical currents that have been present in our cultural hemisphere since the Renaissance. While there is no "Esoteric Tradition" we can, according to Hanegraaff, speak of a so-called "tradition of esotericism":

> Certainly, it is on the basis of its *ideas* that esotericism becomes visible to the historian as a separate field of study, and it is their development over time which enables the historian to speak of a "tradition" of esotericism.[48]

Thus, when we speak of esoteric currents, it is not the esoteric form of thought itself that is being referred to, but rather the esoteric form of thought in its various modes of manifestation.[49] Western esotericism is a passive, nonmanifest construct that is traceable only when active, or manifest in one or more of the esoteric currents; that is, in the empirical data available to us.

> There is not, for us, any esotericism sui generis. Each of the component elements of the form of thought that it has been agreed to call esoteric presents itself only as a theoretical generalization starting from empirical data (under the circumstances, starting from concrete historical ideas).[50]

The relationship between the "active" and "passive" sides of esotericism; that is, the unmanifest esoteric form of thought on the one hand, and the active, manifest form of thought as expressed through the esoteric currents on the other, is by definition a one-sided relation only. The esoteric form of thought, being static, is not subject to historical conditions (since it is an abstract construct), which the esoteric currents on the other hand by necessity are. The constituting components of Western esotericism are the same today as they were during the Renaissance— Faivre does not count with additional components as history evolves.[51] The esoteric currents, being nonstatic and dynamic, constantly change and new currents appear. They show a remarkable tendency to adapt to the historical conditions of our culture, a fact that is easily detectable in many of our contemporary esoteric new religious movements.[52]

The interrelationship between the esoteric currents shows that they are often interpreted by esotericists as dependent, or at least explicatory, of each other. This is most evident in occultism in which the eclectic attitude is taken to its extreme. In discussing the use of certain terms connected to Western esotericism Faivre differentiates between what he calls *Currents* and *Notions*, which he further divides into three groups (Table 1.1).[53] According to Faivre the *Currents* correspond to movements, schools, or traditions, while the *Notions* correspond to spiritual attitudes or to practices.[54]

The division into currents and notions is important as it stresses two interconnected dimensions of Western esotericism—the theoretical (or organizational) and the practical (or experiential). The theoretical dimension, realized in movements, schools, fraternities, organizations, etc., appears to be an important factor in Western esotericism, especially from the eighteenth century onward. The notion that certain societies or groups of initiates are repositories of a sacred knowledge, or gnosis, is indeed a prominent feature of the esoteric mythology. An important aspect of esoteric societies as *transmitters* of gnosis lies in the emphasis of the legitimacy of the "transmutative" knowledge.[55] The theoretical dimension of Western esotericism can be studied from an historical point of view; that is, it is possible to trace a particular school's development from its foundation, to ascertain the identity of its founders and members, and so on. A further characteristic of the esoteric currents is that most of them can be traced back to one or more founding texts, whereas the notions are loosely based on a corpus of literature.

The practical or experiential dimension of esotericism can be traced back to classical or Renaissance esotericism, but during the nineteenth century the importance of this dimension is considerably increased. To a certain extent, the experiential aspect of esotericism can be linked to the notion of gnosis, the revelatory form of knowledge, which, according to Hanegraaff, is the prime characteristic of Western esotericism.

Table 1.1. Terminology relating to Western esotericism according to Faivre.

Currents that are not notions	Currents that also correspond to notions	Notions that are not currents
Hermetism	Alchemy	Hermeticism
Christian Kabbalah	Astrology	Gnosis
Paracelsism	Magic (or *Magia*)	
Rosicrucianism	Occultism	
Theosophy	Perennialism	

Faivre's division of terms in relation to Western esotericism into notions and currents is important as it stresses two important aspects of Western esotericism. Nevertheless, the division might lead to some confusion, as it does not provide any clear criteria of where currents end and notions begin. This is apparent in Faivre's table in which there is a group that correspond to both notions and currents simultaneously. Especially the relationship between groups 1 and 2 is problematic. Faivre is correct in separating the two groups, as they, from a theoretical point of view, clearly refer to two different *types* of terms, or phenomena. However, if we apply Faivre's classification of terminology to the historical esoteric currents and notions, the division becomes problematic. According to Faivre the notions correspond to spiritual attitudes or to practices, as already mentioned. I would argue that the first group, that is, Currents, include these as well. There are for instance spiritual attitudes and practices connected to the esoteric currents referred to as theosophy, a term that Faivre classifies as belonging to the first group, "Currents which are not notions."[56] There seems to be a discrepancy, then, in this division when applied to the historical "manifestations" of esotericism—the division is valid but the criteria for the division are questionable. Nevertheless, Faivre's classification is, if used with care, of great practical use for the scholar when used on a general level.

Western Esoteric Rituals of Initiation

The recent academic interest in Western initiatory societies (often with a focus on Freemasonry) parallels, to a certain extent, the academic interest in Western esotericism. In other words, it is a relatively new field of research, which was previously avoided by the academic community. Freemasonry was often viewed as a subject not worthy of serious research, partly because a large part of the literature dealing with the subject did not meet academic standards. This negative view was aptly described by Yates when discussing the supposed connections between Rosicrucianism and Freemasonry:

> The main reason why serious historical studies on the Rosicrucian manifestos and their influence have hitherto been on the whole lacking is no doubt because the whole subject has been bedevilled by enthusiasts for secret societies. There is a vast literature on Rosicrucianism which assumes the existence of a secret society, founded by Christian Rosencreutz, and having a continuous existence up to modern times. In the vague and inaccurate world of so-called 'occultist' writing this assumption has produced

a kind of literature which deservedly sinks below the notice of the serious historian. And when, as is often the case, the misty discussion of 'Rosicrucians' and their history becomes involved with the masonic myths, the enquirer feels that he is sinking helplessly into a bottomless bog.[57]

Fortunately, the situation has improved considerably in the last seven years. There are today at least three academic chairs devoted to Free-masonry,[58] and important studies have been published on the subject. In addition to this, there exist a number of masonic research organizations that maintain a high scholarly standard in their published transactions.[59] The situation for the scholar has also been improved through a change of attitude among masonic research societies and libraries toward the academic community. Scholars are invited to publish articles in renowned masonic periodicals such as *Ars Quatour Coronatorum* and *Heredom*, and to attend conferences open for both masons and nonmasons. Fur-thermore, most masonic libraries are, contrary to what is often thought to be the case, open for nonmasonic scholars.

Scholars working in the field of Western esotericism have taken an interest in initiatory societies, and it is often assumed that esotericism can be found in this type of society. Yates, for instance, explored the relationship between Rosicrucianism and Freemasonry, and came to the conclusion that the Rosicrucian furor of the seventeenth century prob-ably inspired the founding of "secret societies," such as Freemasonry.[60] Both Faivre and Hanegraaff mention that esotericism can be found in masonic initiatory societies—especially in the high degrees from the second half of the eighteenth century.[61]

Faivre begins his short description of eighteenth-century initiatory societies in *Access to Western Esotericism* with the words: "It is obviously the high degree rites that contain the most esoteric content, therefore Anglo-Saxon Freemasonry is less esoteric in character."[62] After a short discussion of the *Strict Observance* and the *Rectified Scottish Rite*, Faivre makes a distinction between three types of masonic rites: (1) Christian or Western rites, (2) medieval and chivalric rites, (3) neopagan Egyptian rites.[63] Suffice it to say at present that Faivre, while stressing the differ-ence between the Craft degrees and the high or additional degrees, does not state that esotericism is not to be found in the Craft degrees, merely that they contain less esoteric content than the later "High" degree rituals.

In discussing the history of Western esotericism, Hanegraaff states that a Western esoteric tradition known as Christian theosophy, connected to esoteric philosophers such as Jacob Boehme (1575–1624) and Friedrich Christian Oetinger (1702–1782), would later find its way, through German Naturphilosophie, into initiatory societies of the eighteenth century:

> Christian Theosophy came to be closely linked to the emergence of German *Naturphilosophie*, including a strong interest in magic and the "occult" phenomena associated with "the Night-Side of Nature." It flourished, finally, in the so-called Illuminist current of the later eighteenth and the early nineteenth centuries, partly linked to new initiatory societies modelled upon or connected with Freemasonry such as the theurgical Elus Coëns, the Illuminés d'Avignon, the Rectified Scottish Rite, the Order of the Gold and Rosy Cross and the Asiatic Brethren.[64]

Although both Faivre and Hanegraaff state that Western esotericism is to be found in masonic initiatory societies, they do not venture deeper into the subject and do not explain *how* esotericism is actually transmitted in this type of society. Furthermore, they do not discuss the rituals of these societies at all, despite the central position they have for initiatory societies. From an academic perspective, the relationship between Western esotericism and rituals of initiation is thus an unexplored field of research. In the present work it will be analyzed how Western esotericism is transmitted through rituals of initiation and, furthermore, what types of esoteric currents or traditions are transmitted. It is hoped that this will result in a deeper understanding of Western esoteric rituals of initiation, and thereby assist in bringing this type of ritual from the darkness of obscurity, to the light of academic scrutiny.

Concluding Remarks

The academic study of Western Esotericism is a comparatively new field in the history of religions, and it is only in the last ten years that the field has received wide academic recognition. There are several reasons for this belated recognition, but perhaps the most important reason is that Western esotericism has been viewed with suspicion, both by theologians and historians of science. Today, the situation has improved considerably and scholars from a wide range of disciplines are beginning to view Western esotericism as an important part of Western culture.

In this book Western esotericism is approached from a broader (generalist) perspective, which is based on the two research paradigms proposed by Antoine Faivre and Wouter Hanegraaff. These two paradigms can be described as esotericism as a "form of thought" (Faivre), and esotericism as gnosis (Hanegraaff). More specifically, this book will be dealing with the relationship between Western esotericism and rituals of initiation as used by masonic initiatory societies.

Chapter 2

Rituals of Initiation, Secret Societies, and Masonic Initiatory Societies

Ritual as a Field of Research

Scholars such as Asad, Boudewijnse, Bremmer, and Snoek have studied the usage of the term ritual and their research reveals how the word ritual has been used to denote quite different things.[1] The terms rite and ritual derive from the Latin *ritus* and *ritualis* (belonging to ritual). The Latin word *ritus* means "custom" and was primarily used in juridical and religious language. *Rituale* can be found in the first edition of *Rituale Romanum* of 1614 where the word implies the prescribed order where the religious services of the Catholic Church should be acted out. The English word "ritual" first appears in the middle of the seventeenth century and the meaning of the word is "the prescribed order of performing religious services or the book containing such prescriptions." The action or behavior prescribed by the ritual was called "ceremony" or "liturgy." In the first edition of the *Encyclopaedia Britannica* (1771), ritual is described as "a book directing the order and manner to be observed in celebrating religious ceremonies, and performing divine service in a particular church, diocese, order, or the like." The entry for Ritual was unchanged up to and including the seventh edition of 1852. The following three editions did not include an entry for ritual. The eleventh edition of 1910, however, did. This time the entry, written by R. R. Marett, had swollen to five columns and the word had acquired a totally different meaning. I here quote Asad:

> [R]itual is now regarded as a type of routine behaviour that symbolizes or expresses something and, as such, relates differentially to individual consciousness and social organization. That is to say, it is no longer a *script* for regulating practice but a type

27

of practice that is interpretable as standing for some further *verbally definable*, but tacit event.[2]

The word ritual, from 1852 to 1910, changed from denoting a *text*, to denoting *action* and *behavior*, or in the words of Boudewijnse: "It is only since the turn of the century that anthropologists and historians of religion have started to use ritual as the general term for repetitive, symbolic behaviour."[3] The old meaning of the term did not, however, disappear from the scene and it can be found in *Meyers Enzyclopädisches Lexicon* from 1977. During the twentieth century there have been two different interpretations of the term in existence—and often it is not clear which one of the two meanings of ritual scholars intend when using the word. Asad was the first scholar to draw attention to the general changes in the use and meaning of the term "ritual," but he did not, according to Boudewijnse, explain when and how the change in scholarly conception had been brought about.

Boudewijnse argues that it is the Reformation that draws attention to the phenomenon of rituals, and more precisely those of the Roman Catholic Church, and that they were valued in a negative manner. In the nineteenth century the term is used by Orientalists in order to refer to the Rig-Veda, etc., and in France the use is even more common where it is often applied to the ancient Egyptian religion (*rituel funéraire égyptien*), and to Freemasonry (*rituel maçonnique*). In 1871 Edward B. Tylor, in *Primitive Culture*, divided religious rites in two theoretical divisions. According to Tylor, religious rites are in part expressive and symbolic performances, and in part means of intercourse with and influence on spiritual beings. In his *Myth, Ritual, and Religion* (1877) Andrew Lang was one of the first to use the word ritual when referring to religious action. In W. Robertson Smith's influential *Lectures on the Religion of the Semites* (1889) we find that rite, ritual, and ceremony are used interchangeably but without a clear definition of what the author actually meant by the terms.[4] It is clear however that he is referring to action and not to texts and, further, that ritual is of primary importance to myth: "The conclusion is, that in the study of ancient religions we must begin, not with myth, but with ritual and traditional usage."[5] Throughout the book Robertson Smith stresses the primacy of ritual over myth, and according to him the primary ritual of Semitic religions is the sacrifice.

So far as myths consist of explanations of ritual their value is altogether secondary, and it may be affirmed with confidence that in almost every case the myth was derived from the ritual, and not the ritual from the myth; for the ritual was fixed and the myth variable, the ritual was obligatory and faith in the myth was at the discretion of the worshipper.

But it is of the first importance to realise clearly from the outset that ritual and practical usage were, strictly speaking, the sum total of ancient religions. Religion in primitive times was not a system of belief with practical applications; it was a body of fixed traditional practices, to which every member of society conformed as a matter of course.[6]

The last sentence is crucial in understanding Robertson Smith as he was a pioneer in what later became known as the sociology of religion. Boudewijnse remarks "Robertson Smith took a crucial step. By placing religious practice in the context of long-term social traditions and disconnecting it from individual mental states, he connected it to the collectivity. As such, religious practice—ritual—became a *social* fact." One year later, 1890, saw the publication of the first edition of James G. Frazer's famous *The Golden Bough: A Study in Comparative Religion* in which the word ritual is used constantly. Boudewijnse sums up:

[The] use of the term 'ritual' seemed inspired by its original meaning of a script for behaviour: Because it had the connotation of 'rules' and 'prescriptions.' In short, recognition of the aspect of 'rules' as characteristic of 'religious action' as a separate category of behaviour, may have instigated adoption of the term 'ritual' to refer to 'ordered sequences of religious acts,' 'acts based on (a) ritual,' later to be called 'ritual acts,' which, with the passage of time, became 'ritual.'[7]

The so-called "ritual turn," which is the process by which the word "ritual" came to denote ritual *action* instead of *text*, did, however, not necessarily mean that ritual (understood as action) became a subject of scholarly interest. On the contrary, none of the quoted scholars showed any interest in ritual as symbolic behavior worthy of study in its own right. The exception to this is Van Gennep in his important book *Les Rites de Passage* (1909), that I will return to later in greater detail. The study of ritual as an important field of research dates from the 1960s and can be attributed to three important factors: the rise of ethnology; the English translation of Van Gennep's *The Rites of Passage* (1960); and the work of Victor Turner, especially *The Ritual Process* (1969). During the 1970s the term "ritual" became more and more inclusive and was not only concerned with "religious behaviour" anymore. A prime example of this trend is *Secular Ritual,* which appeared in 1977.[8] Catherine Bell comments:

> [R]itual behaviour... now includes high mass in a Greek Ortho-dox church, the swearing in of the president, school graduation ceremonies, and the special talismanic actions taken by a pitcher as he gets ready to throw a baseball. This is not to say that scholars do not see any differences among these rites but simply that what they share has become a greater theoretical interest than what seems to distinguish them—at least for the time being.[9]

From the 1960s it became apparent for a number of scholars that there existed a number of terms related to the phenomenon of "ritual," but that their respective meanings were undefined. Some authors tried to make a distinction between "ritual" and "ceremony" where ceremony came to be used for secular rather than "religious rituals."[10] This divi-sion, however, proved to be of little use as the division of sacred and profane came to be heavily criticized, especially during the 1980s. In 1971 Spiro suggested that the term *rite* should be understood as "the minimum significant unit of ritual behaviour," and a *ceremony* as "the smallest configuration of rites constituting a meaningful ritual whole," and finally a *ceremonial* as "the total configuration of ceremonies per-formed during any ritual occasion." In 1987 J.A.M. Snoek proposed yet another approach, which to a large extent is an elaboration of Spiro's approach but which further includes ritual (understood in two different senses) and Rite with a capital R, for the total of a cult (such as the Russian Orthodox Rite).[11] In 2000 Ronald Grimes suggested that the usage of the word "ritual" should be dropped, and that it instead should be replaced by "rite" for "ritual" in the old sense, and "ritualization" for the extended scope.[12] We can thus discern a number of trends in the usage of the term ritual and related terms such as rite and ceremony.[13]

Rites de Passage

When searching for "Rituals of Initiation" in the *Encyclopaedia Britannica,* one only finds a note that states "see Rites de Passage." In 1909 Arnold van Gennep published his book *Les Rites de Passage,* a work that has had a profound impact on all the later studies of rites of initiation. It is, however, important to stress the fact that Van Gennep did not exclu-sively base his research and subsequent findings on rites of initiation, but rather on various kinds of rites that all tended to ritualize the passing from one state of being (or status) into another. Thus, he paid great attention to the ritualization of pregnancy and childbirth, the reaching of puberty, marriage, and death—events that often are referred to as *life-crises*. But he also discussed recurrent events such as the phases of the moon and the seasonal changes. Earlier research by Heinrich Schurtz *Alterklassen und Männerbünde* (1902) and Hutton Webster *Primitive Secret Societies* (1908) had already divided initiations into two groups—Puberty rites and initiations into secret societies.[14] Van Gennep distinguished between physiological puberty and social puberty and considered that the term "puberty rites" should be dropped since they are performed at social, rather than physiological puberty.

Van Gennep reached the conclusion that all these various types of rites had a common structural denominator. They all marked the transition from an old state to a new one by a three-phased scheme. First, there occurred a separation from the old social position or state of being. Second, a marginal (or liminal) state in which the candidate found himself between the old and the new states. Third, aggregation or incorporation into the new state. These three phases are composed of rites of separation, rites of transition, and rites of incorporation, respectively. In his discussion of Van Gennep's structural theory concerning rites of passage, Max Gluckman has the following to say concerning the emphasis of the three kinds of rites:

> Van Gennep stressed that in different situations various of these three stages might be emphasized: thus rites of separation are prominent in funerals, while rites of incorporation are marked in weddings, and rites of transition at initiatory ceremonies. The phase of transition sometimes developes an autonomy of its own, and becomes a "liminal" (threshold) period between two more firmly established states. This liminal period tends to be 'sacred,' for he saw social life in early civilizations as constant movements between 'the sacred world' and 'the profane world.'[15]

However, Gluckman did not read Van Gennep correctly who actually stated the precise opposite:

> A première vue, il semblerait que dans les ceremonies funéraires, ce sont les rites de séparation qui doivent prendre la place la plus importante, les rites de marge et d'agrégation par contre n'étant que peu développés. Cependent l'étude des faits montre qu'il en est autrement, et qu'au contraire les rites de séparation sont peu nombreux et très simples, que les rites de marge ont

une durée et une complexité qui va parfois jusqu'à leur faire reconnaître une sorte d'autonomie, et qu'enfin de tous les rites funéraires, ce sont ceux qui agrègent le mort au monde des morts qui sont le plus élaborés et auxquels on attribue l'importance la plus grande.[16]

The division between the sacred and profane was a very popular theory among historians of religion; perhaps most explicitly expressed in the works of Mircea Eliade. However, today the general trend is to view the duality between the sacred and profane with caution, since it is very hard, if not impossible, to see any clear-cut borders between the two spheres.[17] The problem with Van Gennep lies in the fact that he uses the term "initiation rites" ambiguously. On the one hand, he uses it explicitly to refer to puberty rites, on the other hand, he uses it from time to time for all *rites de passage* where the object concerned is a person.

Victor Turner was highly influenced by Van Gennep's three-phase theory, and paid special attention to the marginal phase (or rather liminal phase as he preferred to call it). In the article "Betwixed and Between: The Liminal Period in Rites of Passage" from 1964, and his influential book *The Ritual Process* from 1969 he expounded his theories on initiation, but to him the term initiation almost exclusively denoted the puberty rites and the curative cults of the Ndembu. According to Turner, it is in the liminal phase, when the candidate is "betwixt and between" the old and the new states, that the most decisive event of the initiation occur. It is in this phase that the officers of the initiation transmit a *gnosis*, or sacred knowledge, to the neophyte. The sacred knowledge is supposed to transform the candidate's innermost being, to turn him or her into a new being. This sociological and/or psychological change (depending on the type of the initiation) is often connected to the idea of a "second birth" or resurrection after a symbolical death. The concept of death in rites of initiation that follow the scheme of the *rites de passage*, is as a rule a dominant part of the first phase, that is, the separation from the old state of being. In the third phase the candidate emerges from the realm of death (i.e., the liminal period) and is incorporated into the new state. Eliade states that the initiatory death is central for *every* initiation:

The central moment of every initiation is represented by the ceremony symbolizing the death of the novice and his return to the fellowship of the living. But he returns to life a new man, assuming another mode of being. Initiatory death signifies the end at once of childhood, of ignorance, and of the profane condition.[18]

However, it is my opinion that Eliade's statement that "the central moment in every initiation is represented by the ceremony symbolizing the
death of the novice and his return to the fellowship of the living" should
be questioned. First, death is not central in *every* initiation, even though
it is a common characteristic of rites of initiation that are structured as
rites de passage. Second, not all rites of initiation are *rites de passage*, and
vice versa, not all *rites de passage* are rites of initiation. Third, the use of
a symbolic death in rites of initiation does not necessarily have the same
function and meaning in all instances where it occurs. For instance, the
masonic third-degree initiation of a Master Mason, which includes a
symbolical death centered on the legend of Hiram Abiff[19], does not fulfill
the same function as the ones aimed at in Australian puberty ceremonies, on which Eliade to a large extent based his research.

According to Turner the liminality is usually connected to an ab-
normal state, which falls outside structured society. It is a state where
"normality" is turned upside down. Basing his studies on research done
among the Ndembu, Turner reached the following conclusion:

> Thus, liminality is frequently likened to death, to being in the
> womb, to invisibility, to darkness, to bisexuality, to the wilder-
> ness, and to an eclipse of the sun or moon.[20]

The neophytes (i.e., the ones who undergo the initiation) are usually
acting in a passive or humble manner. They have to obey their instruc-
tors, and "accept arbitrary punishment without complaint." A further
characteristic is that the neophytes tend to "develop an intense comradeship and egalitarianism" apart from the ordinary societal bonds.[21] It is
interesting to note *why* the neophyte, according to Turner, must separate from the old state of being. It's simply because the new knowledge
that is being transmitted during the liminal period is viewed as changing
the *persona* of the candidate, and therefore has to *replace* the candidate's
former knowledge.

> The neophyte in liminality must be a *tabula rasa*, a blank slate,
> on which is inscribed the knowledge and wisdom of the group,
> in those respects that pertain to the new status.[22]

Liminality is not, however, exclusively connected with the second phase
of a *rite de passage*. The term can also be applied to other phenomena,
which in one way or another either fall outside the societal structure, or
even form the basis of an "anti-structure." Turner enumerates such
diverse phenomena as "subjugated autochthones, small nations, court

jesters, holy mendicants, good Samaritans, millenarian movements, 'dharma bums,' matrilaterality in patrilineal systems, patrilaterality in matrilineal systems, and monastic orders."[23] These liminal occurrences interested Turner from a sociological perspective:

> Yet all have this common characteristic: they are persons or principles that (1) fall in the interstices of social structure, (2) are on its margins, or (3) occupy its lowest rungs.[24]

According to Turner, the primary function of these liminal phenomena is to maintain and strengthen the social structure(s) by forming an anti-structure. The liminal persons or principles indirectly set the standards for the normal or structured society. That which is not liminal is normal, and therefore part of the structured sphere of society. An important distinction among *rites de passage*, which Turner makes, is that between *rituals of status elevation* and *rituals of status reversal*. These rituals are closely connected with two kinds of liminality.

> (. . .) - first, the liminality that characterizes *rituals of status elevation*, in which the ritual subject or novice is being conveyed irreversibly from a lower to a higher position in an institutionalized system of such positions. Secondly, the liminality frequently found in cyclical and calendrical ritual, usually of a collective kind, in which, at certain culturally defined points in the seasonal cycle, groups or categories of persons who habitually occupy low status positions in the social structure are positively enjoined to exercise ritual authority over their superiors; and they, in their turn, must accept with good will their ritual degradation. Such rites may be described as *rituals of status reversal*.[25]

The first group, *rituals of status elevation*, is of primary importance for the present investigation into the nature of Western esoteric rituals of initiation. Turner states that apart from "life crises rites" (i.e., rites connected to birth, puberty, marriage, and death), he would like to add "the rites that concern entry into a higher achieved status, whether this be a political office or secret society."[26] Turner further states that these rites can either be individual or collective, but that they usually tend to be performed for individuals. Comparing this with the Western material we find that initiations performed within esoteric orders are exclusively individual, even though some aspects of them might be collective.[27] Rituals of status reversal are mostly connected to either calendarical rites or rites of group crises, and these "almost always refer to large groups and quite often embrace whole societies."[28]

Rites of Initiation

The word "initiate" derives from the Latin *initiare* and means "to begin or to originate." The two most frequent usages of the word are to admit new members into a society or club and to teach fundamentals of something to someone. The word "initiation" usually means to admit someone into something. Initiation is thus often used synonymously with rite of initiation.[29]

The scholarly usage of the composite term "rite of initiation," and its twins ritual and ceremony of initiation, is limited to the act of admitting someone into an organization or office. In other words, the problem we often are faced with of understanding whether rite, ritual, and/or ceremony is used to denote action or prescription, does not apply to the usage of rite, ritual, and ceremony of initiation. This derives from the fact that scholars unfortunately tend not to observe the difference between the prescription, and the actual performance, of the initiation. Further, the act of admittance can in certain cases be in the form of Van Gennep's *rite de passage*, but does not necessarily have to be so. Again, this has led to some confusion, as it is common to find that rites of passage are used as synonymous with rites of initiation.

Anthropological studies of rites of initiation shifted from a focus on the ideas and beliefs of the practitioners, to a focus on social significance of the religious action. Significantly, this shift of focus coincided with the so-called "ritual turn" discussed above, that is the word ritual denoting *action* instead of *text*. The icon of nineteenth-century anthropological thinking, James Frazer, claimed in the *Golden Bough* that initiation is "the central mystery of primitive society."[30] According to Frazer, who had the evolution theory firmly rooted in his comparative approach to religion, society has undergone an evolution from magical, to religious, and finally to scientific thinking—an evolution from primitive to civilized, that is, nineteenth-century Victorian scientific-positivist thinking. He thought that religious practices such as initiation rites contained magical elements that had survived from the so-called primitive magical phase of human evolution. In discussing Frazer's notion of survivals, La Fontaine states:

> He included within his purview initiation into adult status of both boys and girls, which, he argued, was the most archaic form, since it was the most widely distributed, initiation into secret societies or cults, which he claimed as a later development, and finally, induction into office in such Ancient Greek cults as the Eleusinian mysteries, from which, he argued, developed first the idea of priesthood, and then divine kingship. The

central feature which underlay all these apparently different phenomena was the idea that they all concerned a passionate interest in, and desire to control, life, death and all the forces of nature. The development of rites followed from the progressively greater understanding of the natural world and showed changing techniques designed to produce the desired result: the enhanced fertility of people, animals and crops.[31]

The chief methodological error of the evolutionists was the theory of a universal social evolution. Societies develop in different ways, depending on a number of different aspects. More importantly in the present context, however, is that the evolutionists actually considered themselves capable of knowing how "the primitive savage" had been thinking. In other words, it was considered possible to reconstruct the "primitive" ideas and beliefs underlying religious practices, such as rites of initiation. Early social anthropologists, such as Robertson Smith and Durkheim, objected to this, and instead emphasized the importance of the social dimension for understanding religious practices. According to the social anthropological school, religious beliefs were secondary to religious practices or actions that were understood as "the means of reviving and strengthening the basic moral precepts on which social life is founded."[32] However, whether one chose to emphasize religious beliefs or action in understanding religion, the classification of various types of rites of initiation remained the same. In the sixth chapter of his *Rites de Passage*, Van Gennep discusses five different types of initiation rites, which closely follows Frazer's division of initiations into three groups, but in which Van Gennep further divides Frazer's third group into a number of subgroups: admission into age groups; admission into secret societies; ordination of a priest or magician; enthroning of a king; consecration of monks, nuns, and sacred prostitutes. He then continues to discuss admission into six different social groups: totem groups; fraternities; religious brotherhoods; classes, castes, and professions; Christianity, Islam, and the ancient mysteries; passage from one religion to another.

In 1964 the International Association for the History of Religions (IAHR) organized a conference exclusively devoted to the topic of "Initiation," which illustrates the general interest in this phenomenon not only among social anthropologists and ethnologists, but also among historians of religion. Although Mircea Eliade was unable to attend the IAHR conference on initiations in 1964, his paper entitled *L'Initiation et le monde moderne* was included in the publication of the transactions of the conference. This paper was printed as the first of a total of twenty-eight contributed papers, and thus had the function of an introduction to the academic field of initiations. Eliade divides initiations into three different categories, or *trois grandes catégories d'initiation*. Eliade's division of initiations into three groups is the perhaps most used division, or at least the one most referenced. The same division is to be found in Eliade's *Rites and symbols of initiation* and in the *Encyclopaedia of Religion* published in 1987. In the first category we find rites that are connected to the passing from childhood to adolescence. It is the same type of rites of initiation that Turner termed "life crises rites," and according to Eliade these rites are always in the form of *rites de passage*. The second category of initiations brings the candidate into a secret (or closed) society. These initiations are usually made on a voluntary basis, as opposed to the initiations of the first category that almost exclusively are an integral part of a society, which leaves little room for personal objections. Usually the candidates cannot apply for membership of a secret society, but are instead invited to join by the society itself. There are various ways of determining whether a person is qualified to join a secret society. For instance, the right to become a member of a *Dancing Society*, a North American secret society, is hereditary.[33]

One prime characteristic of secret societies often mentioned is that they usually claim to possess some sort of secret knowledge. Sometimes this knowledge can consist of a deeper understanding of the religion that is being practiced by the society at large. A common characteristic of secret societies is that they often (but not always) are restricted to a single sex. Eliade expresses his view of secret societies thus:

> What, in my view, is original and fundamental in the phenomenon of secret societies is the need for a fuller participation in the sacred, the desire to live as intensely as possible the sacrality peculiar to each of the two sexes.[34]

Western esoteric rituals of initiation are firmly connected to the notion of secret, or—more adequately—closed, societies as will presently be shown. An important aspect of Western esoteric rituals of initiation is that there are two types of rituals connected to initiatory societies. First, the initiation or admission into the closed society *per se*; that is, a ritual that makes the candidate "one of us" as opposed to "one of them," the demarcation between fraternal brothers and outsiders or profane (lit. outside or before the temple). Second, graded initiations that move the candidate through a system of degrees *within* the society. These degrees have very little to do with the relationship with the profane, but instead have a decisive effect on the relationship with fellow initiates. As the initiate moves higher up the hierarchy or deeper into the closed circles, he is expected to partake in more closely guarded secrets. The effect on his or her relationship with the members of the closed society will be connected to the degree he or she holds. In the context of closed societies or orders that transmit Western esotericism, the degree-structures are often highly elaborate. The *Rite of Memphis* for instance, is composed of 90 working and 6 official degrees, amounting to a total of 96 degrees.

The third and final group of initiations that Eliade distinguishes is that of the *Heroic and Shamanic Initiations*. According to Eliade the prime characteristic of this group is a psychological state that differs from the two preceding groups. The keyword to this state is *ecstasy*. The heroic initiation is connected to a martial ordeal that arouses the candidate to the "fury of the berserkers."[35] The shamanic initiation is, according to Eliade, connected to an ecstatic state that must be achieved in order for the initiate to be recognized as a shaman:

> There are three ways of becoming a shaman: first, by spontaneous vocation (the "call" or "election"); second, by hereditary transmission of the shamanic profession; and, third, by personal "quest," or, more rarely, by the will of the clan. But, by whatever method he may have been designated, a shaman is recognized as such only after having received two kinds of instruction. The first is ecstatic (e.g., dreams, visions, trances); the second is traditional (e.g., shamanic techniques, names and functions of the spirits, mythology and genealogy of the clan, secret language). This twofold teaching, imparted by the spirits and the old master shamans, constitutes initiation.[36]

As interesting as the shamanic initiation may be, it is far from the type of initiation that is to be found in Western esoteric rituals of initiation. All rites of initiation, in one way or another, influence the psychological state of the initiate, but not in the extreme sense as it is expected to be the case in the shamanic initiation. Neither is there any demand on the candidate in these initiations to reach an ecstatic state in order to be recognized as being initiated.[37] In "Some introductory remarks on the significance of initiation" Bleeker offered a classification of initiations into six different categories. The classification will be quoted at length since it differs from Eliade's classification primarily in the width of his concept of initiation:

> 1) the initiation into the tribal community, an initiation in which all young people, both the boys and usually also the girls, take part. Initiation means in this case, that the initiated are intro-

duced to the knowledge of the myth and to the rules and the customs of the tribe.

2) the initiation into certain societies of men or women. This ceremony is generally celebrated by rites, which have either a symbolic or a realistic character, in which latter case they can consist of cruel ordeals.

3) the initiation into a closed society which possess an esoteric truth, sometimes in the form of a secret doctrine.

4) the participation in a type of cult which dramatizes a religious truth of such a mysterious character that only privileged people are allowed to attend to it.

5) the initiation into an office, which requires certain personal qualities or extraordinary knowledge, such as the function of the shaman, the king or the prophet.

6) the initiation into religious truth, which happens when a man embraces a certain belief or is converted.[38]

Compared to Eliade, Bleeker is including far more under the term initiation. The first, fourth, and sixth groups points to an understanding of initiation that goes beyond the three types that Eliade formulated. Group two, three, and five correspond, however, directly with Eliade's first, second, and third group, respectively. During the 1964 IAHR conference on initiation some sort of consensus on the meaning of initiation was reached, as Bleeker states in the preface to the proceedings:

As the meeting progressed, the meaning and implications of initiation became gradually clearer until it was generally agreed, though no official conclusions were formulated, that the following three important aspects should be distinguished:

i) The so-called 'rites de passage' which sometimes function as rites of initiation.

ii) Rites of initiation in the strict sense of the word, i.e., rites introducing people into closed religious societies.

iii) Initiation in the sense of introduction into the mysteries of religion.[39]

This classification differs from those of Eliade and Bleeker as it focuses on the actual rite of initiation and not on what the initiate is initiated *into*. There is thus a difference made between a *rite de passage* and a rite of initiation, even though the former can function as the latter.

The academic literature dealing with rites of initiation is vast, and covers a wide spectrum of different types, both geographical and historical. Significantly, though, only two authors have dealt with Western rites of initiation at any depth—one from a sociological perspective, and the other from an anthropological one. Noel P. Gist's *Secret Societies*, published in 1940, includes, among other things, an analysis of basic themes found in Western rituals of initiation.[40] Jean La Fontaine's well-known work *Initiation* from 1985, discusses the first three degrees of Freemasonry at some length, and compares these to the rites of initiation of the Chinese Triad society.[41] Despite all the apparent differences in works dealing with rites of initiation, including Gist and La Fontaine, there is one common feature that stands out—the undisputed connection between rites of initiation and secret societies. But what do scholars mean by the term Secret Society? And furthermore, how does this term relate to Western esoteric rituals of initiation?

Secret Societies

Secret societies—a term that connotes different things to different interpreters. To some it gives an impression of mysticism, hidden truths, and romantic quests for esoteric knowledge. For others, it suggests something sinister, dangerous, or, indeed, evil. Yet again, to some others the term simply means childish boy-clubs for men. There is a strong tendency among scholars dealing with so-called "Secret Societies" to refer to a remarkable variety of phenomena with the term. This tendency, or rather rule, has been present in works dealing with this phenomenon for more than a century. Thus, in the highly influential work by Heckethorn, *The Secret Societies of All Ages and Countries*, originally published in 1878, we find such divers phenomena as the mysteries of ancient India, China, Egypt, Greece, the Templars, Rosicrucians, and Freemasons treated as if it were a coherent and identical phenomenon, namely as "Secret Societies."[42] Obviously, one would assume, the idea of dealing with such a wide range of phenomena under one single heading should give the scholar a reason to pause, to reflect whether this phenomenological approach is sound or indeed reasonable. Is it legitimate to argue that, for instance, the Mafia, the Ku Klux Klan, the Triad societies, the ancient mystery cults, and Freemasonry constitute one and the same phenomenon? I would argue that it is *not* legitimate, that it is methodologically inadequate to pull certain phenomena out of their historical, geographical, sociological, religious, and psychological (etc.) contexts, and then equate them with a myriad of other phenomena that have been extracted in a similar manner. By adopting this phenomenological approach one is approaching the phenomena in an overly simplistic way, concentrating on apparent external similarities while ignoring differences and the deeper aspects.

Unfortunate as it may be, this trend is still very much in practice, as is evident by examining for instance the standard *Encyclopaedia of Religion*. Under the entry "Secret Societies," George Weckman mentions several distinctly different phenomena, such as the Melanesian Dukduk society; the Poro society in Sierra Leone; the Mau Mau society in Kenya; Chinese secret societies such as White Lotus, Dragon Flower, and Big Sword, but also the Boxers; the Triad societies in Hong Kong; Native American groups such as the Kwakiutl; Freemasons; Ku Klux Klan; Rosicrucians; the Mafia; the medieval Knights Templar; the Thugs of India; and finally, the Assassins of Persia.[43] Now, all of these different groups fall under the same heading, that is, "secret societies," which can be interpreted as implicitly meaning that, for instance, the Ku Klux Klan constitutes basically the same phenomenon as the Rosicrucians.[44] Such a claim needs to be challenged. Even a casual look at the aims of these two groups, of the doctrines they are transmitting, their organizational structures, etc., leaves in my opinion no doubt that we are dealing with two distinctly different phenomena. What, then, is the *raison d'etre* of including such a variety of organizations under the notion of secret societies? The main argument for doing so is the occurrence of what is often referred to as a "ritualistic usage of secrecy." Secrecy is, however, a tricky phenomenon. I will return to this in connection with masonic initiatory societies.

There exists a number of classifications or divisions of secret societies. But, as we will see, these are usually not as reliable as one might hope. Heckethorn makes an initial demarcation between religious and political secret societies. He then proceeds to make a more detailed division into seven groups:

1. Religious: such as the Egyptian or Eleusinian Mysteries.
2. Military: Knights Templars. 3. Judiciary: Vehmgerichte.
4. Scientific: Alchymists. 5. Civil: Freemasons. 6. Political: Carbonari. 7. Anti-Social: Garduna.[45]

This classification is rather arbitrary. For instance, in order to label the "Alchymists" as "Scientific" one is forced to ignore the spiritual aspect

of alchemy. It is also questionable whether there ever existed any organized secret societies of alchemists. Further, labeling Freemasonry as
"Civil" is an extreme simplification of this multifaceted phenomenon. In
fact, Freemasonry can be interpreted in so many different ways that it
is almost impossible to find one adequate and representative term by
which all the various aspects are included. There are religious, moral,
mystic, esoteric, "civil," etc., aspects of Freemasonry.

As mentioned, in 1940 the University of Missouri published an
important study that has a direct bearing on the present subject. It is a
sociological study of secret societies or fraternalism in the United States
by Noel P. Gist.[46] At the outset Gist limits the scope of the work by
defining his use of the term "secret society":

> For the purpose of this investigation a secret society may be
> defined as any social grouping not based on blood relationship
> which possesses some ritualistic element of secrecy, the knowl-
> edge of which is confined to initiated members.[47]

The key notion of Gist's definition is, thus, the ritualistic element of
secrecy. We shall return to secrecy in due course. According to Gist, it
is possible to discern a functional division between different groups that
make use of ritualistic secrecy. All in all, thirteen categories are enumer-
ated by Gist, but he emphasizes that there are no clear-cut borders
between these categories, and that several of the societies can be as-
signed to two or more of the following categories.

> 1) Benevolent and philanthropic societies; 2) Insurance societies;
> 3) Revolutionary and reformist societies; 4) Patriotic societies;
> 5) Professional and occupational societies; 6) Religious orders;
> 7) Mystical and occult societies; 8) Military societies and orders
> of knighthood; 9) College "social" and recreational societies;
> 10) Honor societies; 11) Abstinence societies; 12) Convivial
> societies; 13) Criminal societies[48]

The category of foremost interest for the present study of Western esoteric rituals of initiation is the seventh, or "Mystical and occult societies." To this category Gist counts Rosicrucian orders and the *Esoteric
Section* of the *Theosophical Society*. Other orders that outwardly, that is,
by their names, warrant classification into this group, but which in their
essence are rather conventional and whose elements of mysticism or
occultism may be limited to their names only, include: *the Ancient Arabic
Order of Nobles of the Mystic Shrine, the Mystic Order of the Veiled Proph-*

ets of the Enchanted Realm, the Mystic Nobles of Granada, and the *Mysterious Order of the Witches of Salem.* It is important to note that Gist does not consider for instance the masonic *Ancient and Accepted Scottish Rite* as a mystical society, even though their eighteenth degree is related to Rosicrucianism, which Gist apparently considers to belong to the mystical societies.[49] While discussing the category of Mystical and Occult Societies, Gist makes the following remark:

> While secret in the sense that they withhold portions of their teachings and rituals from those excluded from their portals, these societies appear to differ both in structure and function from the common types of secret orders: their rituals, their symbols, their doctrines, and their objectives place them on the periphery of the world of secrecy rather than definitely within its sphere.[50]

This is a statement that needs to be questioned. Many so-called Rosicrucian orders that Gist include in the category of Mystical and Occult Societies do not differ in their structure from other Western initiatory systems, particularly not when we look at the structure of their rituals of initiation (for instance, *Der Orden des Gold- und Rosenkreuzes* of the eighteenth century, *The Societas Rosicruciana In Anglia,* and the inner Order of the Golden Dawn, the *R.R. et A.C.*).

The basic criterion of secret societies as viewed by Gist, that is, the ritualistic use of secrecy, contains the important aspect of dealing with something in a *ritualistic* manner. Treating secrecy ritually is apparently different from ordinary or profane use of secrecy since it tends to imply some sort of spiritual dimension of secrecy. However, in the already mentioned *Encyclopaedia of Religion,* the secrecy of secret societies tends to be regarded as strictly profane:

> The term *secret society* can be used to describe all groups whose membership or very existence is unknown to nonmembers or that keep certain of their practices or conceptions hidden from nonmembers no matter how public or recognized they are as a group.[51]

This definition is highly problematic when we try to apply it to masonic societies. First, membership in masonic initiatory societies is far from always held secret. Second, the idea of keeping certain practices or conceptions hidden from nonmembers is really an all too common practice to be considered as pertaining exclusively to "secret societies." For instance, tactics within a soccer team are rarely disclosed to outsiders; this does, however, not mean that Liverpool FC is a secret society. However, Weckman further discusses five "distinguishing features" of a religious secret society. First, the secret society is a "voluntary or selective group within a natural community." This implies that it is up to the society whether or not a person will be allowed to join. Second is the idea of secrecy, which, however, does not have to include the existence of the society, nor its membership. Instead, the secrecy may pertain to their "activities, rituals, texts, doctrines, myths, and offices." The third major feature is the practice of initiation. Related to initiation is the fourth characteristic, the hierarchical structure of the society. The fifth and last point is the occurrence of a certain myth concerning the origins of the society that is "central to its self-consciousness." These five distinguishing features are to be found in all of the initiatory societies whose rituals of initiation are analyzed in this book.[52]

Secrecy and Masonic Initiatory Societies

Freemasonry is often regarded as a prime example of a secret society, but many contemporary masonic writers question this.[53] Instead, they often describe masonry as a society with secrets in order to emphasize that masonry is not an anti-social movement. More than a few scholars have experienced difficulties in getting access to certain masonic libraries and archives, but it should be stressed that the mere strict privacy of a society, be it masonic or otherwise, does not by definition make it a secret society.[54] It is the ritualistic usage of secrecy that is of interest to us in the present discussion.

> Nowadays it is fashionable among Freemasons to claim that Freemasonry is not a secret society. Clearly, that attitude results from the desire to clear Freemasonry of undeserved blames that it would conceal anti-social activities. However, it also betrays that most Freemasons are not aware that the term "secret society" is not only used for groups that try to hide their existence, or of which the members try to hide their membership, but also for groups which guard a secret. And in that last respect, Freemasonry is a secret society.[55]

Snoek highlights the fact that the notion of secret societies often implies something negative in the public mind, and that masons therefore often find themselves in a defensive position in which they seek to distance masonry from the popular conception of a secret society. However, masonic apologetics, anti-masonic polemics, as well as authors writing for a popular audience rarely take into account *how* secrecy is actually used, and *why* it is used the way that it is. Furthermore, the use of secrecy is not limited to secret societies.

Bolle has argued that a central secret, or *mysterium magnum*, is central to any religion.[56] This central secret is, according to Bolle, the very innermost core of a specific religion, and Bolle attaches "significance to the fact that mystics present us with the most detailed formulations when it comes to the central mystery of religions."[57] In my opinion, it is questionable whether the central mystery of religion (presuming there is only *a* mystery and not a number of mysteries) constitutes a secret in the normal sense of the word—that is, knowledge of some sort, held by a group of persons, that is not communicated to the public at large. However, supposing that there is such a thing as a central secret to religion, the obvious question is what this secret actually encompasses.

> Any religion—and not only the ones known as mystery religions—has its central secret, its mysterium magnum. And as soon as we say this, we have to check ourselves once more and remember that the privacy of a group and the mystery of a religion are not the same. When a religion reveals its secret, that secret is not one among many. It is *the* secret.[58]

We are, in other words, not dealing with a socially based secrecy, such as the privacy of a group. Rather, *the* secret appears to be a specific kind of knowledge connected to the *raison d'etre* of the religion itself. In other words, *the* secret that Bolle discusses is the equivalent of such notions as the *essence* of a religion, or the *truth* of a religion. Any sensible historian of religion would hesitate to venture into these topics as they constitute notorious minefields, better left for the philosopher of religion or the theologian to tackle. Nevertheless, secrets *are* fundamental aspects of religions, (but perhaps not in the sense of Bolle's central secret), just as secrets are fundamental aspects of human society at large. The restriction of knowledge is one aspect where power (understood in its social capacity) is maintained, and consequently an important aspect of the structure of society. In religion, secrecy is present in various ways. Significantly, it is in mystical traditions that secrecy is used most extensively. Mystic traditions ranging from the Hindu and Buddhist guarded Tantric texts, the supposed secret teachings of Sakyamuni, the poetry of the Sufis, to the teachings of kabbalists and Christian mystics all have in common that their doctrines are restricted to initiates, and that their discourses are veiled in a symbolic language, which for uninitiated is often difficult to fully comprehend. In the gnosticism of late antiquity the very notion of *gnosis* itself was regarded as a closely guarded secret.

In Western esotericism secrecy is used on different levels, as it were. According to Faivre, it is possible to discern three different ways where secrecy is employed in esoteric discourses.[59] The first group of esoteric texts "seem to be designed to mean something other than what they appear to mean at face value," and the author of such texts "seems desirous to give the impression that he conceals while revealing and reveals while concealing."[60] The dialectical interplay between concealment and unveiling forms an important aspect of Western esoteric rituals of initiation as well, where each degree often points toward a further secret for the initiate to penetrate. This is paralleled by esoteric discourses in which the reader is confronted by numerous references to other texts:

> Even so, the person who makes the effort to read all (or, rather, as many as possible) of the texts hinted at, finds himself nevertheless confronted by a circular discourse made of images and symbols, a veil, as it were. It is as if that veil constituted the message itself. The circularity or paradox is that the text says countless things and, at the same time, says one main thing to which we readers are not privy.[61]

This can be compared with the so-called allusive method, which, according to Snoek, is an intrinsic part of Freemasonry. The allusive method means that a ritual, for instance, always has more than one meaning, but it is only the persons who are initiated that know which other meanings that are definitely intended as well. Or in the words of Snoek:

> The allusive method always refers to more than one layer of meaning. There are not only the primary meaning of the phrase used, and the immediate allusive meaning, but, for someone who is amenable to it, at least one extra meaning is added because the text quoted refers to another text, either from the same, or from another book within the referential corpus.[62]

The idea that the veil constitutes the message itself is, in my opinion, of utmost importance to the understanding of Western esoteric rituals of initiation. A further aspect of this is that the understanding of the rituals changes as the candidates advance through the degrees. In this context, however, it is not so much the ritual itself as the experience of it that constitutes the message.[63] It is the experience of the ritual that constitutes the message—or perhaps more adequately, the experience *and interpretation* of the ritual is the esoteric message. It is often claimed that the secrets of Freemasonry and similar orders are noncommunicable, despite the fact that the rituals themselves have been revealed to the public. In other words, the purpose of the secrecy is not so much a matter of keeping the rituals secret as to keep that which is noncommunicable secret. This conclusion is strengthened by Faivre's second category of esoteric discourses' usage of secrecy, that is, cases where the secret of a text is the noncommunication of something that is not transmissible. Or, in Faivre's words:

> Esoteric transmission cannot, so it seems, unveil secrets. Rather, it is the noncommunication of what is not transmissible that constitutes the secret.[64]

Ergo, the secret of a Western esoteric ritual of initiation is the experience of undergoing the ritual—an experience that by definition is noncommunicable. The experience of undergoing a ritual of initiation is tantamount to that of a mystical experience, and one characteristic of mystical experience is the difficulty in expressing and describing it verbally. Snoek has commented on the masonic secret:

> The secret concerned, however, is nothing unethical, but just the experience of going through the ritual of the first degree, which turns one into an Entered Apprentice Freemason. Like any other experience, this cannot be communicated to someone else in any other way than letting that person go through it as well, which will turn him automatically into a Freemason too. So, this is the kind of secret which cannot be divulged.[65]

Furthermore, previous scholars such as Eliade have stated that a rite of initiation is supposed to change the innermost nature of the initiate and thereby make him or her a new person. In my opinion this is also the case in Western esoteric rituals of initiation, but it is not so much the experience as the *interpretation* of it that has a transmutative effect upon the initiate. Esoteric discourses, and I suggest that this includes esoteric rituals of initiation as well, are essentially interpretative.[66] It is through an act of interpretation of the experience of the ritual, *and the ritual as such*, that the ritual of initiation becomes an initiation in the strict sense of the word. The interaction of experience and interpretation is essential to the understanding of rituals of initiation. Without the experience there is nothing but meaningless symbols for the esotericist to interpret, and without the interpretation the experience fails to become initiatic.

The third and last way where secrecy is used in esoteric discourses, according to Faivre, is a more or less systematic "desoccultation of the occult."[67] In the context of esoteric rituals of initiation, the unveiling of explicitly transmissible secrets can be divided into three different sorts. First, the actual ritual of initiation itself. When studying early masonic exposures from the eighteenth century it is clear that it is the rituals that are considered to be the masons' prime secret. Second, the "traditional secrets," which are communicated during the ritual. These consist of the words, tokens, and grips, steps, and some standardized questions and answers.[68] The main object of the "traditional secrets" is to allow Freemasons to recognize each other. Third, certain legends and teachings connected to each degree, such as the masonic legend of Hiram, which is to be found in the Master Mason degree as well as in a number of additional degrees. The nature of these legends and teachings vary from ritual to ritual, but generally it can be said that they form the mythological setting of the ritual.

One final word needs to be said concerning secrecy in the sense of privacy of a group. In each and every masonic ritual of initiation the initiates take solemn oaths of never divulging what has happened during the initiation, and sometimes the very existence of the society is to be kept secret. At certain historical periods such oaths were unquestionably of utmost importance since masonic societies were persecuted by the authorities. For the most part, especially today, this type of secrecy is not necessary since there is very little persecution conducted against masonry, but the oaths are still used in the rituals. Today, this can be considered as, to use Snoek's words, "part of the elegant game which Freemasonry is," just as the "traditional secrets" are.[69]

Is masonry a secret society? The obvious answer to that question is: yes. However, as we have seen, secrecy plays a dominant role in esoteric discourses in general, and the noncommunicable experience of undergoing a ritual of initiation is universal. In other words, Western esoteric rituals of initiation are intrinsically connected to secrecy, but to a secrecy that ultimately is dependent on the individual initiate's personal experience and interpretation of the ritual. Secrecy is part of every initiation in the sense that it is only by undergoing the initiation that one will take part in it. But it must be understood that secrecy is part of the initiation, and not vice versa. Initiation is the prime characteristic of masonry—not secrecy. Therefore, I am of the opinion that it is more adequate to speak of *Masonic initiatory societies* as this captures what these societies are all about—initiations.

Masonic Initiatory Societies

Throughout this book Masonic Initiatory Societies refer to societies whose activities and structure are centered on rituals of initiation of a very specific type, referred to as masonic rituals of initiation. The word "masonic" is in this context not interpreted in its restricted, or legal, sense as referring exclusively to the society of Freemasons that officially was founded in 1717. Rather, it refers to a certain type of rituals originating from Freemasonry, but not necessarily having any links to an official masonic organization.

During the seventeenth century various masonic lodges existing throughout the British Isles used specific rituals in order to admit new members, but also to differentiate between newcomers and more experienced members within the lodges. In chapter 4 the development of these rituals to a tri-gradal system, from the end of the seventeenth century to around 1730, will be analyzed. Chapter 5 deals with the development of so-called high, or additional, degrees that sprang from the original three Craft degrees. Most of these rituals were restricted to Freemasons, but there gradually appeared more and more orders that had no formal links to Freemasonry whatsoever, even though they used rituals originating from Freemasonry, either directly or indirectly. One of the most influential of such orders during the latter part of the nineteenth century was the *Hermetic Order of the Golden Dawn*, whose rituals are analyzed in chapter 6. During the twentieth century Western esoteric rituals of initiation have been practiced in an unprecedented number, and many of the practitioners are probably unaware of the masonic origin of their rituals. An illustrative example of this are the Wicca rituals created by Gerald Gardner in the 1950s, which are analyzed in chapter 7. Today, Wicca is one of the fastest growing new religious movements in the Western culture.

Masonic initiatory societies have been part of the Western culture for more than three centuries, but it is difficult to ascertain what function these societies have had, and continue to have, in the society at large. From a sociological perspective it is tempting to interpret these societies with Turner's concept of communitas. According to Turner, communitas is generated by liminality in society, and is contrasted to social-structural relationships. It forms anti-structures within the social structure of society at large, and thereby serves to maintain the societal structure. Communitas is characterized as being undifferentiated, equalitarian, direct, and nonrational, but tending to develop structures of its own. Although masonic initiatory societies often promulgate such equalitarian notions as a universal brotherhood, they are at the same time highly hierarchical in their structure. Furthermore, while certain masonic societies had an anti-social agenda, most masonic societies can be characterized as being conservative in their view of societal changes. In fact, all attempts to reach an overall definition of the function of masonic initiatory societies are bound to fail because there is a wide variety of different types of masonic initiatory societies. Each society must be analyzed individually, and placed in its proper historical context. Moreover, one and the same society may answer different needs of different members.

Masonic Rituals of Initiation

It is important to stress the fact that practically no studies of rituals of initiation make any references to masonic rituals of initiation, even less attempt to analyze this particular body of rituals. One may ask what has caused this apparent lack of interest from a scholarly perspective. The reason can by no means be due to a lack of sources as there are literally thousands of manuscripts of masonic rituals of initiation in public and private libraries throughout the world. Printed books and periodicals on the subject of masonry run in the tens of thousands, many of which contain reliable reprints of rituals, and literally millions of both men and women have been initiated into one form or an other of Freemasonry since the early eighteenth century. There is, however, a growing body of literature that deals exclusively with masonic rituals of initiation, but unfortunately this literature often fails to reach a broader academic attention. This specialized type of literature deals to a large extent with the development of masonic rituals, such as the development of the Craft degrees of Freemasonry.

When studying masonic rituals of initiation it might be useful to try to define what the basic components are of this particular form of ritual. The structure of most masonic rituals of initiation closely follows that found in the three Craft degrees of Freemasonry, and this structure can be divided into a number of basic "building blocks" (Table 2.1). These building blocks do not necessarily always follow in the same order, nor are they always present in a masonic ritual of initiation. Nevertheless, these building blocks more often than not form the basic components of masonic rituals of initiation, and they can thus been seen as the skeleton of the rituals to which is added the particular symbols, mythology, and ritual aspects of each individual ritual. Depending on the particular rituals, some of these additions are extremely elaborate, while others are less complex.

Table 2.1. The building blocks of a masonic ritual of initiation.

1) THE OPENING of the Lodge during which the candidate is usually not present.

2) ADMISSION into the Lodge at which the candidate answers a number of questions.

3) CIRCUMAMBULATIONS around the Lodge, often symbolic of an ordeal.

4) OBLIGATION never to divulge the secrets of the degree (often the sign, grip, and word) but often also certain ethical rules, which the candidate swears to observe.

5) FORMAL ADMISSION into the degree.

6) INSTRUCTION in the secrets of the degree, the sign, the grip, and the word, but also in the Order's particular teaching.

7) The giving of one or more VISIBLE TOKENS, such as gloves or apron, sometimes also a new name or motto.

8) CLOSING of the Lodge, during which the candidate is present.

Eighteenth-Century Masonic Terminology

The most common way of referring to the practice of masonic rituals of initiation in early-English eighteenth-century exposures is with terms such as "to admit," "to enter," and "to make" a mason, and in later French exposures rituals of initiation are most frequently referred to as "receptions." One of the earliest usages of the term "admission" can be found in *The Dumfries No. 4 MS.* (c. 1710), and it is later to be found in exposures such as *The Grand Mystery Laid Open* (1726), *The Mystery of Freemasonry* (1730), and *Masonry Dissected* (1730). Although not as common in French exposures, the term is nonetheless to be found in exposures such as *La Réception Mystérieuse* (1738) and *Le Secret des Franc-Maçons* (1742). The term "to enter" (in its variants "entry" and "enter'd") is to be found in *The Dumfries No. 4 MS.* and *A Mason's Examination* (1723). The expression to be "made a Mason" is to be found, for instance, in *The Mystery of Freemasonry.* The later French usage of the term "reception" is to be found in most French exposures of the period, such as *Réception d'un Frey-Maçon* (1737), *La Réception Mystérieuse, Le Secret des Franc-Maçons* (1742–44), and *Le Catéchisme des Francs-Maçons* (1744).

The first usage of the term "ceremony" in reference to masonic rituals in an exposure is to be found in *A Mason's Examination,* and it is then frequently to be found in later English exposures, such as *A Mason's Confession* (? 1727) and *A Defence of Masonry* (1730–1731). The term "rite" is not as frequently used as "ceremony" in the first half of the eighteenth century, but is to be found in *A Mason's Confession*, *A Defence of Masonry*, and the spoof *A Letter from the Grand Mistress* (1724), (in the two former texts the terms "rite" and "ceremony" are used as synonyms). In French exposures the term "ceremony" is used almost as frequently as "reception," and it is thus to be found in exposures such as *La Réception Mystérieuse*, *Le Secret des Franc-Maçons*, *Le Catéchisme des Francs-Maçons*, *Le Parfait Maçon* (1744), and *L'Ordre des Franc-Maçons Trahi* (1745).

Significantly enough, the first instance of the word "initiation" is to be found as late as 1730, in the two exposures *The Mystery of Freemasonry* ("initiated") and Prichard's *Masonry Dissected* ("initiated" and "uninitiated"), which might be a reference to the fact that the Master Mason degree had by now been fully developed. In French exposures "initiation" is used repeatedly from 1738 (*La Réception Mystérieuse*) onward, and masons are referred to as "initiates" from at least the same year.[70]

Concluding Remarks

The study of rites and rituals has been part of the academic study of history of religions and anthropology since the latter part of the nineteenth century. It emerges from the literature of these academic disciplines that rites are an important aspect of human behavior. In this book I have chosen to use the word *ritual* as I am analyzing ritual *texts*—I am not conducting any observations of *live* masonic rites of initiation in a systematic manner. Neither am I basing my research on in-depth interviews with practitioners of this type of rite of initiation. When referring to the actual *ritual performance* of the initiation I have decided to use the word *rite*, while the word *ritual* refers to written scripts.

The present study is devoted to a hitherto neglected form of ritual of initiation that I have chosen to term Masonic Rituals of Initiation. These rituals are to be found within a specific type of organization of Western origin that I call Masonic Initiatory Societies. In chapter 4 I will analyze the role model, as it were, of all Masonic Rituals of Initiation—the Craft degrees of Freemasonry.

Chapter 3

Historical Background

Ancient and Medieval Sources

Western esotericism does not refer to a phenomenon that suddenly appeared at the end of the fifteenth century without historical roots or background. It is an amalgam of various religious and philosophical components reaching back into the Hellenistic world, if not even further back. The most important components were born in the syncretistic milieu around the Mediterranean during the centuries before and after AD. The Platonic and Pythagorean philosophies are two early important influences on Western esotericism, but also the various forms of gnosticism with its emphasis on *gnosis*, the sacred knowledge that could bring salvation for the gnostic, were important sources of inspiration. During the Renaissance the rediscovery of the *Corpus Hermeticum* brought yet another source of inspiration, along with the Jewish mystical system of the kabbalah. Perhaps the most important Neoplatonic philosopher who influenced early esotericism during the Middle Ages was Denys the Aeropagite with his theory of a hierarchy of angels and of the universe. The Aeropagite's worldview continued to be important during the Renaissance, especially for the angelic (or demonic) magic of Pico and Agrippa.

Although the importance of astrology and alchemy declined during the Middle Ages, these "sciences" did not completely disappear from the scene. There were relatively few practitioners during this period because few texts were available. In the twelfth century, however, a new interest in alchemy and astrology followed the translations that began to appear from the Arabic. Robert of Chester translated into Latin the first alchemical treatise that became accessible to Europeans.[1] Soon many other translations followed, which triggered a great interest in these sciences.

Magic during the Middle Ages consisted primarily of so-called popular magic, which in some instances contained practices and beliefs from "pagan" cultures, such as the Norse and the Irish.[2] The most popular form of magic though, was the conjuring of spirits, or necromancy. According to Kieckhefer, the aims of the necromancers fall into three main categories. First, they tried to affect other people's minds and wills. This took the form of driving somebody mad, or causing him or her to fall madly in love. Second, to cause illusions. Examples of illusions are the illusory raising of the dead, or the conjuring of an extravagant feast. Third, the necromancer sought to discern secret things, whether of the past, present, or future. Finding lost or stolen property, to identify the identity of a thief are some examples of this last category.[3] The necromancy of the Middle Ages was very pragmatic in nature, and its textbooks were full of instructions for such diverse aims as "arousing a woman's love," "obtaining a castle," and "invisibility." The necromancer would use demons and spirits with names such as Astaroth, Sathan, Diles, Gana, and Zelantes in their magical conjurations.[4] These demonic names stood in sharp contrast to Ficino's natural magic in the Renaissance.

The "New Platonic Academy" of Florence

In the second half of the fifteenth century there gathered around the Renaissance philosopher Marsilio Ficino (1433–1499) a group of learned men that eventually became known as the "New Platonic Academy" at Florence, supposedly founded in 1462.[5] It was in the intellectual milieu around Ficino and his followers that Western esotericism, as it is viewed today, emerged from the various sources of late antiquity and the Middle Ages. Christian mysticism, Neoplatonism, ancient and medieval magic, gnosticism, and Jewish Kabbalah merged together with the hermetism of the *Corpus Hermeticum*. The importance of hermetism for Western esotericism has been pointed out primarily by the works of Walker and Yates. The *Corpus Hermeticum*, which Ficino translated into Latin in 1471, was regarded to have the mythical Hermes Trismegistus as its author. For about two hundred years the *Corpus Hermeticum* was considered as an ancient text, and Hermes Trismegistus the contemporary of Moses. However, in 1614 Isaac Casaubon (1559–1614), a Protestant from Geneva who lived in England, proved that the Corpus was of a much later date, namely from the first centuries of our era.[6]

For Ficino the so-called hermetic tradition was closely connected with the practice of magic, and as the hermetic philosophy began to spread over Renaissance Europe, a revival of magic followed in its footsteps. According to Yates the magic of the Renaissance was more sophisticated, philosophic, and artistic. The barbarous names and demonic entities that were invoked and conjured during the Middle Ages sharply contrasted to the natural magic of Ficino. For Ficino the universe was made up of mystical links, or correspondences, that continuously interacted. The seven planets influenced the sublunary world with their qualities through the mystical links. The fundamental point in Ficino's magic was that the magician, with knowledge of these mystical links, could manipulate them, and thus cause results according to his will. For instance, the malignant influence of Saturn was considered to cause melancholy, and to avoid this Ficino would seek to attract the influence from a positive planet, such as Venus. In order to do this he would surround himself with objects that were related to Venus through the mystical links. These objects could be natural things such as precious stones, herbs, or animals. They could also be man-made: a painting or a poem that was inspired by Venus was considered as linked to that planet and would accordingly help to diminish the influence of Saturn. Eating food related to Venus, such as white sugar and the white of egg, also greatly assisted the magician in his effort to reach his goal.[7] The use of talismans as a means to attract the influence of planets was viewed as a highly powerful aid, but also a very dangerous one, since the Church condemned its use. Ficino was careful in advising the use of talismans, but, as Yates pointed out, he did discuss talismans in his work *De vita coelitus comparanda*.

According to Walker, the magic of Ficino used the human *spiritus* as its medium through which it worked. The spirit was the link between body and soul, and the human functions of sense-perception, imagination, and motor activity were connected to the *spiritus*. The human *spiritus* was made up of the four elements, and it formed a corporeal vapor that flowed from the brain, where it had its center, through the nervous system. Furthermore, the human spirit was connected to the *spiritus mundi*, which mostly consisted of the fifth element—*quinta essentia* or ether. Ficino considered music as especially connected to the human *spiritus*, since it used the same element as its medium—air. But more important than that, the sound consisted of movements where visionary impressions merely transmitted static images. These two reasons caused sound to affect the spirit more effectively than sight, and since it is in the *spiritus* that magic works, sounds were considered more potent than visual impressions. What the magician saw or felt was thus secondary to what he heard.

Ficino used music in his magical workings. He composed hymns or put music to such texts as the *Orphic Hymns*,[8] which he then used as a prominent part of his magical operations. However, Ficino's theory of music won just a few followers among his contemporary musical theorists, probably due to the magical aspect of his theory. The fear of being associated with magical practices became more and more apparent as the evolution of magic with Pico and Agrippa turned toward angels and demons.[9]

  Ficino had various sources for his magic. The two chief sources were the Christian Mass, and several Neoplatonic texts.[10] Other important sources of inspiration, especially with regard to talismans, were such medieval handbooks on magic (often called *grimoires*), as the writings of Alkindi, Avicenna, Roger Bacon, and the *Picatrix*. For Ficino it was important to maintain that he did not use demons or other entities in his magic. His magic was natural; that is, he restricted his manipulations to the planetary correspondences in nature. He sought the influences of impersonal planetary spirits on the spirit and body (not aiming higher: at the rational soul)—and he was content with that, or so he claimed. These impersonal planetary spirits worked through the *Spiritus Mundi* to affect the human *spiritus*. The great difference between these impersonal spirits and demons was that they were not supposed to possess a soul (as opposed to the demons), and therefore they could not act directly on man's rational soul (which the demons could do).

  One of those who had gathered round Marsilio Ficino in Florence, was the young Giovanni Pico della Mirandola (1463–1494). Pico was highly influenced by the learned Ficino and his magic, but he carried magic further than Ficino had dared. He denied Ficino's thesis that certain sublunary objects were more influenced by the planetary qualities than others and claimed that the celestial influences were of a universal nature that affected the whole sublunary world on an equal basis. It was useless to use certain objects such as stones or herbs to try to influence one's spirit. What Pico ventured to do was exactly what Ficino had avoided, namely, to use demons in his magical operations. Pico claimed, however, to be in possession of a powerful protection in this dangerous form of magic—kabbalah. As one of the first Christians to use the Jewish mystical tradition of kabbalah, Pico introduced it to Western esotericism where it has since held a prominent position.[11] Basically kabbalah views the universe as composed of ten spheres or Sephiroth arranged in a diagram called the Tree of Life. The Tree of Life is the manifestation of God out of the negative existence. By a mystical ascent through the Sephiroth from Malkuth to Kether the kabbalist reaches simultaneously knowledge of God, the universe, and himself. This idea rests upon the basic assumption that man is a microcosm of macrocosm, since he is created in the image of God. Furthermore, kabbalah is also characterized by an emphasis on the importance of numbers and letters, and based on this emphasis various kabbalistic methods have been

developed that are concerned with detecting hidden meanings in religious texts such as the Old Testament. According to Yates, Pico divided
kabbalah into two main branches:

(1) *Ars combinandi*, the art of combining Hebrew letters.

(2) 'A way of capturing the powers of superior things,' or the
powers of spirits and angels.[12]

The second branch is obviously connected with the practice of magic
and capturing the powers of spirits and angels implies the use of demons (i.e., spirits with a personal soul). Pico's practice of magic, which
is not restricted to impersonal spirits, and the use of kabbalah as a
safeguard for the magician, greatly influenced the magic of the Renaissance. It is important to note that Pico's magic, which made use of
supernatural beings, exploited the borderland between magic and religion. Or to quote Yates:

The invoking, or conjuring, of angels forms an intrinsic part of
the system, difficult to define, on the borderline of religious
contemplation and magic.[13]

Walker points out the dangers inherent in the two forms of magic from
the point of view of the Church. The natural or nondemonic magic was
a threat to religion because it claimed to obtain the same results as
religion—without a supernatural agent. The demonic or angelic magic
of Pico was a threat to the Church because it could be viewed as a rival
religion—and the idea of rival religions was of course unacceptable
for the Church, since the Christian revelation was considered unique
and exclusive.[14]

The Spread of Western Esotericism across Europe

The Renaissance linguist Johannes Reuchlin (1455–1522) was the author of two important kabbalistic works; *De verbo mirifico* (1494), and
De arte cabbalistica (1517).[15] The latter work was, according to Yates, to
become the "Bible" of the Christian kabbalists.[16] It was the first full
treatise on kabbalah written by a Christian and it presented a clear
presentation of the Christian kabbalistic theory and practice. Reuchlin
was heavily influenced by Pico, and in *De verbo mirifico* and *De arte
cabbalistica* he presented a "Kabbalistic proof" of the existence of the
holy trinity, which he had picked up from Pico.[17] Reuchlin ascribed great

powers to the Pentagrammaton (IHSUH), which for him was the Christian sacred name, just as the Tetragrammaton (IHVH) was for the Jews. In this name was not only the power and strength of all, but it was also seen as a kabbalistic proof of the truth of the Christian doctrine of the Holy Trinity. Charles Zika sums up the meanings of the word to the Renaissance kabbalists:

> (. . .) by this word man can perform wonderful works beyond human strength, and although constituted in nature, hold dominion over it. This word is a sign of the divine union in so far as it is the source of man's superhuman activity.[18]

In the German-speaking part of Europe, the works of the enigmatic Benedictine abbot Johannes Trithemius (1462–1516) had acquired many followers, most notably Agrippa and Paracelsus. His work *Steganographia*, which was published posthumously in 1606, treated a peculiar art of magic disguised in the form of cryptography. His aim was to enable the magician to have access to a universal knowledge, and to allow him to communicate over great distances. Furthermore, the ultimate goal of Trithemius's occult writings was a mystical vision of God, or the conveyance of the magician's soul from earth to heaven. It was this ultimate goal that, according to Trithemius, separated his peculiar form of magic from the demonic magic of sorcerers and witches, a debased form of magic that Trithemius strongly condemned.[19]

Heinrich Cornelius Agrippa (1486–1535)[20] greatly admired Trithemius and met him in 1509–1510, and even dedicated the first draft of his famous book *De occulta philosophia* to Trithemius. The book was not published until 1533, two years before Agrippa's death.[21] This work is a compendium or handbook in Renaissance esotericism. The natural magic of Ficino and the kabbalah of Pico are combined with the art of alchemy, and thus the three "jewels" of Western esotericism: magic, astrology, and alchemy are linked together. Before Agrippa, hardly any effort was made to link alchemy with magic and astrology. Ficino and Pico, for instance, showed very little, if any, interest in alchemy, but with Agrippa alchemy decidedly entered the world of magic and astrology.[22]

Yates describes Agrippa as "something of an Erasmian evangelical, combining pre-Reformation humanism with an attempt to provide a 'powerful' philosophy to accompany evangelical reform."[23] The idea of using the occult philosophy as a powerful rejuvenating component to Christianity became popular in the sixteenth century. The reformation and the counterreformation caused many esotericists to view the Christian religion as in need of something to regain its vitality and spiritual power.

For Giordano Bruno, for instance, this "something" was the hermetism of the *Corpus Hermeticum*.[24]

The *De occulta philosophia* is divided into three books, according to the threefold nature of the universe: the elemental world, the celestial world, and the intellectual world.[25] The three worlds are set in a hierarchy with the elemental world (the sublunary world) at the bottom and the intellectual world at the top. The influences from God descend through the three worlds "through the angels in the intellectual world, to the stars in the celestial world, and then thence to the elements and all things composed of them in the terrestrial world."[26] Accordingly, the three parts of the book deal with the appropriate magic of each world. The natural magic of Ficino for the natural world, celestial magic, or the art to attract and use influences from the stars for the celestial world, and finally, ceremonial magic that is directed to the angelic spirits of the intellectual world. For Agrippa the magical power was more potent the higher up in the worlds the magician got it. The ceremonial magic of the intellectual world was thus more potent than the celestial magic (also called mathematical magic since it operates with numbers) of the celestial world. The use of celestial and ceremonial magic exposed the magician to the grave danger of being influenced by demons, but Agrippa argued that the use of kabbalah guaranteed the safety of the operator against demons on all levels. This argument Agrippa clearly derived from Pico. Thus Agrippa, just as Pico, aimed higher with his magic than Ficino openly dared to do. Another great difference between Agrippa and Ficino, is that he advocated a "transitive" form of magic, to use Walkers terminology. This means that Agrippa's magic also aimed at influencing other people through the will of the magician, whereas Ficino's magic had been self-centered, not aiming at anyone except the magician himself. Concerning Agrippa Walker has the following to say:

> [Agrippa] exposes what Ficino, rather feebly, had tried to conceal: that his magic was really demonic. He also mixes it up with magic that aims at transitive, thaumaturgic effects, whereas Ficino's effects were subjective and psychological. Finally, and most importantly, by treating magic, pagan religion and Christianity as activities and beliefs of exactly the same kind, he demonstrates strikingly how dangerous Neoplatonic magic was from a Christian point of view.[27]

Agrippa's *De vanitate scientiarum* was published in 1526, five years earlier than *De occulta philosophia*, but written several years after the latter. In this work he examines all man's sciences and finds them all empty (including magic), and that all knowledge is in vain. The only thing that is not in vain is "the Word of God in the Scriptures through which we may come to know Jesus Christ."[28] Superficially, the *De vanitate scientiarum* seems to stand in sharp contrast to *De occulta philosophia* since it clearly states that the very magic that he advocates is empty and in vain. But if we bear in mind that magic or occult philosophy was for Agrippa not a goal in itself, but something that should be used as an aid in the evangelical reform, which ultimately aimed at bringing Christianity back to a closer knowledge of Jesus Christ, we come perhaps closer to understanding the enigma of this man.

The Esoteric Missions of Giordano Bruno and John Dee

There are several similarities between Giordano Bruno (1548–1600) and John Dee (1527–1608). Both were strongly influenced by the Neoplatonism of Ficino and Pico, the kabbalah of Pico, and by Agrippa's *De occulta philosophia*. They were both engaged in a spiritual mission, which was closely connected with Western esotericism, and they both failed in their quests and died viewed as dangerous sorcerers and heretics, with Bruno burned at the stake in 1600.

In her book *Giordano Bruno and the Hermetic Tradition* (1964), Yates has shown how Bruno was influenced by Ficino, Pico, and Agrippa, but also the importance of the *Corpus Hermeticum* for him. She traces the occult practices of Bruno, but, most importantly, she describes the philosophical and religious reform that Bruno proposed. It was a hermetic reform of society, based on the *Corpus Hermeticum*.[29] According to Couliano, the magic of the Renaissance in general—and Bruno's magic in particular—is a science that primarily (if not solely) works in the imaginative faculty of man. Magic is closely connected with eroticism and mnemonics, and it is vital to understand the significance of the latter two in order to fully understand the former. The magic that concerns us here is theoretically a science of the imaginary, which it explores through its own methods and seeks to manipulate at will. At its greatest degree of development, reached in the works of Giordano Bruno, magic is a means of control over the individual and the masses based on deep knowledge of personal and collective erotic impulses.[30]

The reason why Eros and magic are so closely connected, according to Couliano, is that they work in the same substance—the universal pneuma.[31] The universal pneuma is another term for the *Spiritus Mundi*, which is connected to the human *spiritus* or spirit. Magic, a phantasmic process, makes use of the continuity of the individual *spiritus* and the *spiritus mundi*. The goal of Bruno's magic is control over the imaginative faculty of the operator himself, as well as control over other individuals and crowds. The fundamental tool of the operator (or manipulator) is Eros—that which we love. The prior condition to magic, is faith.[32] The performer and the subject must believe in the efficacy of the magical act in order for it to work. Without this faith, magic is useless. The magician must create in his own imagination an idea that he truly believes in, and then transmit this imaginative idea into the subject's imagination. Couliano argues that the work of Bruno entitled *De vinculis in genere* in fact is a handbook that sums up Bruno's magic.[33]

The Neoplatonism and kabbalah of John Dee was heavily influenced by Giovanni Pico della Mirandola. Another influence on Dee's conception of the universe was Agrippa and his idea of dividing the universe into the natural, celestial, and supercelestial (intellectual) worlds. Yates argued in her work *The Occult Philosophy in the Elizabethan Age* (1979) that Dee sought to cause a religious reform based on a hermetic-kabbalistic philosophy.[34] Dee's mission failed and the Renaissance magus turned into Faust and Neoplatonism became suppressed. Dee did, however, leave an important testament among his published works that later turned up in the so-called Rosicrucian manifestos at the beginning of the seventeenth century. This testament is the *Monas Hieroglyphica* published in 1564.[35] According to Yates, the *Monas Hieroglyphica* is a statement of Dee's entire philosophy. The central point in this work is a certain figure—the hieroglyphic monad itself. The Rosicrucian manifestos, issued in the German-speaking world, were heavily influenced by Dee and one of them contains a version of the hieroglyphic monad. Yates makes a short analysis of this figure:

> Dee's monas is a combination of the signs of the seven planets, plus the symbol for the zodiacal sign, Aries, representing fire. It must have some astral significance; alchemical operations seem implied through the fire sign; it is also some kind of mathematics or geometry; but above all it is Cabala. It is related to 'the stupendous fabric of the Hebrew letters.' It is a 'Cabalistic grammar.' It can be mathematically, cabalistically, and anagogically explained.[36]

Dee himself regarded this work as highly important, and according to Peter J. French, Dee believed that "he had embodied universal wisdom in his Hermetic treatise, *Monas Hieroglyphica*."[37] Although the hieroglyphic monad itself is composed of simple geometric elements, such as a point within a circle, two lines in straight angle, etc., the symbolism of the monad is highly complex and it has been interpreted in a number of ways. Based on the twenty-two explanatory theorems of the original text, György Szonyi convincingly argues for a two-level interpretation of the monad: on the first level the monad is an astrological cosmogram, which explains the whole of Creation; on the second level it is a talismanic summary of the alchemical transmutation, that is, the spiritual quest that leads from unenlightened seeker to enlightened Magus.[38] The monad, on the latter plane of reference, can thus be interpreted as a visual aid to initiation set within the framework of sixteenth-century esotericism.

There is a very interesting side of Dee's magical operations, usually referred to as "Enochian magic."[39] Between 1581 and 1586, and again for a brief period in 1607, Dee communicated with angels. This communication was performed with the help of various mediums through a crystal, referred to as a "showstone." The most frequently used medium or "skryer" was the alchemist Edward Kelley who would get in contact with angels, and Dee recorded what was being communicated. Dee did not see this practice as a form of magic that was in opposition to his scientific worldview, but rather as a form of divine revelation through the angels. With the help of the angels Dee tried to penetrate deeper into the divine mysteries of the *Book of Nature*, a quest that was fueled by apocalyptic and millenarian speculations on the imminent Day of Judgement and the subsequent establishment of the New Jerusalem. The knowledge that the angels transmitted falls mainly into two categories. On the one hand, in 1583 the angels began to disclose to Dee and Kelley a particular mysterious language. It was considered to be an angelic language and, correctly interpreted, it was the original *lingua adamica* of Adam and Enoch. On the other hand, the angels (or spirits) described spiritual hierarchies. Clulee argues that the conversations they had with angels were in fact a form of magic, but a form that differed from the usual magic of the Renaissance. It is far removed from both the philosophical magic and occult philosophy of the Renaissance as well as from the natural magic he seems to have derived from Roger Bacon. Despite the similarity of the angelology and demonology to material from someone like Agrippa, there is no hint here of the Neoplatonic/Stoic theory of the spirit as the vehicle of magical influence, or of the role of the imagination, or of the sympathetic use of the divine qualities in lower things to draw down the influence of higher things. There is just the idea of the world populated by hosts of spirits, and magic as the straightforward theurgic conjuration of them.[40]

Even though Bruno and Dee failed in their individual efforts to reform religion and society, their ideas did, however, have some influence through the Rosicrucian manifestos. These manifestos triggered off a new interest in Western esotericism, an esotericism that was closely connected to the idea of secret brotherhoods and magical orders.

Christian Rosenkreutz and the Rosicrucian Manifestos

In Germany there appeared in 1614 a text entitled *Fama Fraternitatis* that today is generally regarded as the first Rosicrucian manifesto. Bound together with this text was another short work entitled *The General Reformation of the Whole Wide World*.[41] In the following two years two more texts appeared, *Confessio Fraternitatis* (1615) and *The chemical wedding of Christian Rosencreutz* (1616).[42]

The *Fama Fraternitas* describes how a certain C. R.[43] traveled in his early teens to the east, and there "got acquainted with the wise men of Damascus in Arabia, and beheld what great wonders they wrought, and how Nature was discovered unto them."[44] In Fez he learned mathematics, physics, magic—"for in those are they of Fez most skilful"— and the art of kabbalah. After some of years of studying these sciences he went to Spain where he hoped to share what he had learned in the Orient. This failed, however, because of their reluctance to learn something new and thereby admitting that their previous knowledge was full of errors. He was laughed at, so he left Spain and tried to spread his knowledge in other countries, but everywhere he met with the same reactions. He finally settled down in the German-speaking world where he founded a brotherhood called the *Fraternity of the Rosy Cross*, centered around a building called *Sancti Spiritus*. Originally the fraternity consisted of four members, but the number increased gradually. Central to their study was a certain "magical language and writing, with a large dictionary, which we yet daily use to God's praise and glory, and do find great wisdom therein." There was also a mysterious book called *Liber M*, which C. R. had translated and brought with him from Damascus. This book Paracelsus had—according to the *Fama*—studied "diligently," although not being a member of the fraternity. The brethren bound themselves to maintain six articles that formed their code of living.

> First, That none of them should profess any other thing than to cure the sick, and that *gratis*. 2. None of the posterity should be constrained to wear one certain kind of habit, but therein to follow the custom of the country. 3. That every year upon the day C. they should meet together in the house S. *Spiritus*, or write the cause of his absence. 4. Every brother should look about for a worthy person, who, after his decease, might succeed him. 5. The word C. R. should be their seal, mark, and character. 6. The Fraternity should remain secret one hundred years.[45]

One hundred twenty years after the death of C. R. (i.e., 1604) his grave was rediscovered by the brethren and thus a prophecy that was inscribed upon the door of the vault with his grave was fulfilled.[46] In his tomb there were several objects and books of great importance. After a description of the tomb, its objects, and the body of C. R., the *Fama* continues by inviting new members to the fraternity with a promise that joining will be beneficial "in goods, body, and soul."

The two most important themes in the *Fama* are on the one hand the idea of a "general reformation of the world," and on the other hand, the important claim that this reformation is closely connected to a secret fraternity—the *Fraternity of the Rosy Cross*. The rediscovery of the vault is seen as analogous to the rediscovery of a certain important knowledge for Europe: "For like as our door was after so many years wonderfully discovered, also there shall be opened a door to Europe (when the wall is removed) which already doth begin to appear, and with great desire is expected of many." Yates concludes the following concerning the Rosicrucian reform:

> This very peculiar document, the *Fama Fraternitatis*, thus seems to recount, through the allegory of the vault, the discovery of a new, or rather new-old, philosophy, primarily alchemical and related to medicine and healing, but also concerned with number and geometry and with the production of mechanical marvels. It represents, not only an advancement of learning, but above all an illumination of a religious and spiritual nature. This new philosophy is about to be revealed to the world and will bring about a general reformation. The mythical agents of its spread are the R. C. Brothers.[47]

Inherent in the need for a reformation lays a critique of the spiritual state of Europe. The reform, or redemption as Faivre calls it, would not occur through the churches, "but by means of a universal spiritual science in which heart and mind are united."[48]

The *Confessio* is basically a restatement of the *Fama*. It criticizes the spiritual (and political) state in Europe, especially the Pope. It further argues for the need of a reformation, which the Fraternity of the Rosy Cross is about to set in motion. It tries to justify why the fraternity publicly announces its existence, and once again invites new members to join, as long as they are worthy of it. The ones who merely seek fortune or personal gain will not be able to get in contact with the fraternity. It also hints at the great secrets that they possess, chiefly a certain magical language, and a book that contains all the books in the world, but also a promise of a means by which one is able to know all that is possible to know. This last promise seems to echo the aim of Trithemius' magic.

> Were it not excellent you dwell in one place, that neither the
> people which dwell beyond the River Ganges in the Indies could
> hide anything, nor those which live in Peru might be able to
> keep secret their counsels from thee?[49]

The second Rosicrucian manifesto, the *Confessio* of 1615, has published
with it a tract in Latin called "A Brief Consideration of More Secret
Philosophy." This "Brief Consideration" is based on John Dee's *Monas
Hieroglyphica*, much of it being word-for-word quotations from the *Monas*. This discourse is indissolubly linked to the Rosicrucian manifesto,
which follows it, the *Confessio*. And the *Confessio* is indissolubly linked
with the first manifesto, the *Fama* of 1614, the themes of which it repeats. Thus it becomes evident that the "more secret philosophy" behind the manifestos was the philosophy of John Dee, as summed up in
his *Monas Hieroglyphica*.[50] According to Yates, Dee's influence on the
Rosicrucian manifestos was the result of his mission in Bohemia in the
1580s, where he had tried to spread his reforming religiosity based on
hermetic, magical, and alchemical teachings,[51] (to which should be added
the influence of the kabbalah).

The third, and last manifesto issued, was the *Alchemical Wedding
of Christian Rosencreutz* in 1616. This imaginary novel was written by
Johann Valentin Andreae (1586–1654) in his early teens.[52] It is basically
an alchemical allegory spanning over seven days where Christian
Rosenkreutz attends a wedding between a king and a queen, the alchemical reincarnation and union of the male and female principles in
man.[53] In the first edition of this work there was printed in the margin
Dee's mystical sign, the *Monas* itself. It is also a spiritual allegory over
the processes of regeneration and change within the soul.[54] But most
importantly for the present study, the *Alchemical Wedding* is in fact
describing an initiation.[55] Suffice to say at present though that we here
have a document, even though a fictive one, which describes an initiation that transmits the "secret knowledge" that the *Fraternity of the Rosy
Cross* claimed to possess—a knowledge that primarily was based on
John Dee. And, as has been shown in this short survey, Dee derived his
esoteric knowledge from the likes: Agrippa, Pico, and Ficino.

Concluding Remarks

Western esotericism is a form of thought that was formed during the
Renaissance out of various antique and medieval sources. The two most
important factors that helped to popularize and spread esotericism
throughout Europe were on the one hand the hermetism/hermeticism
of the *Corpus Hermeticum*, which Marsilio Ficino had translated into

Latin, and on the other hand the Kabbalah that, to a large extent, Giovanni Pico della Mirandola had brought to the Christian attention.

Western esotericism spread across Europe and gathered such diverse followers as Trithemius, Agrippa, Bruno, and Dee. Esotericism was looked upon as a powerful philosophy that could be used in reforming religion and society. Giordano Bruno and John Dee set out on personal missions to propagate this spiritual reform. At the beginning of the seventeenth century three small pamphlets heavily influenced by Dee appeared in Germany. These texts are known as the Rosicrucian manifestos, and they call for a general reformation of the world through a secret philosophy that a certain *Fraternity of the Rosy Cross* claims to possess.

The Rosicrucian manifestos caused a great interest in this mythical fraternity, and as a result, a boom of secret and closed societies emerged. Most of these societies worked out systems of initiation, which transmitted the esoteric form of thought through symbols and allegories. The rituals of initiation that were employed are the focus of the present study. With this chapter's brief introduction to Western esotericism as a key, it is now time to unlock the mysteries of the esoteric societies, and venture into their world of secret temples and lodges, and, most importantly, lift the veil of their rituals of initiation.

Chapter 4

The Craft Degrees of Freemasonry

The Emergence of Freemasonry

Scholars today tend to regard 1717 as a purely artificial date for the inception of Freemasonry. The year is only important in masonic history as it was that year in which the Premier Grand Lodge was formed in London by four existing lodges, but the history of Freemasonry as such stretches farther back into history. The history of Freemasonry has always been an important aspect of masonic literature. In fact, *The Constitutions of the Free-Masons* (often referred to as *Anderson's Constitution*) published in 1723, the decidedly single most formative and influential masonic text, begins with a lengthy history of the order, which is based on medieval masonic constitutions, so-called *Old Charges*.[1] James Anderson (1679–1739), a Scottish Non-Conformist minister of poor means, was commissioned by the Grand Master John Montagu (1690–1749) and the Grand Lodge on September 29, 1721, to digest a number of *Old Charges* and present a new constitution.[2] The history contained in Anderson's Constitution was important to the post-1723 masons' self-understanding since the work was read at their reception into the order.

TO BE READ

At the Admission of a NEW BROTHER, when the *Master* or *Warden* shall begin, or order some other Brother to read as follows:[3]

The history that the new initiates encountered at their initiation was a legendary one, beginning with Adam, "created after the image of God, *the great Architect of the Universe*," at the date Year of the World I, or 4003 before Christ. The history is not so much a history about the *Fraternity of Accepted Free Masons*,[4] as a history of the craft of masonry.

Masonry is identified as architecture, which by Anderson is considered the noblest science of the Seven Liberal Arts. Anderson then goes on to describe how masonry was taught and passed on through biblical times all the way to seventeenth-century England. The purpose of Anderson was probably not to offer an objective history of Freemasonry, but rather to glorify masonry, and to provide the Grand Lodge with "a past that would prove its outstanding importance."[5]

The form of Anderson's history has clear similarities with that connected to the Renaissance *Philosophia Perennis*.[6] The *Philosophia Perennis* was seen as a "true philosophy" that was transmitted through a chain of initiates, of which the most commonly recognized included Enoch, Abraham, Noah, Zoroaster, Moses, Hermes Trismegistus, the Brahmins, the Druids, David, Orpheus, Pythogoras, Plato, and the Sibylls.[7] In a similar manner, geometry and masonry,[8] were according to Anderson, transmitted through Adam, Cain, Seth, Noah, Japhet, Shem, Ham, the Chaldees and the Magi, Mitzraim, Abram, Moses (labeled "General Grand Master-Mason"), Solomon ("Grand Master of the Lodge at Jerusalem"), Hiram ("the most accomplish'd Mason upon Earth"), Pythagoras, Euclid, Ptolomeus Philadelphus, Archimedes, Vitruvius, Augustus ("Grand-Master of the Lodge at Rome"), etc. The notion of masonry as a secret tradition that has been handed down through the ages is tightly connected with the legendary history of Freemasonry as such. An illustrative example of this is found in *The Perjur'd Free Mason Detected*, published in 1730:

> But under these Discouragements there were always found A
> Few, Fate so directing, who associating together, with the ut-
> most Secresy and Fidelity constantly instructed one another in
> the Rules of Art, and preserved their Councils from the Eyes of
> all Men; binding themselves to one another by an inviolable
> Oath of Secresy, and a Word or Token of Amity and Fellowship;
> by which Means they have preserv'd the Knowledge of *Masonry*
> in all its most exquisite and accomplish'd Parts, and handed it
> down to us even to this Day.[9]

The *Old Charges* that Anderson founded his history upon (which he called Gothic Constitutions), is the name given to a collection of manu-scripts, of which the earliest, the *Regius* MS, dates from *c.* 1390. Accord-ing to Hamill, some 127 versions have been traced of which 113 are still in existence.[10] They follow the same basic pattern: a) An opening prayer. b) A legendary history of the mason craft tracing it from biblical origins to its establishment in England. c) A code of regulations for Masters,

Fellows, and Apprentices covering both craft practices and morals.[11] d) Arrangements for large-scale "territorial" assemblies at which attendance was obligatory. e) Procedures for the trial and punishment of offenders. f) Admission procedures "for new men that were never charged before," including an oath of fidelity.[12] The Old Charges are important for our understanding of early Freemasonry in a number of ways. First, they form a historical link between the medieval operative masons and the later nonoperative masons because the texts were used by both categories.[13] Thus, they give credence to the theory that modern Freemasonry has developed out of medieval operative masonry. Second, many features of modern Freemasonry can be found in these texts, and so it is possible to account for some of the procedures found in early nonoperative masonry. Third, the elaborate legendary history gives us a picture of just how elevated the masonic craft was perceived to be by both operative and nonoperative masons alike. Fourth, and most important to our purpose, the Old Charges are crucial to our understanding of masonic rituals of initiation as they contain the earliest references to the admission procedures that later developed into this particular type of rituals.

Until quite recently it was assumed among scholars that nonoperative masonry developed out of medieval guilds of stonemasons in England during the seventeenth century. The importance placed on the English origins of Freemasonry is apparent in influential works such as *The Craft—A History of English Freemasonry* by John Hamill.[14] However, new research shows that the development in Scotland during the same period probably played a more significant part than previously assumed. David Stevenson has provided enough material evidence to allow for a reevaluation of Scotland's part in the transition of masonry from an operative organization into nonoperative Freemasonry.[15] Apart from providing a wealth of masonic "firsts" to be found in Scotland—such as the earliest attempts at organizing lodges at a national level, earliest examples of "nonoperatives" joining lodges, earliest evidence connecting lodge masonry with specific ethical ideas expounded by use of symbols, earliest references to the Mason Word, earliest "masonic catechisms" expounding the Mason Word and describing rites of initiation, earliest evidence of the use of two degrees or grades within masonry, earliest evidence of the emergence of a third grade[16]—Stevenson argues that the formation of Freemasonry took place in Scotland, and not in England.

> The Medieval contribution, of craft organisation and legend, provided some of the ingredients essential to the formation of freemasonry, but the process of combining these with other

ingredients did not take place until the years around 1600, and it took place in Scotland.[17]

Furthermore, Stevenson does not only place the formation of Freemasonry in Scotland around 1600, but even identifies what he believes to be the individual responsible for the creation of Freemasonry:

He [William Shaw] set out to reorganise the mason craft in Scotland and endow it with a new stature and meaning: and in doing so he created freemasonry.[18]

William Shaw (c. 1550–1602) had been appointed the king's master of works in 1583, which meant that he was in charge of all the major building projects in Scotland. Shaw was apparently not merely interested in the administrative and financial aspects of his appointment, but also took an active part in the architectural considerations of the building projects and, furthermore, had far-reaching ambitions to reorganize the masonic craft. In two separate Statutes from 1598 and 1599, Shaw set out rules that were to be observed by the masons in Scotland. From a ritual perspective the first Shaw Statute appears to be the most important one, as this statute apparently regulated the form of admitting new members to lodges. According to Stevenson, the rites of the new organization, though they presumably grew out of older medieval rites, were based on the Mason Word, and "there is no pre-seventeen-century evidence for the existence of the Word."[19] Even though the First Shaw Statutes do not state how the actual rituals should be performed it is clear that a minimum number of members had to be present and that the skill and worthiness of the candidates were tried.

Early Freemasonry and Western Esotericism

It is often assumed that Western esotericism only enters the world of masonry by the middle of the eighteenth century—through the so-called high or additional degrees—and that the early Craft masonry, as it was practiced on the British Isles, was merely moral in character. There is evidence, however, that as early as the first half of the seventeenth century masonry was often perceived of as linked to what we today call Western esotericism. In fact, the earliest printed reference to the Mason Word in *The Muses Threnodie* of 1638, connects the "Brethren of the Rosie Cross" with the Mason Word:

> For what we do presage is not in grosse,
> For we be brethren of the *Rosie Crosse*;
> VVe have the *Mason word*, and second sight,
> Things for to come we can foretell aright;[20]

In the same manner, the earliest-known printed reference to Accepted Masons is also to be found in connection to esoteric topics. In a "divertissement" published in *Poor Robin's Intelligence* for October 10, 1676, the "Company of accepted Masons" is mentioned in an ironical manner together with the "Ancient Brother-hood of the Rosy-Cross" and the "Hermetick Adepti":

> These are to give notice, that the Modern Green-ribbon'd Caball, together with the Ancient Brother-hood of the Rosy-Cross; the Hermetick Adepti, and the Company of accepted Masons, intend all to Dine together on the 31 [*sic*] of *November* next, at the Flying-Bull in Wind-Mill-Crown-Street; having already given order for great store of Black-Swan Pies, Poach'd Phœnixes Eggs, Haunches of Unicorns, & c. To be provided on that occasion; All idle people that can spare so much time from the Coffee-house, may repair thither to be spectators of the Solemnity: But are advised to provide themselves Spectacles of Malleable Glass; For otherwise 'tis thought the said Societies will (as hitherto) make their Appearance Invisible.[21]

The "Modern Green-ribbon'd Caball," or the Green Ribbon Club, was a political club formed around 1675, probably by Anthony Ashley Cooper, 1st Earl of Shaftesbury (1621–1683). The primary purpose of the club appears to have been to gather political opponents to the court, in what can be called a "debating and intelligence resort."[22] The "Hermetick Adepti" most likely referred to a group of alchemists, since the English word "Hermetick" in the seventeenth century was often used as synonymous with alchemy. As we shall see, alchemy came to be regarded as an important part of masonry, even before the latter part of the eighteenth century when the so-called alchemical degrees were developed on the continent. However, it was through Rosicrucianism that the public eye most often viewed early masonry as part of what we today call Western esotericism. The first English expositor and defender of Rosicrucianism was Robert Fludd[23] (1574–1637), who in 1616 published his *Apologia Compendiara Fraternitatem de Rosea Cruce*. Fludd's interpretation of Rosicrucianism, as well as his interpretation of alchemy, became more spiritualized over the years. English Rosicrucianism during the seventeenth century differed from its German and French counterparts, as it blended with alchemy in a far more outspoken manner. The first English edition of the *Fama* and *Confessio* was published in 1652, in a translation by the alchemist and mystic Thomas Vaughan (1621–1665).[24] According to Waite, it was Vaughan who two years previously, in 1650, had published the first printed English reference to the Rosy Cross in England (twelve years after the publication of *The Muses Threnodie* in Scotland).[25] References to Rosicrucian themes can, however, be found earlier in one of Ben Johnson's masques of 1626, and in Francis Bacon's *New Atlantis* (1627), which "presented a utopian dream of an ideal scientific and religious society based on an order of priest-scientists pursuing the search for knowledge, a dream which included adaptations of many Rosicrucian motifs."[26]

A further reference, albeit a casual one, to Rosicrucians and masons is to be found in a poem entitled *The Knight*, printed as a pamphlet in 1723:

> And in the *Rosi-crucian* Trade,
> He knew all has been writ or said,
> And might for an *Adeptus* pass,
> As most Men think indeed he was.
> Well vers'd he was in all the Fancies
> Of *Hydro-pyro-geo-mancies*,
> And many learned Things could tell
> Of Knots and Charms, and the Night Spell,
> Which make the Devil stand as Warden,
> To watch a Deer-park or a Garden
> A Charm for Masons and for Sclaters,
> That could be writ in Golden Letters,
> He had, which, when they us'd their Calling,
> Would keep them from all Harm by Falling;
> In coming down make no more Haste,
> *Than going up, Probatum est.*[27]

By the mid-1720s, we find the first printed references to a supposed Rosicrucian influence on masonry. The references to Rosicrucianism, in connection to masonry, had up until then been restricted to casual remarks, with no clear arguments as to the supposed connection between the two. In a mock advertisement printed in *The Daily Journal* of December 27, 1725 it is claimed that "Masonry" had received a "new light from some worthy Rosicrucians":

Friday, Dec. 24. 1725.

The Brethren of the *Shears* and *Shopboard* are hereby Informed, that their Whimsical kinsmen of the *Hod* and *Trowel,* having (on new Light received from some worthy *Rosicrucians*) thought fit to change both their *Patron* and *Day,* and unexpectedly taken up our usual Place of Meeting: The Worshipful Society of *Free* and *Accepted* TAYLORS are desired to meet on Monday next, the 27th Instant, at the FOLLY on the Thames, in order to Chuse a Grand Master, and other Officers, and to Dine.

You are desired to come *Cloathed,* and *Armed* with, *Bodkin* and *Thimble.*[28]

According to Knoop, Jones, and Hamer this is the first known reference of suggested Rosicrucian influence on masonic development. In an anonymous letter printed in *The Daily Journal* of September 5, 1730, it is claimed that the English Freemasons were ashamed of their true origin, which according to the anonymous author was to be found in the building activities of Edward III at Windsor in the fourteenth century, and instead "took great pains to persuade the world" that they derived from, and were the same as, the Rosicrucians:

It must be confessed, that there is a Society abroad, from whom the English Free-Masons (asham'd of their true Origin, as above) have copied a few Ceremonies, and take great Pains to persuade the World that they are derived from them, and are the same with them: These are called *Rosicrucians,* from their Prime Officers, (Such as our Brethren call *Grand Master, Wardens,* &c.) being distinguished on their High Days with Red Crosses. This is said to be a worthy, tho' they affect to be thought a mystical Society, and promote chearfully one another's Benefit in a very extraordinary Manner, they meeting for better Purposes than Eating and Drinking, or glorying like *Batts,* those amphibious Birds of Night, in their Wings of *Leather.* On this Society have our Moderns, as we have said, endeavour'd to ingraft themselves, tho' they know nothing of their most material Constitutions, and are acquainted only with some of their Signs of *Probation* and *Entrance,* insomuch that 'tis but of late Years, (being better inform'd by some *Rosicrucian*) that they knew John the Evangelist to be their right Patron, having before kept for his Day that dedicated to John the Baptist, who, we all know, lived in a Desart, and knew nothing of the *Architecture* and *Mystery*, which, with so much Plausibility, they impute to the Author of the *Revelations*.[29]

From then onward, right up to the present age, one often finds claims in masonic literature that masonry derives from the Rosicrucians.[30] A standard argument for this theory is the oft-quoted entries in the diaries of Elias Ashmole (1617–1692), the antiquarian. In two separate entries he mentions his admittance into masonry in 1646, and a subsequent attendance in a masonic lodge thirty years later.[31] On the basis of certain Rosicrucian manuscripts in Ashmole's collection, now at the Bodleian Library, it has often been claimed that Ashmole was a Rosicrucian himself. Ashmole had copied out by his own hand an English translation of the *Fama* and the *Confessio*, to which he had affixed a petition to be allowed to join the Rosicrucian Fraternity.[32] This is not the place, or the time, to enter into the discussion whether or not Ashmole was a Rosicrucian, but the fact that Ashmole was a mason, and that he took such a large interest in the *Fama* and the *Confessio* as to copy it by hand, shows that the two were not seen as incompatible with each other as early as the seventeenth century, at least not in this particular case. In fact, one of the earliest Rosicrucian texts published in England, a tract called *Summum Bonum* from 1629, deals with Rosicrucian matters in what appears to be a very "masonic manner." In the tract, the Rosicrucian brotherhood is not perceived of anymore as a real secret brotherhood to which one can apply for membership, but rather as a spiritual brotherhood. According to Waite, the *Summum Bonum* defines the brotherhood as a "Company of Spiritual Builders" that is set out to build a "Spiritual Palace, a House founded on the Rock, the Holy Place of a Holy Priesthood."[33] Furthermore, the "corner-stone of this building is Christ, while those who are integrated in the House are the Living Stones thereof."[34] By interpreting the Rosicrucian brotherhood as a company of spiritual builders the author of *Summum Bonum* echoes a characteristic masonic theme, that of the masons building a new, spiritual temple. For instance, in the dedication of *Long Livers* published 1722, the translator-editor Eugenius Philalethes Jr. writes:

Remember that you are the Salt of the Earth, the Light of the World, and the Fire of the Universe. Ye are living Stones, built up a spiritual House, who believe and rely on the chief *Lapis Angularis*, which the refractory and disobedient Builders disallowed, you are called from Darkness to Light, you are a chosen Generation, a royal Priesthood.[35]

The "Salt of the Earth,"[36] the "Light of the World,"[37] and the "Fire of the Universe"[38] might, apart from their biblical references, refer to alchemical concepts. In the light of the fact that English Rosicrucianism of the seventeenth century was heavily influenced by alchemy, it is perhaps not so surprising that masonry was not only viewed as connected to Rosicrucianism, but to alchemy as well. The following quotation from *Long Livers* provides us with an illustrative specimen of alchemical writing of the period, in which we find a number of typical symbols:

> And now, my Brethren, you of the higher Class, permit me a few Words, since you are but few; and these few Words I shall speak to you in Riddles, because to you it is given to know those Mysteries which are hidden from the Unworthy.
>
> Have you not seen then, my dearest Brethren, that stupendous Bath, filled with most limpid Water, than which no Pure can be purer, of such admirable Mechanism that makes even the greatest Philosopher gaze with Wonder and Astonishment, and is the Subject of the eternal Contemplation of the wisest Men. Its Form is a Quadrate sublimely placed on six others, blazing all with celestial Jewels, each angularly supported with four Lions. Here repose our mighty King and Queen (I speak foolishly, I am not worthy to be of you) the King shining in his glorious Apparel of transparent incorruptible Gold, beset with living Sapphires; he is fair and ruddy, and feeds amongst the Lillies; his Eyes two Carbuncles the most brilliant, darting prolifick, never-dying Fires; and his large flowing Hair, blacker than the deepest Black, or Plumage of the long-lived Crow; his Royal Consort vested in Tissue of immortal Silver, watered with Emeralds, Pearl and Coral. O mystical Union! O admirable Commerce![39]

As we have seen, there are numerous printed references from the seventeenth and early eighteenth centuries in which masonry, both operative and nonoperative, are perceived of as linked to Rosicrucianism and/or alchemy. Why then did the authors of these texts believe that there was some sort of connection between masonry and these particular aspects of Western esotericism? I assume that one reason lies in the fact that masonry was a closed society into which one could only enter by undergoing a secret ritual of initiation. The parallel to the *Fraternity of the Rosy Cross* as proclaimed in the *Fama* and the *Confessio* (as well as in the writings of the English Rosicrucians of the period) is striking, to say the least. In the same manner, alchemy was seen as something reserved for initiates, for persons who could decipher the alchemical symbols. Furthermore, the masonic initiation could have been interpreted as the alchemical idea of transmutation, which often implied a spiritual refinement of the alchemist himself. This is of course mere speculation on my part, but the fact nonetheless remains that masonry was often seen as compatible with what we today call Western esotericism. It is now time to turn our attention from how masonry was perceived from the outside, to how masonry actually worked on the inside—it is time to analyze the ritual evidence.

The Pre-1730 Ritual Evidence

The development of the masonic Craft degrees, as we know them today, was a long and gradual process. We know very little of the development from operative rituals of admission into the later rituals of initiation of nonoperative masonry, but the information we have shows that the nonoperative rituals owed much of their form and content to the earlier operative rituals. As mentioned, the development was a gradual process, a process that had its perhaps most formative period during the seventeenth century and the first three decades of the eighteenth. With the publication of Samuel Prichard's *Masonry Dissected* in 1730 the development of the Craft degrees had reached its completion in the sense that there were now three degrees: Entered Apprentice, Fellow Craft, and Master Mason. Prior to 1730 the Craft rituals had consisted of only two rituals, Entered Apprentice and Fellow Craft or Master Mason. However, by 1730 the Entered Apprentice ritual had been split into two degrees, Entered Apprentice and Fellow Craft, thus inserting a new degree between the two former ones. The old second degree became the third degree, called Master Mason.[40]

The sources of our knowledge of the pre-1730 rituals consist of eight manuscripts and six printed texts, of which the earliest, *The Edinburgh Register House MS*, is from 1696.[41] All these texts are in the form of a catechism, that is questions and answers, whose apparent object it is to verify whether or not a person is an initiated mason. From these questions and answers we can extract much information to reconstruct rituals of initiation that were in use during this period. From 1737 onward, especially in France, the exposures are more descriptive in nature and thereby give us more information about how the rituals were actually performed.[42] From 1760 we find the same type of descriptive exposures in England.[43]

Discussing the evolution of the early catechisms Knoop, Jones, and Hamer divide the documents into four groups. (1) *Edinburgh Reg-*

ister House and *Chetwood Crawley MSS* that probably represent Scottish operative working in the later decades of the seventeenth century. (2) *A Mason's Confession* that professedly represents Scottish operative working in the third decade of the eighteenth century. (3) The main body of the catechisms that supposedly or professedly exhibit the ceremonies of accepted or nonoperative masons during the first three decades of the eighteenth century. (4) Samuel Prichard's *Masonry Dissected* from 1730 in which we find the first known description of the three-degree system.[44] The printed texts, usually referred to as exposures since they profess to expose the secrets of Freemasonry, closely follow the manuscript versions. The conditions of the manuscripts themselves reveal that they probably were used as *aide-mémoire* by masons; that is, they were used by masons in order to remember the rituals that in these days were only transmitted orally.

The earliest manuscript catechism, *The Edinburgh Register House MS* from 1696, contains, in a rough manner, most of the major elements of a masonic ritual of initiation. The manuscript consists of two parts. In the first part, "SOME QUESTIONES THAT MASONS PUT TO THOSE WHO HAVE Y^E WORD BEFORE THEY WILL ACKNOWLEDGE THEM," there are fifteen questions aimed at verifying whether a person is a mason, or Entered Apprentice, and two questions whether he is a "fellow craft." After an affirmative answer to the question whether one is a mason, one is asked to explain the "first point":

> What is the first point? Ans: Tell me the first point ile tell you the second, The first is to heill and conceall, second, under no less pain, which is then cutting of your throat, For you must make that sign, when you say that [.][45]

From the answer it is possible to identify three common features of later masonic rituals. First, the practice to give the Mason Word, either by lettering it, or by dividing it in two parts, so that the candidate and an officer together give the whole word. Second, the cutting of the throat refers to the penalty of breaking the oath of the first degree. Third, "you must make that sign" is an allusion to the earliest form of the Entered Apprentice sign, which is made by holding the hand right and across the throat, and then making a smart move with the hand as if cutting the throat.[46] In the second part of the manuscript, this part of the ritual is further explained:

> Here come I the youngest and last entered apprentice As I am sworn by God and St Jhon by the Square and compass, and common judge to attend my masters service at the honourable

lodge, from munday in the morning till saturday at night and to keep the Keyes therof, *under no less pain then haveing my tongue cut out under my chin and of being buried, within the flood mark where no man shall know, then he makes the sign again with drawing his hand under his chin alongst his throat which denotes that it be cut out in caise he break his word.*[47] [my emphasis]

The fourth to the thirteenth questions deal with the nature of the lodge in which the candidate was "entered." A "true and perfect lodge" is made of seven Masters and five Entered Apprentices, or five [Master] Masons and three Entered Apprentices, and is supposed to be located a day's journey from a "burroughs town." After stating the name of the lodge in which the candidate was entered (in this case the lodge of Kilwinning), it is explained that the lodge stands east and west as the temple of Jerusalem—and it was in the porch of Solomon's temple that the first lodge was held. The temple of Jerusalem, apparently an important symbol in masonic rituals as early as 1696, develops in the first three decades of the eighteenth century into one of the most important characteristics of the Craft rituals, especially with the emergence of the third degree from 1730 onward. The building site of Solomon's temple becomes the mythological scene of the rituals, and early on there are speculations concerning the nature of the new temple that the masons are set out to build. The lodge that was supposed to have been located in the porch of Solomon's temple was seen as the first masonic lodge, and Solomon's temple was considered to be the "model" on which a new—spiritual—temple was to be built.

In the lodge there are three "lights": in the northeast, southwest, and the east, whose symbolism is explained as "The one denotes the master mason, the other the warden The third the setter croft [should probably be Fellow Craft]."[48] Furthermore, there are three "jewels" in the lodge: "Perpend Esler a Square pavement and a broad oval." The three lights and jewels of the lodge remain important symbols in masonic lodges to this day, but the interpretation and the exact nature of these symbols have varied over the years.

Questions fourteen and fifteen deal with the key to the lodge, which is described as a "well hung tongue" that lies in "the bone box." The key to the lodge is to be found "Three foot and an half from the lodge door under a perpend esler, and a green divot. But under the lap of my liver where all my secrets of my heart lie."[49] In a later catechism the bone box is explained as being the mouth, the bones being the teeth. It is interesting to note that there are only two questions that deal with the Fellow Craft degree, of which only the second provides any information about the ritual. This can perhaps be explained by the probability that the second degree was not as developed ritually as that of the first degree. The only information that the *Edinburgh Register House MS* give us is the following:

> How many points of the fellowship are ther Ans fyve viz foot to foot Knee to Kn[ee] Heart to Heart, Hand to Hand and ear to ear. Then make the sign of fellowship and shake hand and you will be acknowledged a true mason. The words are in the I of the Kings Ch 7, v, 21, and in 2 chr: ch 3 verse last.[50]

The Five Points of Fellowship are a combination of a posture, which has to be made by two persons together, and the manner in which the word is communicated, that is one has to stand in a certain position when communicating the word. From 1730 onward the sign of the Five Points of Fellowship is only used in the third degree, in the "raising" of Hiram. The words from the Old Testament are Jachin and Boaz, the names of the two pillars placed at the entrance to the temple of Solomon. Later documents show that Jachin was the Entered Apprentice word, while Boaz was that of the Fellow Crafts.

The second part of the manuscript, which follows after the catechism, briefly describes the ritual itself, or "THE FORME OF GIVING THE MASON WORD." The title of the second part is itself important as it clearly states what appears to be the object of the masonic rituals in this period. In other words, the central feature of the masonic rituals was the transmission of the Mason Word, a word identified with Jachin in the Entered Apprentice degree, and Boaz in that of Fellow Craft.[51] The three main ingredients of the ritual as described in the manuscript appear to be an ordeal, an oath, and the communication of the traditional secrets. The ordeal is in the form of acts whose object is to frighten the candidate. The oath is taken with the right hand on the Bible (in most later documents specified to be opened at the Gospel of St. John), while kneeling.

> Imprimis you are to take the person to take the word upon his knees and after a great many ceremonies to frighten him you make him take up the bible and laying his right hand on it you are to conjure him, to sec[r]ecie, By threatening that if [he] shall break his oath the sun in the firmament will be a witness agst him and all the company then present, which will be an occasion of his damnation and that likewise the masons will be sure to murder him, Then after he hes promised secrecie They give him the oath a[s] follows[52]

Through the oath the candidate affirms that he will never reveal, in any way, what he is about to hear and see. After the oath he is "removed out of the company," which presumably means that he is taken outside the lodge, where he is once again frightened "with 1000 ridicolous postures and grimmaces." He is then instructed by the youngest mason, that is, the most recent newly made member, in the traditional secrets and the "words of his entrie" already quoted. After being led inside the lodge again, and having said the "words of his entrie," the word is being communicated by the Master Mason after it has been whispered from one member to another. The text then goes on to describe the procedure in making a "master mason or fellow craft." After all the Entered Apprentices have left the lodge the one who is "to be admitted a member of fellowship" is put to his knees in order to take a new oath. As in the previous degree, he is then led outside the lodge where he is instructed in the "postures and signes of fellowship," but this time there is no mention of trying to frighten him. He then enters the lodge again and shows what he has learned, after which he receives the word while standing in the special posture together with the communicator of the word, that is in the position of the Five Points of Fellowship.

> Then the master gives him the word and gripes his hand after the masons way, which is all that is to be done to make him a perfect mason.[53]

The fact that the *Edinburgh Register House MS* contains the main features of the Entered Apprentice and, to a lesser extent, the Fellow Craft rituals, is important, as it shows that later masonic rituals are conservative when it comes to the basic components of the rituals. The other pre-1730 catechisms, though in essence in accordance with the *Edinburgh Register House MS*, exhibit a variety in details, both in regard to divergent interpretations and innovations. For instance, the *Chetwode Crawley MS., c.* 1700, gives an alternative explanation of the three lights that are to be found in a lodge: "The one denotes the Master mason, The other the Words [should probably be Ward(an)s] and the Third The ffellow-Craft."[54] As to innovations, the first reference to what has become perhaps the most characteristic regalia of Freemasonry in the public mind—the leather apron and gloves—is found in the earliest-known printed catechism, *A Mason's Examination* from 1723. The text mentions that all of the fraternity receive a pair of men's and women's gloves, and a leather apron.[55] In the same catechism we also find the earliest-known use of Hebrew letters:

Q. Are you a Free-Mason? A. Yes, indeed, that I am.

Q. How shall I know it? A. By the Signs and Tokens רסם, from my Entrance into the Kitchen, and from thence to the Hall.[56]

The entrance into the kitchen denotes the Entered Apprentice degree, while the entrance into the hall denotes the Fellow Craft degree. The first reference to the letter G in a ritual context is to be found in the *Wilkinson MS, c.* 1727: "Q. What is the Center of y[r] Lodge[?] A. the letter G. Q. What does it Signify[?] A. Geometry, or the fifth Science."[57] Later on in the development of the rituals of Freemasonry, the letter G becomes a standard feature, which not only stands for geometry, but in many cases for God as well. Most of the catechisms are presented in what appears to be skeleton form, which means that they are devoid of speculations and elaborations on the significance of the rituals themselves. There are, however, some exceptions to this. The *Dumfries No. 4 MS., c.* 1710, is the earliest catechism that contains a more speculative and religious approach to the rituals. After a prayer and a short preface, the MS. contains a large section on the history of masonry, based on the legendary history found in the Old Charges. The practice of masonry is called a Royal Secret—which in those days was not an idle term—and it is stated in the text that the mason should be "true to god and the holy catholick church." The strongly religious character of the MS. can be seen from the following quotation:

Q what is meant by y[e] brassen see yt Hiram framed & supported it by 12 oxen 3 looking towards y[e] north 3 towards y[e] south 3 towards y[e] west 3 towards y[e] east A It was appointed to bath & wash y[e] preists in at yt time But now we finde it was tipe of Christs blood whose blood was to purg sin & to wash y[e] elect & y[e] 12 oxen a type of y[e] 12 apostles who opposed all heathenism & athism & sealed y[e] cause of christ w[t] there blood Q what meant y[e] golden dore of y[e] temple Qr they went in to sanctum sanctorum A it was another type of Christ who is y[e] door y[e] way and the truth & y[e] life by whome & in whom all y[e] elect entreth into heaven[58]

The author of the text further explicitly identifies the temple of Jerusalem with Christ, and to a certain extent with the Church. Furthermore, the "mistery of the golden door of the temple" is explained as "Christ is the dore of life by w[e] we must enter into eternal happiness [. . .]."[59] The identification of Christ with the temple was, however, by no means an unusual one. On the contrary, the new temple was a common metaphor for Christ.[60] The religious aspect of early Freemasonry can also be seen in how the Master of the lodge sometimes was interpreted. In the *Institution of Free Masons, c.* 1725 we can see that God was considered to be the Master of the lodge: "Who rules & governs the Lodge & is Master of it? A. Iehovah the right Pillar."[61]

The earliest known MS. Catechism to recognize three classes of masons, with its own secrets, is *The Trinity College, Dublin, MS.*, dated 1711. In the text it is stated that the Master's Word is the somewhat peculiar word "matchpin."

> The Masters sign is back bone, the word matchpin. The fellow craftsman's sign is knuckles, & sinues ye word Jachquin. The Enterprentice's sign is sinues, the word Boaz or its hollow.[62]

From 1730 onward the quest for a lost Master's Word becomes an important feature of the third degree, as will be discussed presently. In the post-1730 third-degree legend an old Master's Word, YHVH, is replaced by the word Macbenac at the time of Hiram's murder. The word is supposed to mean "the flesh falls from the bones" in allusion to the decomposed state of Hiram's corpse. It is still unclear from where the word Macbenac derives, but the pre-1730 texts reveal that different words were used as the new Master's Word. The above quoted "matchpin" is an early example. Another example of a Master's Word is "Mahabyn," which is to be found in the *Sloane MS. 3329, c.* 1700.

> Anoth^{er} they haue called the mast^{ers} word and is Mahabyn which is allways divided into two words and Standing close With their Breasts to each oth^{er} the inside of Each oth^{ers} right Ancle Joynts the mast^{ers} grip by their right hands and the top of their Left hand fingers thurst close on ye small of each oth^{ers} Backbone and in that posture they Stand till they whisp^{er} in each oth^{ers} eares ye one Maha- the oth^{er} repleys Byn.[63]

A variant of "Mahabyn" is the word "Maughbin" mentioned in *A Mason's Examination*, printed in 1723. The word "Maughbin" also bears a close resemblance to "Matchpin."

> An enter'd Mason I have been,
> *Boaz* and *Jachin* I have seen;
> A Fellow I was sworn most rare,

And know the Astler, Diamond, and Square:
I know the Master's Part full well,
As honest *Maughbin* will you tell.[64]

The most interesting early catechism in connection to the third, or
Masters degree, is the *Graham MS.* from 1726. Apart from its religious
character the manuscript includes an early version of the Hiram legend,
in which Noah has the part that after 1730 is ascribed to Hiram.[65] According to this early version Shem, Ham, and Japheth go to the grave
of Noah to try to find anything that might lead them to the "vertuable
secret which this famieous preacher had." The three men had agreed
that if they didn't find the secret itself, then the "first thing that they
found was to be to them as a secret." When they came to the grave they
found nothing save the dead body in a state of decay. When they tried
to pull at one of its fingers it came off, and the same thing happened
when they tried with a joint, then another, the wrist, and finally the
elbow. They then proceeded to raise the body of Noah with what evi-
dently are the Five Points of Fellowship in an almost identical manner
to the raising of Hiram in later ritual texts.

> [so they] Reared up the dead body and suported it setting ffoot
> to ffoot knee to knee Breast to breast Cheeck to check and hand
> to back and cryed out help o ffather as if they had said o father
> of heaven help us now for our Earthly ffather cannot so Laid
> down the dead body again and not knowing what to do—so one
> said here is yet marrow in this bone and the second said but a
> dry bone and the third said it stinketh so they agreed for to give
> it a name as is known to free masonry to this day so went to their
> undertakings and afterwards works stood: yet it is to be believed
> and allso understood that the vertue did not proceed from what
> they ffound or how it was called but ffrom ffaith and prayer so
> thus it Contenued the will pass for the deed[.][66]

In the next section I will analyze the legend of the third degree in more
detail, and I will show that the interpretation of the legend during the
1730s most likely can be explained from a Western esoteric standpoint.
Even though the early catechisms show a variety of details, the main
features of the Entered Apprentice degree can already be found in *The
Edinburgh Register House MS* from 1696. It is, however, noteworthy that
all the catechisms from this period, 1696–1730, focus on the Entered
Apprentice degree, while the descriptions of the Fellow Craft degree
remain sparse. One possible reason for this is that during the initial, but

formative, period of development of the masonic rituals of initiation, it was the first degree that was seen as the most significant ritual. However, a more likely explanation is that secrecy about the first degree may have been less strict because it was regarded less important. Be that as it may, the catechisms from this period do not contain any clear references to Western esotericism, contrary to what might have been expected from how masonry was perceived by outsiders during the same period. There are thus no references to Rosicrucianism or alchemy, which, as we have seen, were often considered to be linked with masonry. However, references to kabbalah can be found in *The Grand Mystery Laid Open*, published in 1726. These references are important as they are the first explicit references in masonic catechisms to not only kabbalah, but also to Western esotericism in general. Furthermore, it is significant that we find kabbalistic influence on masonic rituals in the 1720s as it was during this period that the third degree ritual developed into the form published by Samuel Prichard in 1730—a form influenced by kabbalistic speculations.

> Have the six Spiritual Signs any Names? Yes, but are not divulged to any new admitted Member, because they are Cabalisttical? What are these Signs, The first Foot to Foot, the second is Knee to Knee, the third is Breast to Breast, the fourth is Hand to Back, the fifth is Cheek to Cheek, the sixth is Face to Face. Who is the Grand Master of all the Lodges in the World? *INRI*. What is the meaning of that Name? Each distinct Letter stands for a whole Word, and is very mysterious. How is the Master of every particular Lodge called? Oakecharing a Tocholochy.[67]

The form of kabbalah alluded to in the text is probably that of notariqon. I have dealt elsewhere with kabbalistic speculations concerning letters and numbers in connection with rituals of initiation, and the above quotation, as well as the next, can be viewed as good examples of kabbalistic influence.

> Why do you hold the Holy Bible at your Breast? for the Enjoyning Secrecy, and because in it is contained the Grand Secret of Masonry. Who was the first Mason? Laylah Illallah. Who invented the secret Word? Checchehabeddin Jatmouny. What is it? It is a Cabalistical Word composed of a Letter out of each of the Names of Laylah Illallah as mentioned in the Holy Bible.[68]

In a contemporary text, *A Letter to the Grand Mistress* published in 1724, masonry is virtually identified as kabbalah.[69] The text itself is probably a spoof, but it is evident that the author had considerable knowledge of Freemasonry, and masonic rituals of initiation. It is perhaps interesting to note that the author claims that without a "Key to *Raymundus Lullius*" it is impossible to come to the "Quintessence of *Free-Masonry*."[70] Ramón Lull (1235–1316) had a number of influential alchemical works attributed to him, and was in alchemical literature considered to be an important adept of the art of alchemy. Lull was also considered to be an authority on the Art of Memory,[71] which, according to Stephenson, was important to William Shaw and the formation of Freemasonry. Unfortunately, the author of *A Letter to the Grand Mistress* never specifies what the key to Lull actually might have been.

The Master Mason Degree
and the Ritual Enactment of the Hiramic Legend

Samuel Prichard's *Masonry Dissected*, first published in October 1730, is the perhaps most influential of all masonic exposures published in the eighteenth century, and the text ran into no less then thirty editions. According to the title page of the pamphlet, Prichard had been a mason himself, a "late Member of a Constituted Lodge," and his object of publishing the exposure was explained in "The Author's Vindication of himself from the prejudiced Part of Mankind":

> I was induced to publish this mighty Secret for the publick Good, at the Request of several Masons, and it will, I hope, give entire Satisfaction, and have its desired Effect in preventing so many credulous Persons being drawn into so pernicious a Society.[72]

Prichard's assertion that he had published the pamphlet at the request of several masons appears to be quite odd, to put it mildly. Why would masons themselves want to publish their "mighty Secret" and thereby prevent persons from joining their "pernicious" society? If there is any truth in Prichard's claim, then perhaps it is possible to get to the motive of these masons by looking at the result that *Masonry Dissected* had upon the later development of masonic rituals. The obvious result of Prichard's text is the establishment of the three degrees and the rituals connected thereto. As there existed no official ritual handbooks at this time—all rituals were supposed to be learned by heart—what better way might there be of implementing a new degree then by making it readily available by publishing it? Could the development of the third degree, and the peculiar mysticism connected thereto, have been the deliberate effort of a group of masons who deemed it necessary to reform the masonic system of initiation? Unless new information comes to light, we can never reach a conclusive answer to these questions. It is, however, interesting to note a peculiar part of Prichard's vindication, which seems to imply that the old form of masonry needed to be "repair'd by some occult Mystery," or would soon be annihilated:

> [. . .] but it is very much doubted, and most reasonable to think it will be expended towards the forming another System of Masonry, the old Fabrick being so ruinous, that, unless repair'd by some occult Mystery, will soon be annihilated.[73]

It is tempting to interpret the "occult Mystery" as the legend of Hiram. *Masonry Dissected* was, however, not only instrumental in establishing the tri-gradual system[74], but also had a formative effect upon the Craft degrees as a whole. The Fellow Craft catechism of *Masonry Dissected* differs from earlier catechisms most notably in two respects. First, the "Five Points of Fellowship" is dropped from the Fellow Craft degree, and instead figures prominently in the Master degree. Second, the mystery of the letter G becomes the main focus of the Followcraft degree, as shown by the following quotation:

> The Repeating of the Letter G.
>
> Resp.   In the midst of Solomon's Temple there stands a G,
> A Letter fair for all to read and see,
> But few there be that understands
> What means that Letter G.
> Ex.   My Friend, if you pretend to be
> Of this Fraternity,
> You can forthwith and rightly tell
> What means that Letter G.
> Resp.   By Sciences are brought to Light
> Bodies of various Kinds,
> Which do appear to perfect Sight;
> But none but Males shall know my Mind.
> Ex.   The Right shall. Resp. If Worshipful.
> Ex.   Both Right and Worshipful I am,
> To Hail you I have Command,
> That you do forthwith let me know,
> As I you may understand.
> Resp.   By Letters Four and Science Five
> This G aright doth stand,
> In a due Art and Proportion,

You have your Answer, Friend.

N.B. Four Letters are Boaz. Fifth Science Geometry.

Ex.   My Friend, you answer well,
If Right and Free Principles you discover,
I'll change your Name from Friend,
And henceforth call you Brother.

Resp.   The Sciences are well compos'd
Of noble Structure's Verse,
A Point, a Line, and an Outside;
But a Solid is the last.[75]

It is thus explained that the letter G stands for Geometry. Geometry, the fifth of the Seven Liberal Arts, has always been an important symbol in Freemasonry, and the Old Charges show that it was an important aspect of operative masonry as well.

The catechism of the Master degree follows the same basic structure as the pre-1730 catechisms of the Entered Apprentice and Fellow Craft or Master Mason degrees. It begins with an affirmative answer to the question whether the candidate is a Master Mason, an affirmation that is checked through the posing of a number of questions. The answers reveal that the candidate was "pass'd" a Master in a "Perfect Lodge of Masters," which is made up of three Masters.[76] He came to be "pass'd Master" by the help of God, the "square" and his own industry, "from the square to the Compass." The square and compass have a prominent place in masonic symbolism and have different interpretations.[77] He furthermore states that he has seen *Jachin* and *Boaz* and that he was made a, most rare, Master Mason with Diamond, Ashler, and the Square. By having seen the two pillars is meant that he has undergone the previous two degrees. It is then stated that the word *Machbenah* will make him free. Then follows the earliest known version of the legend of Hiram, which begins with the question of what the candidate is going to do in the West. He answers that he is going to "seek for that which was lost and is now found," which he explains to be the Master Mason's Word. The word had been lost by "Three Great Knocks, or the Death of our Master Hiram." During the building of Solomon's Temple Hiram was the Master Mason, and one day at high noon, when he was surveying the works as was his custom, he entered into the temple. There he was attacked by three "ruffians," who were supposed to be Fellow Crafts. The ruffians had placed themselves at each of the three entrances and thereby trapped Hiram inside the temple. One by one, they demanded that he should give them the Master's Word, but he replied that "he did not receive it in such a manner, but Time and a little Patience" would bring it to them. Each of them gave him a blow with a setting maul, setting tool, and a setting beadle, respectively. The last blow killed Hiram and the ruffians carried his body out of the temple through the west door, and hid him "under some Rubbish till High 12 again." During the night they carried his body to the "Brow of the Hill, where they made a decent Grave and buried him." Hiram was, however, missed already the same day, and King Solomon ordered fifteen "Loving Brothers" to search for him. They agreed that if they did not find the Word in him or about him, the first Word that came to them should be the new Master's Word. Then one of the brothers who was more tired than the others sat down in order to rest himself. When he took hold of a shrub it came easily up, and he saw that the ground had been broken. He called the other brothers and they found Hiram's grave, which was covered with moss and turf. They covered the grave again and placed a "sprig of Cassia,"[78] at the head of the grave, and then went to tell King Solomon what they had found. Solomon ordered that Hiram's body should be taken up to be buried decently, and that fifteen Fellow Crafts, with white Gloves and Aprons, should attend his funeral. Then follows the crucial part of the ritual:

> Ex. How was *Hiram* rais'd? R. As all other Masons are, when they receive the Master's Word.

> Ex. How is that? R. By the Five Points of Fellowship.

> Ex. What are they? Hand to Hand, Foot to Foot, Cheek to Cheek, Knee to Knee, and Hand in Back.

> N.B. *When* Hiram *was taken up, they took him by the Fore-fingers, and the Skin came off, which is called the Slip; the spreading the Right Hand and placing the middle Finger to the Wrist, clasping the Fore-finger and the Fourth to the Sides of the Wrist; is called the Gripe, and the Sign is placing the Thumb of the Right Hand to the Left Breast, extending the Fingers.*

> Ex. What's a Master-Mason nam'd. R. *Cassia* is my Name, and from a Just and Perfect Lodge I came.

> Ex. Where was *Hiram* inter'd? In the *Sanctum Sactorum.*

> [. . .]

Ex. Give me the Master's Word.

R. Whispers him in the Ear, and supported by the Five Points of Fellowship before-mentioned, says *Machbenah,* which means *The Builder is smitten.*[79]

The Five Points of Fellowship, which previously figured in the "Fellow Craft or Master Mason" degree, assume an important part in the third degree ritual as it now becomes connected to the raising of Hiram. The initiates are identified with Hiram, and thus experience a ritual death. It should, however, be noted that the raising of Hiram is not a resurrection such as encountered in, for instance, the myths of Osiris or the Gospel accounts of the resurrection of Christ. It is only in certain later masonic High degree rituals that Hiram resurrects in the true sense of the word. The raising of Hiram in *Masonry Dissected* implies the raising of Hiram's body by the fifteen Fellow Crafts from the grave that the three ruffians had made. The identification of the initiate with Hiram, through Hiram's death, is nonetheless an important initiatory act—an identification that becomes even more important by the fact the Hiram, and thus the initiate, becomes buried in the *Sanctum Sanctorum* of the temple. I will have the opportunity to return to this topic shortly.

The publication of *Masonry Dissected* provoked the publication of responses in which the honor of Freemasonry was defended, and the integrity of Samuel Prichard was questioned.[80] One such answer was the anonymous *A Defence of Masonry,* published in 1730–1731. Apart from a polemic treatment of Prichard's motives in publishing *Masonry Dissected,* the text includes an interesting discussion of masonry's apparent relationship to ancient mysteries.[81]

> The Conformity between the Rites and Principles of *Masonry* (if the *Dissection* be true) to the many Customs and Ceremonies of the Ancients, must give Delight to a Person of any Taste and Curiosity, to find any Remains of Antique Usage and Learning preserved by a Society for many Ages, without Books or Writing, by oral Tradition only.[82]

Masonry is particularly likened to the Pythagoreans, the Essenes, and the Druids—but more importantly masonry is connected to Kabbalah. Significantly enough, Kabbalah is specifically connected to the Mason Words, and it is thus the literary Kabbalah, or gematria, which is seen as compatible with masonry:

> The *Cabalists*, another Sect, dealt in hidden and mysterious Ceremonies. The *Jews* had great Regard for this Science, and thought they made uncommon Discoveries by means of it. They divided their Knowledge into *Speculative* and *Operative*. *David* and *Solomon*, they say, were exquisitely skilled in it, and no body at first *presumed* to *commit it to Writing*; but, what seems most to the present Purpose, the Perfection of their Skill consisted in what the *Dissector* calls *Lettering of it*, or by ordering the *Letters of a Word* in a particular manner.[83]

Is it possible to discern any traces of kabbalah in the Hiramic legend? A cursory survey leads to a negative answer to the question: there are no *obvious* references to kabbalah such as, for instance, any speculations concerning the emanations of God (the theory of the *Sephiroth* deriving from the *Sepher Yetzirah*); no references to the feminine aspect of the Divine, the *Shekinah*; no speculations concerning numbers, *gematria*, *inter alia*. Nevertheless, the chief aspect of the legend, the search for a lost word, offers an intriguing parallel with zoharic speculations concerning the loss of the proper way to pronounce the name of the Lord, the Tetragrammaton (*YHVH*). According to kabbalistic tradition, the proper mode of vocalization, or of pronouncing the Divine Name was a guarded secret that was reserved for the Holy of Holies within the temple of Jerusalem. The second siege of Jerusalem by Nebuchadnezzar in 586 BC that resulted in the destruction of Solomon's temple and the beginning of the so-called Babylonian Captivity of the Jews that was to last until 538 BC, had the consequence that the High Priest no longer had the opportunity to pronounce the name of God.[84] This subsequently led to the tragic consequence that the true way of pronouncing the holy name passed into oblivion. Thus, we find in the zoharic tradition a search for the lost name, or rather the true way of pronouncing a known name. A. E. Waite (1857–1942), one of the most influential masonic and esoteric amateur scholars of the first half of the twentieth century, has written extensively on the parallel between the zoharic and the masonic search for something lost. Even though Waite lacked a proper academic training, accounting for his writing being "diffuse, often verbose, and peppered with archaisms,"[85] his firm belief that the originators of masonry were versed in kabbalistic doctrine is worth considering:

> For myself I believe that the mystic hands which transformed Freemasonry were the hands of a Kabalistic section of Wardens of the Secret Tradition; that their work is especially traceable in the Craft Legend; and that although in its present form this

Legend is much later and a work of the eighteenth century, it represents some part or reflection of those Zoharic preoccupations which began in England with Robert Fludd, Thomas Vaughan, were continued through Henry More, and were in evidence both in France and Britain before and about the period of the French Revolution.[86]

In order to understand Waite's arguments concerning the Craft Legend (i.e., the legend of Hiram), it is vital to be familiar with his conviction that the object of the masonic initiation is a *Unio Mystica* with God.[87] For Waite the loss of the Master's Word, which occurred at the moment of the murder of Hiram within the uncompleted Temple, and the subsequent masonic search for this lost word, has its parallel in the zoharic tradition. According to Waite, the early Christian kabbalists of the Renaissance held that the search for a lost name within the zoharic tradition, in reality was about finding Christ. The originators of the masonic tradition, who had knowledge of the zoharic search, incorporated the theme of a search for something lost (in this case the Master's Word) to represent the search for Christ. To Waite, *Verbum Christus Est*, the lost Master's Word is Christ.[88] This claim would be unintelligible if not understood against a Kabbalistic background. The old Master's Word was the name of the Lord, *YHVH*. According to Christian Kabbalistic tradition, the name of God conceals the name of Jesus, and thus it is "Kabbalistically" proved that Christ is the Savior. By including the Hebrew letter ‫ש‬, Shin, (which by its shape was considered by Renaissance kabbalists to allude to the trinity) in the name of the Lord, Yod He Vau He, the name of Jesus emerges *YHSVH*, Yeheshuah or Jeheshua.[89] This Kabbalistic proof has been held in high esteem among Christian kabbalists such as Pico della Mirandola (1463–1494) and Johannes Reuchlin (1455–1522).

The question now arises: to what extent are the two traditions related? Recent research by Snoek tends to substantiate the theory that the search for the Master's Word is indeed influenced by the zoharic quest for the proper way of pronouncing the name of the Lord. Admittedly, Snoek does *not* mention the zoharic similarities, but his findings are nonetheless confirming the kabbalistic connection. In two separate articles Snoek has made a thorough study of the Hiramic legend and therein reaches several important conclusions.[90] According to the legend of Hiram, the old Master's Word was lost at the occasion of Hiram's murder, and a new Master's Word was adopted, *viz. Makbenak*—believed to mean "the flesh falls from the bones."[91] The old Master's Word was the name of God in Hebrew, Tetragrammaton, pronounced as

Jehovah,[92] which is the same name that figures in the zoharic tradition. The notion that the old Master's Word was *lost* at the time of Hiram's death, is indeed perplexing, to say the least, since it is clearly stated in the legend itself that the old Word was *YHVH*. Snoek has unraveled this knot by clearly showing that in the early English versions of the legend there was never a question of *losing* the Word, but that which was lost was rather the way of *pronouncing* the Word.[93] According to the early versions of the legend the Master's Word could only be pronounced by the three Masters together, *viz.* King Solomon, King Hiram, and Hiram Abiff. This is the reason why Hiram *could* not, as opposed to *would* not, reveal the word. Since Hiram had not passed on his knowledge before being killed, the proper way of pronouncing the Master's Word was lost.[94] We have thus two traditions, the zoharic and the masonic, where a central theme is the loss of the proper way of pronouncing the name of the Lord, *YHVH*. To me, it seems highly unlikely that the choice of the old masonic Master's Word would have been made without the influence from Kabbalistic speculations on the name of God. Especially since the speculations concerning *YHVH* are not limited to the zoharic tradition, but are an important aspect of the Christian Kabbalah as well.

There is a further dimension connected to this common theme, namely that of *Unio Mystica*. Snoek has demonstrated in the mentioned articles that Hiram in the early versions of the legend became identified with the Lord. This identification is, in my opinion, of incalculable importance when trying to understand the early masonic initiation:

> It should be clear by now that placing the name of God on the tomb of Hiram was a functional equivalent to his being buried in the *Sanctum Sanctorum*. Both make clear that Hiram is in fact Jahweh. It is precisely that which renders the third degree ritual an initiation of a very well-known kind: the candidate is identified with a hero, who turns out to be (a) God. In that way, the ritual *Unio Mystica* between the candidate and the divinity is expressed and realized.[95]

Viewing the legend of Hiram in the light of Snoek's findings, shows that the legend in its original form was an "initiation myth," as opposed to the later versions where the legend adopts the function of a "moralistic story." The link to the zoharic tradition becomes stronger when the initiatic aspect of the legend is stressed. At the core of the Jewish Kabbalah lies the fundamental aim of the individual experience of the Godhead, or a *Unio Mystica*.[96] It is this fundamental aim that links the two traditions together in a *functional* manner. Both traditions center on a direct identification with, or experience of the Godhead. With this in mind, the masonic adoption of the zoharic theme of the loss of knowledge whereby the Lord's name is being pronounced, becomes more understandable than if the Hiramic legend is being used in a merely moralistic sense, as is the case in its later versions.

To conclude, let us return to the question posed at the outset of this part. Is the masonic legend of Hiram influenced by kabbalah? As we have seen, the masonic legend of Hiram centers on the loss of how to pronounce the name of the Lord, *YHVH*. The same topic (centered on the identical name) is found within the zoharic and Christian Kabbalistic traditions. This might be viewed as a coincidence, albeit a highly odd one, if it weren't for two important factors. First, the legend of Hiram is the most central and important legend within the masonic system of initiation. Consequently, it is highly unlikely that the content of the legend would have been chosen arbitrarily. On the contrary, early versions of the legend show that it centered on an initiatic theme where the candidate was identified with God through Hiram. Which brings us the second factor, namely the kabbalistic experience of the Godhead. Since the aim of the Master degree initiation was not merely moralistic, but rather initiatic in the strict sense of the word, it aimed at the same goal found in kabbalah, that is, a *Unio Mystica*.[97] Adding these factors to the identical theme of the loss of how to pronounce the name of the Lord, it becomes fairly safe to assume that we can trace kabbalah as a theme in the legend of Hiram.

Concluding Remarks

In this chapter I have endeavored to trace the development of the Craft degrees of Freemasonry during its formative period of the first three decades of the eighteenth century. The publication of Samuel Prichard's *Masonry Dissected* in October 1730 marked the end of the development from a two-degree system to that of a system consisting of three degrees: Entered Apprentice, Fellow Craft, and Master Mason. Furthermore, I have discussed how early Freemasonry was perceived by the public during this period, with special focus on the identification of Freemasonry with Western esotericism. The sources show that it was in particular with Rosicrucianism that Freemasonry was linked in the public eye. The masonic catechisms, however, reveal that references to esoteric currents on the whole were quite rare, but that the few references that can be found tend to be kabbalistic in nature. In particular, the third degree legend of Hiram can, in my opinion, be interpreted as being influenced by the kabbalistic search for the lost way of pronouncing the name of the God.

Even though *Masonry Dissected* was an important factor in implementing the three-degree system, it was not until after the establishment of the United Grand Lodge of England in 1813 that masonic rituals became standardized in England. In France, on the other hand, attempts to standardize the rituals occurred much earlier and in 1782 the *Rite Ecossais Rectifié* was standardized, and the *Rite Moderne* in 1786. The development of the Craft degrees after 1730 went through two main phases. The first phase, covering the period 1737 to 1751, took place mainly in France. The French exposures of this period[98] differ from the earlier English exposures primarily through the fact that they are much more elaborate and give more information on how the rituals actually were performed. Furthermore, they include new features, such as elaborate toasting and table procedures, and the use of tracing boards and passwords. In England, the enormous success of *Masonry Dissected* caused the Grand Lodge to take drastic measures in order to prevent nonmasons from sneaking into lodges. One of these measures was the reversal of the degree words. In 1751 a rival Grand Lodge was formed by a number of Irish lodges working in London, which called itself the Grand Lodge of the Antients since they considered themselves as working with older, and thus more genuine, rituals. The Antients referred to the Premier Grand Lodge as the Moderns in reference to the fact that the latter had changed the rituals. The second phase of the development of the Craft degrees is illustrated by a number of English exposures printed during the period 1760 to 1769.[99] These exposures, such as *Three Distinct Knocks* published in 1760 and *Jachin and Boaz* from 1762 contain information about the development of the Craft degrees after 1730.

The most significant development of masonic rituals of initiation after 1730 is not, however, to be found within the Craft degrees. Far more significant is the appearance of the so-called High degrees.

Chapter 5

High or Additional Degrees
of Freemasonry

Introduction

Chapter 4 revealed how the masonic system of initiation developed from
originally two degrees, to a system of three degrees by 1730. Even
though the three Craft degrees continued to be modified and elaborated, the basic components and the structure of the degrees was firmly
established. It did not take long, however, before new rituals began to
appear on the masonic scene. These new rituals were often considered
to be complements to or elaborations of the Craft degrees. In fact, the
masonic lodges of the second half of the eighteenth century experienced a virtual "ritual-boom," especially in France and the German-speaking countries. Many of these new rituals were collected into systems or
Rites[1] and these Rites often competed with each other to serve as the
sole custodian of what was claimed to be *the* secret of masonry.[2] The
High degrees are often referred to as Red degrees, while the three Craft
degrees in their turn are referred to as Blue degrees. In order to be
eligible for the High degrees, the candidate has to be a Master Mason.

Templar and Ecossais Rites

In discussing masonic High degrees of the eighteenth century, a distinction needs to be made between what is known as the Templar degrees,
on the one hand, and the Ecossais (or Scottish) degrees on the other
hand. It has been established that the Ecossais degrees come from
London[3], whereas the Templar degrees have a French origin.[4] These
two types of High degrees are the most characteristic degrees of the
eighteenth century.[5]

The earliest reference to Ecossais or Scottish masonry in England is a "Scots Masters Lodge" held at the Devil's Tavern, Temple Bar, London in 1733. This lodge met on the second and fourth Monday of each month, and the lodge was active until 1736 when it was erased from the list of lodges. In 1735 a total of twelve masons were "made" Scots Masters at the Bear Inn, Bath, Lodge No. 113. Five years later, in 1740, there were at least three more references to masons being made, or "rais'd," Scots Masters.[6] Ecossais masonry appears to have spread to the Continent at an early stage and references to this type of High degree masonry in Berlin date from at least 1741, and in France from around 1743.[7]

While the Ecossais Degrees to a large extent are occupied with the construction of a new Temple (an implicitly Christian theme), the Templar Degrees center on the legend that Freemasonry derived from the medieval Knights Templar. The order of the Knights Templar, founded in the first decade of the twelfth century, was disbanded by Philip IV "The Fair" of Bourbon (1268–1314) and Pope Clement V (1264–1314) in the first decade of the fourteenth century, but according to a masonic legend the Templars survived in the highlands of Scotland and later reappeared to the public as the Order of Freemasons. The first person to present this theory of continuation was the Scotsman Chevalier Andrew Michael Ramsey (1686–1743) who lived as an expatriate in Paris. Ramsay was the orator of the lodge Le Louis d'Argent, whose Worshipful Master was Charles Radclyffe (1693–1746). In a famous oration given at the lodge in 1737, Ramsay stated that Freemasonry was founded by the medieval crusaders in the Holy Land, or *Outremer*.[8] He did not explicitly identify the crusaders who, allegedly, founded Freemasonry as being the Knights Templar, but as Pierre Mollier has pointed out, the identification of the Crusaders with the Templars was not far away:

> A partir du moment où l'on établissait un rapport entre Franc-Maçonnerie et Chevalerie, de surcroit si cette Chevalerie était celle des croisades, les Templiers n'étaient plus loin! En fait, ils apparaissant déjà en filigrane dans le Discours de Ramsay. En effet, dans le contexte des croisades, à qui d'autre qu'aux Templiers peut s'appliquer la défense de « *Cette promesse sacrée* [qui] *n'étoit pas un serment exécrable, comme on le débite* »?[9]

Ramsey's oration proved to be a milestone in the development of masonic rituals of initiation and soon rituals began to appear that incorporated Ramsey's thesis. It was in the milieu of the Jacobite Parisian Lodges that the masonic Templar degrees first developed, perhaps as early as 1737.[10]

The best-known propagator of Templar degrees in Germany was Baron Karl Gotthelf von Hund (1722–1776), and it is often claimed that he had been initiated into a Templar degree in France in 1743.[11] On the basis of this initiation, he set up the *Rite of the Strict Observance*, which consisted of three additional degrees: Scottish Master, Novice, and Knight Templar or Knight of the Temple. The name of the Rite had "the double meaning of following strictly the rules of the Order as well as distinguishing it from the then current German Freemasonry."[12] Von Hund furthermore introduced a peculiar feature in the structure of his Rite, namely that of the Unknown Superiors or *Superiores Incogniti*.[13] These Unknown Superiors ruled, through von Hund, the *Rite of the Strict Observance*, and the members of the Rite were expected to strictly observe the decrees of these superiors. It has been suggested that the actual head of the Rite was none other than the young pretender Bonnie Prince Charlie, Charles Edward Stuart (1720–1788). The political implications for masonry (especially in connection with the Scottish Rites) during the eighteenth century have been the subject of much debate and speculations. Although it is clear that many Jacobite exiles were active in masonic lodges, it remains an open question to what extent Jacobite interests actually shaped masonic rituals of initiation.[14] In 1772 the *Strict Observance* merged with the so-called Clerics (Klerikat) created by Johann August Starck (1741–1816), but this agreement ended in 1778. Four year later, in 1782, the *Strict Observance* was officially brought to an end at the Convent of Wilhelmsbad and replaced by the *Rectified Scottish Rite* (see below).

Many of the High degree Rites that were founded during the eighteenth century have passed into oblivion, but there still remain a number of important Rites to this day. The most important of these are the *Ancient and Accepted Scottish Rite*, the *Rectified Scottish Rite*, and the *Swedish Rite*. By far the largest of these Rites in terms of the number of initiates is the *Ancient and Accepted Scottish Rite* (AASR), which has a total of thirty-three degrees including the three Craft degrees.[15] The Rite is a collection of French eighteenth-century rituals and it contains both Ecossais and Templar degrees.[16] There are also other influences such as chivalry, alchemy, and Rosicrucianism.[17] The Rosicrucian symbolism is mostly concentrated in the eighteenth degree, Knight Rose-Croix, while the twenty-eighth degree, Knight of the Sun, contains alchemical symbolism.[18] In 1801 the Scottish Rite was officially founded in Charleston, South Carolina (Table 5.1).

The *Rectified Scottish Rite* was founded around 1774 by Jean-Baptiste Willermoz (1730–1824), a tradesman in silk living in Lyons.[19] Willermoz had become a mason in 1750 and six years later he founded the lodge "Parfaite Amitie," which was constituted by the Grand Loge de France.

Table 5.1. The degree system of the *Ancient and Accepted Scottish Rite*.

Lodge of Perfection	Chapter	Areopagus
4° Secret Master	15° Knight of the East or Sword	19° Grand Pontiff or Sublime Ecossais of Heavenly Jerusalem
5° Perfect Master	16° Prince of Jerusalem	20° Worshipful Grand Master
6° Intimate Secretary	17° Knight of the East and West	21° Noachite or Prussian Knight
7° Provost and Judge	18° Knight Rose-Croix	22° Knight of the Royal Axe or Prince of Libanus
8° Intendant of the Building		23° Chief of the Tabernacle
9° Master Elect of the Nine		24° Prince of the Tabernacle
10° Illustrious Elect of Fifteen		25° Knight of the Brazen Serpent
11° Sublime Knight Elect of the Twelve		26° Scottish Trinitarian or Prince of Mercy
12° Grand Master Architect		27° Knight Commander of the Temple
13° Knight of the Royal Arch		28° Knight of the Sun
14° Grand Elect of the Sacred Vault or Sublime Mason		29° Grand Scottish Knight of St. Andrew
		30° Knight Kadosh

Tribunal	Consistory	Supreme Council
31° Inspector Inquisitor Commander	32° Sublime Prince of the Royal Secret	33° Sovereign Grand Inspector General

In 1767 he was initiated into *L'Ordre des Élus Coëns* (see below) and in 1773 into the already mentioned *Rite of the Strict Observance*. The rituals of the *Rectified Scottish Rite* developed, from the "rather crude" rituals of the *Strict Observance*, over a span of some thirty-four years from 1775 to 1809.[20] The main object of the rituals is said to be the "progressive revelation of the theosophical doctrine and teachings of Martines de Pasqually" who had founded *L'Ordre des Élus Coëns*.[21] It seems that Willermoz remained faithful to the teachings of Martines de Pasqually

Table 5.2. The degree system of the *Rectified Scottish Rite*.

Lodge	Inner Order
1° Entered Apprentice	5° Esquire Novice
2° Fellowcraft	6° Chevaliers Bienfaisants de la Cité Sainte
3° Master Mason	7° Professed
4° Scottish Master	8° Grand Professed

and the *Élus Coëns* and considered them to be the key to the true secret and object of Freemasonry. In fact, *L'Ordre des Élus Coëns* functioned as an inner order of the *Rectified Scottish Rite*, or as a "masonry beyond masonry."[22] Today, the Rite is active in Switzerland, France, and Belgium, and it is explicitly Christian in character. The majority of lodges belonging to the *Rectified Scottish Rite* no longer practice the two highest degrees: Professed and Grand Professed (Table 5.2).

The *Swedish Rite* is the name given to a Rite practiced in Scandinavia and Germany.[23] The degree system consists of a total of eleven degrees, with the last degree restricted to a limited number of initiates (as the case is with most masonic Rites). The Grand Master of the Rite is called the Vicar of Solomon. As a system, this Rite is particularly unified as the rituals of the individual degrees are closely interconnected with each other.[24]

Freemasonry was introduced in Sweden as early as 1735, when the first lodge was established in Stockholm by Count Axel Wrede-Sparre (1708–1772).[25] Wrede-Sparre had been initiated by Charles Radclyffe, Earl of Derwentwater (1693–1746), in Paris in 1731. Six years later, that is, in the same year that Ramsay delivered his famous oration, 1737, Radclyffe gave the Swedish mason Carl Fredrik Scheffer (1715–1786) a charter to open lodges in Sweden. In 1756 the first St. Andrews Lodge, L'Innocente, was founded in Stockholm by Carl Fredrik Eckleff (1723–1786).[26] It worked a fourth and fifth degree. Three years later, 1759, Eckleff founded the first chapter, which worked the sixth to the ninth degrees.[27] These degrees eventually became part of the Swedish Rite. Eckleff was instrumental in shaping what eventually developed into the *Swedish Rite* and it is often assumed that it was he who firmly implemented a Christian basis for the rituals. However, the rituals were of French origin and it was only around 1800 that Freemasonry was opened to Jews in France. It is therefore naturally assumed in the Constitutions issued by Radclyffe that Freemasonry was to be Christian in Sweden. Eckleff's system was further developed by Duke Carl of Södermanland (1748–1818), later King Carl XIII, who revised the rituals in *c.* 1780 and *c.* 1800 (Table 5.3).

Table 5.3. The degree system of the *Swedish Rite.*

St. John's Degrees	St. Andrew's Degrees	Chapter Degrees
I° Apprentice	IV–V° Elect and Very Worshipful Scottish Apprentice and Fellow	VII° Very Illustrious Brother, Knight of the East
II° Fellow Craft	VI° Enlightened Scottish Master of St. Andrew	VIII° Most Illustrious Brother, Knight of the West
III° Master Mason		IX° Enlightened Brother of St. John's Lodge
		X° Very Enlightened Brother of St. Andrew's Lodge
		[XI°] (Knight Commander's degree) Most Enlightened Brother, Knight Commander of the Red Cross

Egyptian Rites

During the latter part of the eighteenth century a new form of masonry appeared, which was partly a reaction against the Ecossais and the Templar Rites. This form of masonry did not place the origins of the Order of Freemasons with the medieval crusades but instead in ancient Egypt.[28] Ever since the Renaissance, Egypt had been seen as the cradle of Western civilization, and during the latter part of the eighteenth century a virtual "egyptomania" flourished.[29] This was enhanced even more with Napoleon's military campaign in Egypt and the vast amounts of Egyptian artifacts subsequently brought back to France by French officers. Perhaps the most important of these objects was the Rosetta Stone, which was found in 1799 at Rosetta (Rashid), east of Alexandria. In 1822 Jean-François Champollion managed to decipher the ancient Egyptian hieroglyphs with the help of this stone.

Although Egyptian masonry never became a real challenge to the predominance of the other forms of High degree masonry, it has remained on the fringes of regular masonry to this day. However, a closer look at the rituals of the Egyptian Rites, such as the *Rite of Misraim* show, as Faivre has pointed out, that Egyptian masonry was not very Egyptian in nature.[30] In fact, most of the rituals that were included in the Egyptian Rites, such as the *Memphis* and *Misraim* Rites, were taken from Ecossais and Templar Rites. There is, however, one aspect that sets Egyptian masonry apart from the Templar and Ecossais systems, and that is the marked prevalence of Western esoteric influences upon the former. It is clear that the foremost propagators of Egyptian masonry, from the eighteenth century to the twentieth, were part of the Western esoteric movement.

One of the earliest propagators of Egyptian masonry was Karl Friedrich von Köppen (1734–1797) who founded the Order of the *Afrikanische Bauherren* in 1767.[31] This order was based on a short text by Köppen and Bernhard Hymmen (1731–1787), entitled *Crata Repoa*.[32] In this text, the authors presented an alternative history of Freemasonry in which the first Grand Master was identified as the biblical Ham, who had immigrated to Egypt and there taken the name Menes. In Egypt Menes received a secret knowledge, which has been passed on and preserved by generations of Freemasons all the way to the eighteenth century. Allegedly, the Order of the *Afrikanische Bauherren* was based on this secret knowledge. The Rite comprised a total of eleven degrees divided into three groups or Temples.

Another influential system was Cagliostro's *Egyptian Rite*, which was founded in Naples in 1777, with a Supreme Council established in Paris in 1785.[33] Allesandro di Cagliostro (ps. of Giuseppe Balsamo 1743–1795), was one of the most famous and charismatic adventurers of the eighteenth century. He claimed to have been initiated at the pyramids in Egypt and he asserted that he possessed the knowledge to transmute base metals into silver and gold. Other claims included the ability to evoke spirits, and that he had lived for no less than two thousand years. In 1785 he announced that both men and women should be entitled to the mysteries of the pyramids, and he thus opened his Rite to women.[34] Cagliostro's preoccupation with esoteric matters apparently found its way into the initiatory system of his Egyptian Rite, and the Rite included alchemical aspects, the search for a spiritual immortality, and angelic theurgy.[35]

The most famous of all the Egyptian Rites, and certainly the most influential ones, were the *Misraim* and *Memphis Rites*. The first of these Rites, the *Rite of Misraim*, was founded around 1805 in Milan by the Frenchman Lechangeur (d. 1812). It is said that his reason for founding this Rite was that he was denied access to the higher degrees of the Ancient and Accepted Scottish Rite (AASR).[36] He therefore decided to create his own order, which he claimed would be superior to the AASR. It is possible that there is some historical truth to this story, as Egyptian masonry was largely a reaction against the Ecossais and Templar Rites. The order was called the *Rite of Misraim* in reference to the order-legend about the son of the biblical Ham, Misraim. According to this legend, Misraim had a profound part in shaping the religion of ancient Egypt—it was none other than Misraim who was the originator of the secret tradition of Isis and Osiris. Furthermore, the wisdom preserved within the sanctuary of the Rite was claimed to derive from Adam, who had received it directly from God.[37]

A few years later the order came into the hands of three brothers from Avignon, Marc, Michael, and Joseph Bedarride, and it was under their leadership that the order was introduced in France in 1815. The Bedarride brothers tried to get the Rite recognized by the ruling masonic body in France, the Grand Orient. The Rite was comparatively successful for a couple of years and a number of lodges were established throughout France. Internal strife, however, put a stop to further expansion and in 1817 the Supreme Council of the Rite was formally disbanded.[38] Various lodges nevertheless continued to work the degrees of the Rite. The Rite consisted of a total of ninety degrees, divided into four series, which were further subdivided into seventeen classes. The four series were called Symbolic, Philosophic, Mystic, and Kabbalistic.[39]

In 1833 Jacques-Étienne Marconis de Nègre (1795–1868) joined the *Rite of Misraim* in Paris, but he was excluded from the Rite a few months later. He then moved to Lyons where in 1836 he founded a lodge of the *Rite of Misraim*, using another name. The Bedarride brothers apparently did not suspect that the founder of this lodge was the same person who had been excluded a few years earlier in Paris. In May 1838, however, Marconis was expelled once again from the Rite. This time, instead of rejoining under a different name, he set up his own Egyptian masonic Rite—the *Rite of Memphis*.[40] This Rite consisted of 96 degrees, with a 97th degree reserved for the head of the Order, called the Grand Hierophant 97°.[41] Marconis managed to set up lodges of the Rite in Paris, Belgium, and Great Britain (where a Grand Lodge of the Rite was established). In 1856 Marconis traveled to New York where he instituted a Grand Lodge of the Rite, called the "Disciples of Memphis." After a few years Harry J. Seymour became the head of the Rite in the U.S., and in 1867 he reformed the initiatory system of the Rite and reduced the number of degrees from 96 to 33. A few years later the Rite was (re-)imported to Europe via John Yarker (who established a Sovereign Grand Sanctuary in 1872), and eventually formed the basis for the Ordo Templi Orientis. In Italy, the *Rite of Memphis* and the *Rite of Misraim* merged into one system around 1881 through the endeavors of Guiseppe Garibaldi (1807–1882), under the name *Rite of Memphis and Misraim*.[42] There are today a large number organizations that claim to represent the Rites of Memphis and Misraim.

"Esoteric" Freemasonry

Masonic Rites of a more outspoken esoteric bent included Rites and orders such as *L'Orde des Élus Coëns* and the *Rite Ecossais philosophique*, but Rosicrucian Rites and degrees can also be included in this category. The first of these, *L'Orde des Élus Coëns*, or the *Order of the Masonic Knights Élus Coëns of the Universe*, was founded by the theosophist and kabbalist Martines de Pasqually (1708/1709–1774) in the 1760s and it included a peculiar form of theurgy mixed with the philosophy and theosophy of its founder.[43] Although this order possessed all the outward characteristics of a masonic organization such as a hierarchical degree system, rituals of initiation, lodges, and employed a typical masonic terminology, it is perhaps more fitting to label *L'Orde des Élus Coëns* as a religious movement. The reason for this is not only the peculiar religious teachings derived from Pasqually but also the marked religious life that the members were expected to live, which is referred to in the name of the order: "chosen priests," from the Hebrew Kohen, meaning priest. Pasqually's teachings center round the *gnostic* idea of the Fall of Man through which humankind became separated from God. Through the initiatory system of the order the members were expected to reverse the Fall and make an upward journey in which the seven degrees of the order (not counting the three Craft degrees) corresponded to the seven gifts of the Spirit. The final goal of the initiatory process was "reintegration," a return to the primitive and primordial state of man characterized by union with God. The theurgy employed in the order was a means to this goal, through which divine energies were invoked and the communion with good spirits was sought. According to Jean-François Var this theurgy was not aimed at acquiring natural or supernatural powers, and it was part of a religious "cult," which included a liturgy.[44] As mentioned, the initiatory system of the order consisted of a total of ten degrees, of which the preliminary Craft degrees were not seen as part of the Order as such. The degrees were divided into four different classes (again, not counting the Craft degrees), with the degree of Réau-Croix as the highest degree, which constituted a class of its own. After the death of Pasqually in 1774 Caignet de Lester (1725–1778) succeeded him as leader of the order (Grand Souverain de l'Ordre), followed by Sebastian de Las Casas in 1778. Although *L'Orde des Élus Coëns* was formally dissolved in 1781 it continued to have active lodges, most notably the one in Lyons under the leadership of Willermoz.[45]

The *Rite Ecossais philosophique* was the successor of an esoteric Rite called *Rite Hermétique d'Avignon*, founded in 1774.[46] According to Snoek:

The Rite Hermétique was in fact created in the lodge Saint Jean d'Ecosse in Marseille, where some members of the lodge, which was founded in 1774 in Avignon, received its degrees, and it was this lodge of Marseille that constituted the lodge Saint Jean d'Ecosse in Avignon on 31 July 1774.[47]

In 1776 the *Rite Hermétique* was exported from Avignon to Paris, where it changed its name to *Rite Ecossais philosophique*. The history of the development of the degree system[48] of the *Rite Ecossais philosophique* is a complicated matter in itself, but suffice to say that the list offered in *Collectanea* (which I use as my primary source for the True Mason ritual), corresponds with a list made by Thory for the Rite in 1766 (sic!) (Table 5.4).[49] Obviously, the date of the list is an error, since the Rite did not even exist then.[50] It is uncertain when the Rite was dissolved, but it probably occurred sometime between 1844 and 1849.[51] The *Rite Ecossais philosophique* is a good example of the more alchemically oriented masonic systems of the eighteenth century as will be evident to the reader from the degree of True Mason or Académie des Vrais Maçons, analyzed later in this chapter.

Finally, mention should be made of the so-called Rosicrucian degrees and Rites, which also appeared on the masonic scene during the eighteenth century. The prime characteristic trait of this type of degrees and Rites is that they allude in different ways to the Rosicrucian movement of the seventeenth century. As discussed in chapter 3, a Rosicrucian Fraternity never existed as described in the Rosicrucian manifestos but the idea of such a fraternity nevertheless became popular during the seventeenth century. It did not take long before masonry was seen as linked to Rosicrucianism. For instance, in *The Muses Threnodie* (1638) the "Brethren of the Rosie Cross" are described as being in possession of the Mason Word. It needs to be emphasized, however, that the masonic Rosicrucian degrees differ considerably both in content and in their relation to seventeenth-century Rosicrucianism. In order to simplify matters, most (but not all) of the masonic Rosicrucian degrees and Rites of the eighteenth century were focused on alchemy, whereas later Rosicrucian degrees and Rites are more focused on Christian Mysticism.

Table 5.4. The degree system of the *Rite Ecossais philosophique*, ca. 1766 [sic!].

4° Le Vrai Maçon	7° Le Chevalier d'Iris
5° Le Vrai Maçon dans la Voie droite	8° Le Chevalier des Argonautes
6° Le Chevalier de la Clef d'Or	9° Le Chevalier de la Toison d'Or

One of the most influential masonic Rosicrucian Rites to appear on the scene was *Der Orden des Gold- und Rosenkreuzes*, which was founded at the middle of the eighteenth century in the German-speaking world (Table 5.5). This Rite was a masonic offshoot of an alchemical brotherhood called *Der Orden des Gülden und Rosenkreutzes* founded in 1710.[52] The Rosicrucianism of *Der Orden des Gold- und Rosenkreuzes* was heavily infused with alchemy[53] but there was also a political aspect to the Order. Many, if not most, of the masonic Craft lodges of the eighteenth century cherished the ideals of the Enlightenment, whereas the High degree Rites often were more ambivalent regarding these ideals. The members of *Der Orden des Gold- und Rosenkreuzes* were to a large extent conservative in their outlook, and the Order can be seen, to a certain extent, as part of the anti-*Aufklärung* movement active in the German-speaking world during the second half of the eighteenth century.[54]

> Apart from the pursuit of alchemical knowledge, another important characteristic drew people to the new Rosicrucian order: its political stance. Rosicrucianism in the late 18th century became a rallying point for those who were of conservative outlook and who were opposed to the socially radical, rationalistic, and even anti-religious tendencies which were becoming a serious challenge in Germany.[55]

The Order was comparatively successful and lodges were established in the German-speaking countries, Austria, Hungary, and northern Italy.[56] Its success was due not only to the fact that the order functioned as a "conservative focal point," but also because it stressed the importance of religion in times when anti-religious sentiments were popular in certain parts of society. Furthermore, the German character of the Order appealed to persons of a nationalistic orientation. The Order also claimed to possess a secret knowledge (alchemy), which was restricted to its initiates.[57] The initiatory system of *Der Orden des Gold- und Rosenkreuzes* consisted of nine degrees, and one had to be a Master Mason in order to be eligible to join the order.[58]

Table 5.5. The degree system of *Der Orden des Gold- und Rosenkreuzes.*

1° Junior	6° Major
2° Theoreticus	7° Adeptus Exemptus
3° Practicus	8° Magister
4° Philosophus	9° Majus
5° Minor	

Another important masonic Rosicrucian order is *The Royal Order of Scotland,* which was founded in the middle of the eighteenth century, perhaps as early as 1741.[59] The order fell into a twenty-year-long abeyance from 1819 to 1839, but it recuperated and is today a relatively large Rite with numerous Provincial Grand Lodges.[60] It was established in the United States in 1877 with the prolific masonic author Albert Pike (1809–1891) as its first Provincial Grand Master. It consists of two High degrees: the Order of Heredom of Kilwinning, and the Knights of the Rosy Cross. The first of these two degrees gives further explanations of the three Craft degrees, while that of the Knights of the Rosy Cross is characterized by Christian mysticism veiled in Rosicrucian symbolism. According to a legendary history of the Order,[61] the *Royal Order of Scotland* was founded by King Robert the Bruce (1274–1329) in 1314 to commemorate the assistance he received at the battle of Bannockburn on June 24, 1314 from sixty-three Knights Templar. The Knights Templar had showed up unexpectedly at a crucial point of the battle and assisted Robert the Bruce to defeat the English forces of Edward II (1284–1327). The defeat ensured the independence of Scotland until the union of 1707.

The eighteenth degree of the *Ancient and Accepted Rite,* Rose-Croix of Heredom, Knight of the Pelican and Eagle, is probably the most well-known and practiced of all the masonic Rosicrucian degrees. Even though the history of this degree reaches back to the middle of eighteenth-century France, it differs considerably in content from other eighteenth-century masonic Rosicrucian Rites such as *Der Orden des Gold- und Rosenkreuzes.*[62] In 1768 a masonic body was founded in Paris, which called itself the First Sovereign Chapter Rose Croix, and in the statutes, which it issued a year later it is stated that "The knights of Rose Croix are called knights of the Eagle, of the Pelican, Sovereigns of Rose Croix, perfect Prince Masons free of Heredon."[63] The Eagle and the Pelican are symbols of Christ, which alludes to the Christian nature of the degree. The name Heredon, more commonly spelled as Heredom, and sometimes as Harodim,[64] is the name given to a mythical mountain supposed to exist north of Kilwinning, Scotland.[65] According to a masonic myth, associated particularly with Ecossais masonry, the masons were driven away after the destruction of the Temple of Jerusalem and subsequently found their way to this mountain in Scotland. They remained on this mountain until the time of the Crusades.

Rosicrucian degrees thus fall into two main categories, alchemical and Christian, but it needs to be emphasized that there are no clear-cut borders between the two categories. Furthermore, alchemical degrees of the eighteenth century are not by necessity Rosicrucian, as is evidenced by the following example.

True Mason, or Académie des Vrais Maçons

The following ritual, from the *Rite Ecossais philosophique,* is a representative example of a French High degree ritual of the latter part of the eighteenth century. As a ritual, the degree of a True Mason, or Académie des Vrais Maçons, is not particularly elaborate or impressive. Nevertheless, it includes parts that are deeply saturated with Western esotericism, particularly in the form of alchemy and, to a lesser extent, kabbalah.[66] These parts are concentrated in a discourse delivered by the Senior Sage or Surveillant, in the explanation of the tracing board, and in the instruction in the form of a catechism.

The ritual takes place in a lodge, called the Academy, and it is performed by three main officers, called Most Wise,[67] and Senior and Junior Sages, respectively. The Academy is illuminated by three candles placed on the tracing board. The dominant colors of the ritual are black, white, and red; the walls are draped in black, there should be white and red columns, the gloves and the cordons should be white, black, and red.[68] Given the alchemical nature of this ritual, these colors probably refer to the three stages of the alchemical process: Nigredo, Albedo, and Rubedo.

The Academy is opened in the ordinary fashion of masonic rituals of initiation. That is, the chief officer, in this case the Most Wise, asks the two Surveillants or Sages whether the lodge room is properly guarded, and if all present are True Masons. The Academy is then proclaimed to be opened, and one of the brethren, called Sage Academicians, is asked to give a lecture on a chosen subject. It is then announced by the Senior Surveillant that a reception is to be made: "Most Wise, there is a philosopher mason in the preparation chamber, whom the Academy has deemed worthy of being admitted among us."[69]

The candidate, who has been waiting in a chamber of preparation,[70] is divested of all metals, and has his hat, coat, and shoes removed. The sleeves of his shirt are rolled up, his hands are tied behind his back, and finally he is blindfolded. After the usual questions and knock on the door, the candidate is admitted to the lodge room where he is led to the West, facing the Most Wise in the East. There is an "earthenware vessel, into which are poured wine spirits, mercury and salt. These are to be lighted and furnish the only illumination on the academy."[71] The candidate is asked what he desires, and after answering that he wants to be admitted to the Academy, if he is found worthy, the Academicians indicate their consent to his request by rapping once on the floor with their rods, which they are holding.

The candidate is then, in the customary fashion of masonic rituals, led around the lodge. These perambulations, which are three in number, are made in a circle, a square and a triangle. When the perambulations are completed, the blindfold is removed, and the candidate is caused to see the earthen vessel with the fire. After four minutes, he is conducted to the foot of the throne of the Most Wise, and there caused to kneel. The candidate then takes the obligation in this kneeling position. This obligation is a comparatively short and simple one:

> I, ... , promise on my word of honor, and under penalty of having my lips sealed and my bowels cut open, never to reveal either directly or indirectly, to anyone at all, and under any pretext, the mysteries which I will behold, and may the Great Jehovah be my strong and holy guide.[72]

The candidate is then declared a True Mason by the Most Wise, and instructed in the traditional secrets of the degree, that is, the sacred word, the password, the name, the grip, the age, the step, and finally the battery. Of these secrets, perhaps the most significant are the sacred word and the password—Jehovah and Metralon,[73] respectively. The Most Wise proceeds to present the candidate with the apron, gloves, and a wand. The candidate is led to the tracing board, where he gives a discourse he has prepared beforehand.

When the candidate has finished his discourse, the Most Wise responds with a discourse of his own. This discourse begins by stating that the degree of True Mason was created at the time when God brought order out of chaos, and that the degree includes the principles of all other degrees. There have been many Adepts over the centuries, but some of them have been led astray. The profanes who criticize that which they do not understand, "who are lacking a keen mind and industrious hand, (. . .) will lose for themselves all the joys of discovery and labor; and scorn all that they do not possess, power of imagination and courage of doing." The Most Wise continues by urging the brethren to abandon the profanes, or "these off-springs of darkness" and enemies to their own hatred of their vain and inconsequential idea.

> For us true children of light, and sincere friends of humanity, who see in those instructions and the practice, the clear announcement of truth, there will be at last the pleasures which result therefrom.[74]

The discourse ends with a promise that the brethren will guide and help the candidate in "the science," by explaining the obstacles placed in his path and assisting him in his studies. There is also an exhortation to follow in the footsteps of "that great man, whose presence is so dear and useful to us, and whose memory will always be precious to us." One plausible suggestion is that this refers to Hiram, or perhaps Christ. Upon the completion of the discourse, the Senior Surveillant proceeds to explain the symbolism of the tracing board.

> You will see first, wise academician, in the upper part of the tableau a radiant and capital "J" in the middle.
> The triangle represents God in the three persons, and the capital "J" is the initial of the ineffable name of the Great Architect of the Universe.[75]

The ineffable name of the Great Architect indicated by the letter J is, of course, Jehovah, that is, the sacred word of the degree. As discussed in chapter 4, Jehovah or יהוה, is the old Master's Word, which was lost at the time of Hiram's death.

> The shadowy circle signifies the world which God created; the cross within it represents the light by means of which He will develop it.
> The square, the four elements which developed in it.
> The triangle, the three principles, which the mixture of the four elements produced. The circle is surrounded by the waters which God has placed above the firmament.[76]

The reference to the cross is one of the few direct references to Christianity to be found in the ritual. The passage also explains why the perambulations that the candidate had to undergo during the ritual were in the shape of a circle, square, and a triangle. The four elements refer, of course, to the antique idea that all matter is constituted by four elements, *viz.* earth, water, air, and fire.[77] This idea continued as a basic component of alchemical theory long after orthodox science had discarded it. The three principles refer to the alchemical principles of sulfur, mercury, and salt (discussed later in this chapter).

> The starry circle designates the firmament.
> The other circle with the signs and the planets represents the Zodiac.[78]

According to the Ptolemaic worldview, the earth is the center of the universe, and around this centre there are seven planetary spheres in which the seven planets of antiquity (the Moon, Mercury, Venus, the

Sun, Mars, Jupiter, and Saturn) move. The movement of the planets was considered to be caused by the *Primum Mobile*, located either at, or beyond, the firmament of the stars. It is this firmament that is referred to in the previous passage.

> The cross which surmounts them signifies that as God through his great power created the universe, so through his beneficence he redeemed it.
>   The four figures which surround it are the emblems of the atmosphere and the four winds.
>   Man, the sun, the plants which one sees on the surface of the earth are the image of the three divisions of nature, that is, the animal, the mineral and the vegetable, which through the medium of the primal fire and of the central fire, that the great architect placed in continual agitation, come to their perfection.[79]

It is specifically stated in the bylaws of the degree that no mason may be admitted, without being "Christian, pious, discreet and wise."[80] Although the Christian elements of the ritual are almost nonexistent, it is significant to note that as a rule, High degree systems tend to be limited to Christian members. It is therefore quite natural to find a reference to the cross in the ritual. Further, the division of nature into the animal, mineral, and vegetable worlds derives from Aristotle. The primal and central fires most likely refer to the two different types of fire often encountered in alchemical literature.[81]

> The two uppermost letters signify that God created those which stand below; that nature produces and that art multiplies.
>   On the altar of perfumes, we note the fire which is given to matter; the two towers are the two furnaces, wet and dry, through which we must travel.
>   The tube which is in the furnaces, serves to give the temperature of the fire produced by charcoal of oak trees. The fire will well consume the philosopher's stone. Below we see the rod for stirring the fire.
>   And the two figures surmounted by a cross, are nothing other than the two vases of nature and of that royal art, in which one may cause a double marriage of the white woman and the red servant, from which marriage there will be born a most powerful king.[82]

This part of the explanation of the tracing board is entirely devoted to alchemical imagery. The two furnaces, described as wet and dry, through which "we must travel" is a direct reference to the alchemical formula of *Solve et Coagula*, discussed later. The furnace itself is an important symbol, as it is thought that the metal undergoes its mortification and subsequent purification within a furnace, or *athanor* as it is usually called. The furnace is furthermore often identified with the fire that causes the mortification of the metal. It is significant that the coal is specified as being of oak trees, as the oak is a name for the philosophical tree.[83] The philosophical tree symbolizes the entire alchemical process, from base metal to gold, or from unenlightened to enlightened soul. The philosopher's stone is probably the most well-known of all alchemical symbols, and its primary import is the completion or the crowning of the alchemical work. As such, it is considered to possess a number of qualities, such as the ability to transmute metals, cure diseases, prolong life, and to rejuvenate. "Royal art" was the name given to alchemy (but as shown in chapter 4, it was also a name given to Freemasonry), as gold was considered to be the royal metal. A further reference to the "royal" nature of the alchemical process is the "most powerful king" that will be born out of the marriage between the "white woman" and the "red servant." The white woman and the red servant stand for the female and male principles, respectively. The king is another symbol for the philosopher's stone—the goal of the alchemical quest.

Completion of the explanation of the tracing board is followed by the instruction, which is in the form of a catechism. In French masonic eighteenth-century rituals, catechisms used to be practiced at the end of the ritual (just before closing the lodge), or at the table lodge after the initiation. The instruction is of utmost importance because it not only touches on symbols encountered in the ritual, but more importantly also shows exactly the kind of alchemy with which the members of the degree were expected to be familiar. The catechism begins with the following question:

Q.—Who is your father?

A.—Hermes.[84]

Hermes was, of course, seen as the mythical founding father of alchemy, and the above question can therefore be interpreted as that the candidate, being an alchemist, is thereby a "child" of Hermes.[85]

Q.—Did you receive the light?

A.—Verily, Most Wise, the three principles were explained to me.

Q.—Do you know how to proceed with your labors?

> A.—Verily, Most Wise, I know how to stir with the rod, to manipu-
> late the materials and to seal the vapours against esscape [sic!].[86]

Receiving the light is a recurrent theme in masonic rituals of initiation,
but in this context the light probably refers to the knowledge of the
alchemical process, as the answer indicates that the light is connected
to the knowledge of the three principles. The three principles, in their
turn, refer to the three alchemical principles sulfur, mercury, and salt.
The manipulation of the materials, or metals, is a direct allusion to the
practice of alchemy. Furthermore, the sealing of the vapors from escape
is a reference to the usage of hermetically sealed vessels in alchemy.

> Q.—What is the significance of the ten knocks you gave on your
> entry into the academy?
>
> A.—It is the perfect number.
>
> Q.—Why do you say that ten is the perfect number?
>
> A.—Because ten comprehends all the faith and unity of God by
> whom all was created, as well as chaos from which all that exists,
> was produced. Furthermore, he who would be quite happy to
> understand that which is the basic number of formal arithmetic,
> and to understand the nature of the prime spherical number which
> is the half of the ten, will know, says Pic de Mirandole, the secret
> of the fifty doors of learning of the great fifty years of this genera-
> tion, as well as the ruler of similar cycles, which the Cabalists call
> "Ensopht," or Divinity itself, unadorned.[87]

In Christian and Jewish Kabbalah alike, the number ten is seen as a
"perfect number" as it contains God's entire creation in the form of the
ten Sephiroth. The reference to "Ensopht" constitutes the unlimited
Godhead, Ain Soph, from which the Tree of Life with its ten Sephiroth
emanates. Giovanni Pico della Mirandola (1463–1494) was the first to
seek evidence in the Kabbalah for the "truth" of Christianity, and thus
inspired later kabbalists such as Johannes Reuchlin. Pico included his
Kabbalistic arguments for the authenticity of Christianity in his
Conclusiones (1486), a collection of nine hundred questions and answers.[88]
The book was, however, suppressed by the pope.

> Q.—Explain the meaning of your jewel, the colors of the ribbon as
> well as what is attached; the cross and the two letters on the flap
> of you apron; as well as the sun in the center; the letters which are
> on the two sides and the two red stripes with which it is bordered.

A.—The jewel is the representation of mercury, sulphur and salt. The colors of the ribbon and gloves represent the three principal colors which are apparent in the civil government.

The cross on the flap of the apron is the Light, the two letters represent the True Mason.

The sun represents gold, the two letters, the meaning already given. Finally the poppy-red color with which the apron is bordered designates the perfection of the philosopher's stone as black denotes putrification and white sublimity.[89]

The reference to the three colors black, white, and red refers to the three stages in the alchemical process; *nigredo, albedo,* and *rubedo*.[90] In the initial or black state the impure metal is killed or putrefied, that is, it is dissolved into its original form, or *Prima Materia*. According to alchemical theory, there can be no regeneration without corruption, no life without death. This state of dissolution, or mortification, is often symbolized in alchemical imagery with symbols of death and corruption, such as skeletons, skulls, and coffins. In the second or white phase the blackened matter is purified by the mercurial water, the universal agent of transmutation. "The body has been whitened and spiritualized (i.e., the fixed is volatilized) and the soul has been prepared to receive illumination from the spirit. This is the stage at which the alchemist achieves the white stone and the white elixir which has the power to transmute all imperfect metals to silver."[91] This stage can also be interpreted as the spirit's separation from the body, which will reunite when the body is purified and made pure and spotless. This stage is often symbolized by things pure, white, or silver, such as the moon, snow, and virgins. Finally, in the third or red stage, the spirit is reunited with the white matter. This union is often described as a "chemical wedding," and upon its completion the desirable Philosophers' Stone is achieved. Images such as red lions, basilisks, red roses, and the sun often symbolize the *rubedo* phase of the *opus alchymicum*.[92]

Q.—Do you know how to make the universal matter?

A.—I do, Most Wise.

Q.—From what do you produce it?

A.—Eternal and internal fire.

Q.—What does it result in?

A.—The four elements, which are said to be the main principles.

Q.—What are they?

A.—Fire, air, water and earth.

Q.—What are their qualities?

A.—Heat, drought, cold and moisture, the first two coupled with the latter two, bring to the earth the drought and cold.

Water has cold and moisture.

Air has moisture and heat, fire has heat and drought, which are all united on earth, because the elements are circulated like the wind of our father Hermes.[93]

As Abraham states, the idea of the four elements was derived from Empedocles (494–432 BC) and Plato's *Timaeus* (*c.* 360 BC), but came to alchemy through Aristotle's theories of matter.[94] All matter ultimately derives from a *prima materia*, and the four elements are the forms in which it manifests itself.[95] The four elements are not simply the ordinary fire, air, water, and earth in nature, but abstract principles, which emanate from the *prima materia*. The alchemical process of transmutation, or *opus alchymicum*, is based on the fundamental theory that all material objects and matter consist of various proportions of the four elements and that these proportions can be manipulated. However, in order to cause this manipulation, it is first necessary to "kill" (the *nigredo* phase) the original form of the matter one wishes to transmute. The answer to the question of what the qualities of the four elements are displays further familiarity with basic concepts of alchemy: there are four qualities connected to the elements—hot, dry, cold, and moist.[96] Each of the elements has two of these qualities; fire has hot and dry, air has hot and moist, water has cold and moist, and finally earth has cold and dry.

Q.—What does the mxture [sic!] of the four elements and their four qualities of which everything is formed, produce?

A.—The three main principles.

Q.—What names are given them?

A.—Mercury, sulphur and salt.

Q.—What do you mean by mercury, sulphur and salt?

A.—The philosophical, and not the commonly known, mercury, sulphur and salt.

Q.—What is the philosophical mercury?

A.—It is a liquid and spirit which dissolves and refines the sun.

Q.—What is philosophical sulphur?

A.—It is fire and a spirit which destroys and colors that fire.

Q.—What is philosophical salt?

A.—It is a mineral and a substance which congeals and fixes, and accomplishes all this through the medium of the atmosphere.[97]

The three main principles of metals mentioned above were first proposed by Paracelsus (Theophrastus Bombastus von Hohenheim, 1493–1541).[98] According to this theory, all metals are constituted by three main principles; mercury (the spirit), sulfur (the soul), and salt (the body).[99] Mercury and salt, or spirit and body, are seen as two contraries, which are united by the mediating principle of sulfur, that is, the soul. Paracelsus' theory of the *tria prima*, or the first three principles, differs from earlier medieval alchemy in which the metals were considered to derive from two principles, namely sulfur, and mercury.[100] Sulfur was considered to be the male principle, or hot, dry, and active seed, whereas mercury was seen as the feminine principle with its cold, moist, and passive qualities. These two principles were connected to the well-known alchemical formula of *Solve et Coagula*, dissolve and coagulate. This formula, known already by the Greek alchemists, illustrates the fundamental practice of alchemy; that is, the converting of a solid body into a fluid substance (*solve*), and the opposite process of turning a fluid into a dry solid body (*coagula*). The process was to be repeated time and again, and each time the matter to be transmuted was considered to become purer. Mercury was connected to the *solve* aspect of the formula and was thus attributed to the power of dissolving fixed matter; while sulfur was considered to possess the power of fixing and coagulating the volatile substance, and thus to be connected to the second, or *coagula*, part of the formula. Furthermore, the mercury often encompassed the two elements of water and earth, while sulfur encompassed air and water.

Q.—How are these obtained from three principles?

A.—The four elements redoubled, as Hermes said, or the great elements, accordingly to Raymond Lully, which are Mercury, sulphur, salt and glass. The former two act like volatiles, the one being like water and the other like air (or oil), and flee fire which causes the one to be driven off and the other to be consumed. The remaining two substances however being solid and dry, are not affected by fire. The salt defies the heat of fire while glass, or pure earth is not affected except to be melted and refined. Because each element has two qualities the great or redoubled elements, that is to say, mercury, sulphur, salt and glass consist of two of the simple elements, or in other words, each of the four has two elements in different proportions. Mercury has more water than is usually attributed to it; oil or sulphur, more air; the salt has more fire; and glass has more earth. Earth is at last found pure and clean at the center of all the elementary compounds, and it is ultimately freed from all the others.[101]

The answer is an elaboration of Paracelsus' three alchemical principles of mercury, sulfur, and salt.

Q.—What advantages does this give one?

A.—Two kinds, the first spiritual, the second is material.

Q.—What are they?

A.—The spiritual consists of knowing God, nature and himself. The material is wealth and riches.[102]

It is significant that not only the spiritual advantage of alchemy is mentioned but also the material one. This shows that the alchemy taught by the *Rite Ecossais philosophique* to its initiates was not merely of a spiritual character, but of a "chemical" nature as well.

Q.—Has not each of these sciences something which is appropriate and particular to it?

A.—Pardon me, Most Wise, the one is common and trivial and the other mystical and secret. The invisible world of our theology is cabalistic, celestial, astrological and magical, while the elementary is physiological and chemical, which reveals by these discoveries and the separations of fire, the mosa [sic!] hidden and occult secrets of nature of the three kinds of compositions. We also call this latter science hermetic, or the operation of the great work.

Q.—What are the sources where one may search for this latter science?

A.—The purest are Hermes Trismegistus, Arnold de Villenaeue; Raymond Lully, Gaber, Basil Valentine, Bernard Count of Trevisan, Nicholas Flamel, the Philalethes, the Cosmopolitan, the President of the Espagnet and Chevalier, the figures of Abraham the

Jew, Michael Mayer, and many others, whom we will recognize among others.[103]

The names referred to as sources for the alchemical science are all well-known and influential alchemical authors. Hermes Trismegistus is of course the mythical author of the *Corpus Hermeticum*, which was first translated into Latin by Marsilio Ficino in 1471. During the Renaissance, however, Hermes also became known as an adept of alchemy, and a number of alchemical texts were attributed to him, of which the *Tabula Smaragdina* or *Emerald Tablet* is perhaps the most famous. This short text contains the famous dictum "As above, so below," illustrating the esoteric doctrine that man is a microcosm corresponding to the macrocosm.[104]

Arnau de Vilanova (1240–1311) was a physician who translated medical works by authors such as Galen, Avicenna, and Albuzale into Latin, and he is generally seen as a representative medieval Galenism. Even though it is not ascertained whether or not Vilanova actually practiced alchemy, there are many legends about him, which connect him with the practice of alchemy.[105] According to one such legend Vilanova is supposed to have performed his first transmutation in Rome in 1286. There are a number of alchemical works ascribed to him, such as *Epistola super alchemia ad regem Neapolitanum* or *De secretis naturae* and *Exempla de arte philosophorum*, but these are probably apocryphic. The first collected edition of his works was published at Lyons in 1504.

Raymond Lully, or Ramón Llull, (1232–1316) was a Catalan mystic who developed a mysticism combined to a certain extent with Christian mysticism, Sufism and Neoplatonism. The alchemical works ascribed to him are probably all apocryphal and include titles such as *Apertorium artis*, *L'Epistre de l'abbreviation de la pierre benoiste*, *Clavicula Raymundi Lullii*,[106] and *Comendium animae transmutationis artis metallorum*.[107] Alchemical works ascribed to Llull began to circulate during the middle of the fourteenth century and these pseudo-Llullian works later became standard features in the alchemical corpus. In addition to alchemy, Llull's name also became associated with magic and kabbalah with works such as *De auditu cabbalistico* attributed to him.[108]

The alchemical works of Geber were extremely influential, and his theory of sulfur and mercury was predominant until Paracelsus modified it in the beginning of the sixteenth century. Works attributed to Geber include *Of the investigation or search of perfection* and *Of the sum of perfection, or of the perfect magistery*.[109] The name, Geber, is taken from the Arab scholar Jabir ibn Hayyan (*c*. 721–*c*. 815).

Basilius Valentinus was supposed to have been a fifteenth-century Benedictine monk, to whose name a number of alchemical tractates are ascribed. The most influential of these are *Die Zwölf Schlüssel*, or *Twelve Keyes*,[110] which was first published in 1599, and *The Triumphant Chariot of Antimony* (1604), which was first published in English in 1660. The true identity of Basilius Valentinus has not been settled, but it has been suggested that he was a late-sixteenth-century author, possibly the first publisher of Valentinus' works, Johann Thölde (1565–1614).

Bernard of Trevisan, the Earl of Trevisa in Italy, or Trevisanus (b. *c.* 1460) was another early influential alchemist, whose works include *La parole delaissee* (1618), *Le Text d'Alchymie et le Songe-Verd* (1695), and *Treatise of the Philosophers Stone* (1684).[111]

Nicolas Flamel (1330–1418) was a public writer and artisan who after his death became regarded as an alchemist, who together with his wife Perrenelle supposedly succeeded in transmuting mercury into gold, in 1382. The reason that Flamel came to be regarded as an alchemist probably stems from the fact that he left a large legacy after his death and because he had ordered certain allegorical motifs to be painted on arcades at the cemetery of the Holy Innocents.[112] According to the legend, he had bought a rare manuscript entitled the "Book of Abraham the Jew," in the ritual referred to as the "figures of Abraham the Jew." This manuscript allegedly contained seven emblematic drawings that outlined the alchemical process. A number of versions of what claim to be Abraham's figures have been published, called the *Hieroglyphic Figures of Flamel*.[113]

The "Philalethes" can refer to either Eugenius Philalethes, or to Eirenæus Philalethes—but it is more likely that the reference is to the former, as the "Cosmopolitan," which is also mentioned in the ritual, is another name for the latter. Eugenius Philalethes was the pseudonym of Thomas Vaughan (1621–1665),[114] well-known for his translation of the *Fame and Confession of the Fraternity of the R. C.* published in 1652. His alchemical works include *Anthroposophia Theomagica*, *Anima Magica Abscondita*, and *Magia Adamica*, all three first published in 1650.[115] Vaughan's alchemical writings were influential not only in England, but on the Continent as well, and his works were translated into French, German, and Latin. The emphasis of his alchemical work is more on the spiritual, or metaphysical, side than on the purely physical. As such, the alchemy of Vaughan can, at least to a certain extent, be seen as a form of mysticism. Eirenæus Philalethes, on the other hand, was probably the pseudonym of the influential scientist George Starkey (1628–1665). Starkey was born in Bermuda and educated at Harvard College. In 1650 he immigrated to London to collaborate with one of the most important persons in the development of modern chemistry—Robert Boyle (1627–1691).[116] The alchemy of Starkey (if indeed he is the true author behind the name of Eirenæus Philalethes), differs considerably from his name-sake Eugenius Philalethes,' in that it focuses on the physical or chemical aspect of the alchemical work.[117]

Jean d'Espagnet (*c*. 1564–1637) was an influential alchemist, and is quoted at length by Joseph Pernety in his *Les Fables Égyptiennes et Grecques* (1786). His alchemical works include *La Philosophie Naturelle* and *Arcanum Hermeticæ*, both which were included in the influential collection *Bibliotheca Chemica Curiosa* (1702).[118] Finally, we have Count Michael Maier (1569–1622), the German alchemist and Rosicrucian apologist. Maier moved in high circles and was, among other things, the confidant of the Emperor Rudolph II and a frequent attendee at the court of James I. His most famous alchemical treatise, considered to be a classic of alchemical literature, is *Atalanta Fugiens* published in 1618. The work contains 50 emblematic figures illustrating the alchemical process.[119]

When the instruction is done, the ritual ends in the following manner:

> The most wise then says: Behold, wise Academician, what the senior Surveillant and I have to say for your instruction. We urge that you study diligently, and we wish you much happiness in all that you do, and wish you a rapid progress in that science which is the sole and honorable aim of Masonry.[120]

The lodge is then ritually closed, and as a last act all present say together: "Glory, laud and honor to the Creator; peace, benediction and prosperity to true Masons!"[121]

The ritual of True Mason is an excellent example of how alchemical doctrines are transmitted through a masonic ritual of initiation. The alchemical doctrines transmitted, especially during the explanation of the tracing board and the instruction, summarize in a condensed form the most important symbols and theories of eighteenth-century alchemy.[122] Furthermore, the list of alchemical authors at the end of the ritual contains the most celebrated and influential names in alchemical literature. As such, the ritual of the True Mason was truly initiatic in the sense that it initiated its adepts in the Arcanum of alchemy. This would naturally depend on whether the candidate already was familiar with alchemy.

Concluding Remarks

The High degrees of Freemasonry were enormously successful and a large number of Rites were established during the eighteenth century.

A number of these Rites, such as the *Ancient and Accepted Scottish Rite* and the *Swedish Rite*, are active to this day. Others, such as *Der Orden des Gold- und Rosenkreuzes*, ceased to exist a long time ago. Perhaps the most striking characteristic of this form of ritual is its diversity, which includes such types as Chivalric, Templar, Ecossais, and Egyptian High degrees. Their common denominator is that, in various ways, they contain elaborations of the Craft degree rituals. Furthermore, it is particularly in certain types of High degrees that Western esotericism is explicitly transmitted. As an example of such a ritual, I analyzed the True Mason ritual of the *Rite Ecossais philosophique*, which in essence contains a complete exposition of eighteenth-century alchemy.

In the nineteenth century the more outspoken esoteric High degree systems, such as the Rites of Memphis and Misraim, the *Antient and Primitive Rite*, and the *Swedenborgian Rite* existed on the fringes of the masonic world. Some of the masons involved in these more obscure systems, such as William Wynn Westcott, would be responsible for creating masonic initiatory societies that came to exist outside the fold of traditional Freemasonry, of which *The Hermetic Order of the Golden Dawn* is one of the most famous examples.

Chapter 6

The Hermetic Order
of the Golden Dawn

Introduction

The Hermetic Order of the Golden Dawn—created in 1888—and the rituals of initiation that the order used are of incalculable importance for the subsequent development of Western esoteric rituals of initiation. Through the elaborate rituals of initiation the candidates were exposed to a composite form of Western esotericism, which by scholars is termed Occultism.[1] The foremost characteristic of Occultism is its composite nature, that is, the belief that a wide variety of phenomena are linked together, and further, that these phenomena to a certain extent are explanatory of each other. Thus, in the rituals of the Golden Dawn, there are references to not only alchemy and astrology, but to Tarot, kabbalah, geomancy, ritual magic, and Rosicrucianism *inter alia*, as well. The practice of linking esoteric phenomena to one another is by no means an innovation restricted to Occultism. On the contrary, it is an intrinsic part of the esoteric form of thought as expressed by Faivre under the heading of "Correspondences," and to a lesser degree "the Practice of the Concordance."[2] What was new in Occultism, and perhaps most clearly expressed in the rituals of the Golden Dawn, was the marked extent to which this was carried out. It was not merely a matter of inclusiveness, but rather a conscious syncretistic approach to esotericism as a whole. The candidates of the Golden Dawn were expected to become proficient in a remarkably wide variety of esoteric practices before they were admitted to the next degree. The prescribed courses of study show that the candidates had to learn the symbolism and technicalities of alchemy, astrology, kabbalah, and the Tarot.[3] Gerald Yorke (1901–1983) summed up the importance of the Golden Dawn as follows:

The Hermetic Order of the Golden Dawn (G.D.) with its Inner Order of the Rose of Ruby and the Cross of Gold (R.R. et A.C.) was the crowning glory of the occult revival in the nineteenth century. It synthesised into a coherent whole a vast body of disconnected and widely scattered material and welded it into a practical and effective system, which cannot be said of any other occult Order of which we know at the time or since.[4]

Despite the syncretistic assimilation of a vast area of esoteric knowledge there were no tendencies toward a muddled or chaotic system of initiation afforded by the Golden Dawn. On the contrary, every degree and all the teachings transmitted were part of a coherent whole, a precise yet simple structure, namely that of the kabbalistic Tree of Life. At the core of the initiatory system of the Golden Dawn lies the Tree of Life with its ten spheres or *Sephiroth* and twenty-two connecting paths. The degrees were connected individually to a certain *Sephira* and the candidate symbolically journeyed from *Malkuth* upward to *Tiphareth*, which was attributed to the grade of Adeptus Minor (Table 6.1).[5] At each initiation the Temple was rearranged in order to adequately illustrate the particular *Sephira* to which the degree was attributed. To a large extent the temple was nothing but a symbolic representation of the Tree of Life. It is this connection to the Tree of Life that makes the initiatory system of the Golden Dawn unique in the sense that it was the first of its kind and marks the beginning of a new trend in Western esotericism.

The use of the Tree of Life as the structural core of Golden Dawn's initiatory system should be considered in the light of the historical context of the last decades of the nineteenth century in Britain. The particular

Table 6.1. The degree system of *The Hermetic Order of the Golden Dawn*

Ipsissimus 10° = 1□	Kether
Magus 9° = 2□	Chokmah
Magister Templi 8° = 3□	Binah
Adeptus Exemptus 7° = 4□	Chesed
Adeptus Major 6° = 5□	Geburah
Adeptus Minor 5° = 6□	Tiphareth
Philosophus 4° = 7□	Netzach
Practicus 3° = 8□	Hod
Theoricus 2° = 9□	Yesod
Zelator 1° = 10□	Malkuth
Neophyte	

form of kabbalah that flourished in esoteric circles during this period had drifted away considerably from the originally Jewish Kabbalah and its Christian counterpart. Even though literary kabbalah still held a prominent position within Occultist Kabbalah, the emphasis was no longer on interpreting the Holy Scripture, but rather to reduce significant words into numbers and thereby reach a fuller understanding of their import by relating them to words of similar numerical value. Far more significant, however, was the use of the Tree of Life as a model of the universe to which every conceivable phenomenon whatsoever could be applied. In a sense, the linear scheme of the Tree of Life became a method whereby it was possible to reach order out of an apparently chaotic mass of phenomena, without necessarily any further knowledge of kabbalistic doctrine. The knowledge of kabbalah, which the chief exponents of Occultist Kabbalah possessed, was to a large extent limited to secondary sources.

In 1896 there appeared an English translation of Éliphas Lévi's seminal work *Transcendental Magic* in which the Tarot was connected to the Tree of Life. The works of Éliphas Lévi had not only been instrumental in the French "Occult Revival" of the latter half of the eighteenth century, but had also influenced the occult scene in Britain. The translation of Lévi's chief works into English disseminated his theories on various esoteric topics firmly into British Occultism[6]. Arguably, the main thesis was the connection of the Tarot with the Tree of Life.

> But Lévi's most startling innovation was in connecting the Cabala with the Tarot. Modern occultists take this connection so much for granted that it tends to be forgotten that there is absolutely no historical evidence that the two were in any way related. (. . .) In his *Doctrine et rituel de la haute magie* he connects the twenty-two trumps with the twenty-two letters of the Hebrew alphabet and the four suits with the four letters of the tetragrammaton or Name of God and the ten numbered cards of each suit with the ten Sephiroth.[7]

Even though the Golden Dawn is to be credited with a number of innovations within British Occultism, it is nonetheless a child of its time and thus mirrors the interests and trends of Western esotericism in Britain at this particular point in history. The ritual of initiation that will be analyzed in this chapter is not only a prime example of which esoteric doctrines were in vogue in the last decades of the nineteenth century, it is above all of utmost importance for the understanding of a large part of the rituals that are found in contemporary or modern esotericism.

History

The history of *The Hermetic Order of the Golden Dawn* is, like that of the majority of closed societies in the west, of a twofold nature; factual and legendary.[8] In Anderson's *Constitutions of Free-Masons* published in 1723 it is assumed that Adam was skilled in the art of geometry and it is implied that masonry ultimately stems from Adam, "our first Parent."[9] In my opinion, this should not be viewed as a simple fraud or an attempt at deceiving would-be members, but rather as an expression of a certain form of thought in which legitimacy can be founded on spiritual rather than historical grounds. More often than not, stories regarding the foundation of closed societies are by its members interpreted symbolically rather than literally. This idea pertains directly to the idea of transmission, which Faivre considers as one of the constituting aspects of Western esotericism.

According to the official/legendary[10] history of the Golden Dawn, William Wynn Westcott (1848–1925), a high-ranking Freemason and prominent member of the *Societas Rosicruciana In Anglia* (SRIA)[11], obtained some documents from another mason, Rev. A.F.A. Woodford (1821–1887), one of the founding members of the research Lodge Quatuor Coronati, No. 2076. The stories differ on how Woodford came into possession of these documents, but he supposedly identified the documents, which were written in cipher (hence referred to as the Cipher MS.), as being pseudo-masonic rituals of a Rosicrucian provenance. The Cipher MS. was sent to Westcott by Woodford on August 8, 1887.[12] Westcott deciphered the rituals and enlisted the help of S. Liddell Mathers (1854–1918) who rewrote them into workable form. Among the papers was an address to a certain Fräulein Anna Sprengel in Germany (Soror Sapiens Dominabitur Astris), who was supposed to be a Rosicrucian adept and member of "Die Goldene Dämmerung," that is, the Golden Dawn. After a brief correspondence with her, Westcott was chartered to open a Temple of the Golden Dawn, which was to be ruled by a triumvirate: Westcott, Woodman, and Mathers.

However, in all probability the Cipher MS. was composed by Kenneth Mackenzie (1833–1886)[13] with the intention of improving the rituals of the *Royal Order of Sikha and the Sat B'hai*, an order founded by an Indian Army Officer, Captain James Henry Lawrence-Archer (1823–1889). Mackenzie, however, soon lost interest in this order and instead got involved with the British branch of the *Swedenborgian Rite* under the leadership of John Yarker (1833–1913). After Mackenzie's death in 1886 the rituals found their way into Westcott's possession.[14] The correspondence with Fräulein Anna Sprengel, through which the Golden Dawn was chartered, was a fraud. The German branch of the Golden Dawn is considered by scholars to have never existed, except perhaps in the imagination of Westcott.[15] One can only speculate as to why Westcott went to such lengths to forge a story of origin for the Order, but it seems highly unlikely that Westcott sought personal advantages through the formation of the Golden Dawn. Being a longtime mason and deeply familiar with esoteric literature, he was undoubtedly well-acquainted with the importance of legitimacy in transmitting esoteric teachings in general and in the formation of initiatory societies in particular. Furthermore, legendary stories of origin were quite common in the mileau of nineteenth-century British initiatory societies. For instance, the *Societas Rosicruciana In Anglia* and the *Red Cross of Constantine*, both founded by Robert Wentworth Little (1840–1878) had completely legendary stories of origin. Westcott's endeavor was to afford the Golden Dawn an apparently legitimate foundation upon which to grow, but history would prove this foundation highly unstable, as it would be the cause of a disastrous conflict just twelve years later.

Nonetheless, on February 12, 1888, the Hermetic Order of the Golden Dawn was officially chartered in England to W. W. Westcott, S. L. Mathers, and Dr. William Robert Woodman (1854–1918), Supreme Magus of the SRIA, by Soror S.D.A. of Germany (her signature on the charter made by Westcott). On March 1, 1888, the Isis-Urania Temple No. 3 was officially opened in London.[16] Initially, male members were recruited from the SRIA, but soon candidates were drawn from elsewhere, such as the ranks of the Theosophical Society. In less than a year some sixty members had joined the order. Soon other temples were chartered in Britain: Osiris Temple in Weston-super-Mare, and Horus Temple in Bradford. The apparent success of this newly founded order caused misgivings in certain circles, most notably in the *Theosophical Society* who set up an *Esoteric Section* as a countermove.[17] Blavatsky was, however, not content with the formation of the *Esoteric Section*, but rather ordered her members not to join any other occult order and to give up their existing memberships. Diplomatic negotiations then followed between the two orders that ended in their mutual acceptance of one other. Some minor dissensions within the order followed, but as a whole the order continued to expand. In 1893 the important Amen-Ra Temple of Edinburgh was chartered, followed by Ahathoor Temple in 1894 in Paris, where Mathers and his wife Moina had moved in 1892.

1892 marked a new phase in the history of the Golden Dawn, as it was only now that the Inner Order, or *Rosae Rubeae et Aureae Crucis*, was ritually worked. The rituals of the Inner Order were written by Mathers and their central leitmotif was the legend of Christian

Rosenkreutz, the legendary founder of the Rosicrucian Brotherhood. True to the legend of Rosenkreutz, a Vault of the Adepts, that is, Rosenkreutz's tomb, was central to the rituals of the inner order. This vault was seven-sided, adorned with numerable astrological and alchemical signs, and painted with Golden Dawn's characteristic "flashing colours."[18] However, the Inner Order did not only differ in the emphasis on Rosicrucianism, but also in the important fact that its members were expected to put their theoretical magical knowledge into practice. The Adepts, as the members of the Inner Order were referred to, saw themselves as magicians in the proper sense of the word. In the heyday of Golden Dawn, around 1896, some 300 members had joined the ranks of the order, of which about 60 eventually were initiated into the Inner Order—the existence of which was kept secret to members of the Outer Order.

As time went on Mathers became the sole Chief of the Golden Dawn, as Westcott had been outmaneuvered. However, in the late 1890s Mathers' behavior became more and more eccentric and his autocratic rule soon caused dissension among members of the Inner Order in London. In 1900 this dissension culminated in an outright revolt against Mathers, which, in essence, he had brought upon himself. On February 16, he had written a letter to Florence Farr (1860–1917), who was acting as his representative in the Inner Order in London. In his letter he cautioned her not to reveal the contents, but the charges contained were so grave that it became the source for an investigating committee appointed by some Inner Order members. The object of the letter was apparently to justify Mathers' autocratic rule, which he tried to accomplish by denouncing any importance that Westcott might have had in the formation of the order. What Mathers actually did was not only to denounce Westcott but also to state that the order was based on a fraud.

> [Westcott] has NEVER been *at any time* either in personal, or in written communication with the Secret Chiefs of the Order, he having *either himself forged or procured to be forged* the professed correspondence between him and them, and my tongue having been tied all these years by a previous Oath of Secrecy to him, demanded by him, from me, before showing me what he had either done or caused to be done or both.—You must comprehend from what little I say here, the *extreme gravity* of such a matter, and again I ask you, both for his sake and that of the Order, not to force me to go farther into the subject.[19]

The investigating committee, led by William Butler Yeats (1865–1939), confronted Westcott with these allegations, but Westcott made a poor defense for himself, stating that all his witnesses were dead. Mathers tried to disband the committee since he, as Chief of the Order, had not consented to its formation in the first place. His demands were ignored and the London Adepti further declared themselves independent of his rule. In a desperate attempt to resume power Mathers sent Aleister Crowley as his envoy to London, but Crowley only managed to worsen the conflict even more, if indeed that were possible.

Thus ends the saga of the Golden Dawn, but various factions of the order continued its rituals in more or less adapted forms.[20] Today there are a number of organizations that claim to represent the "genuine" Golden Dawn, but as to the validity of their claims, a scholarly investigation is yet to be made.

A Note on Sources

The rituals of the Golden Dawn were never printed, but copied by hand by its members. A number of manuscripts of these rituals are in various private and institutional libraries.[21] Part of the rituals came to the attention of the public in 1900 when a court case was conducted against a certain Mrs. Horos and her husband. The couple had obtained some of the Golden Dawn rituals by Mathers and used them in setting up their own order, *The Theocratic Society*, which they used as a cover for luring young women and girls into their fold and then sexually abusing them. The first printed edition of the rituals of the outer order was issued by Aleister Crowley in *The Equinox* Volume I, Number II (1909), in a special supplement entitled "The Temple of Solomon the King, Book II." At the end of the article, Crowley announced the publication of the Inner Order rituals in the coming issue. Mathers tried to restrain Crowley from publishing these rituals by posing a court injunction—in vain. *The Equinox* Volume I, Number III (1910) contained the ritual of the 5° = 6° grade of Adeptus Minor in "The Temple of Solomon the King, Book III." The rituals that Crowley had published were, however, in an abbreviated form, and important information is thus lacking in this version. Between the years 1937 and 1940 Israel Regardie (1907–1985) published *The Golden Dawn. An Account of the Teachings, Rites and Ceremonies of the Order of the Golden Dawn*. Regardie, who had been initiated in the *Stella Matutina*, included a wealth of information on the Golden Dawn in his four thick volumes, but the rituals that he printed were not the ones of the original Golden Dawn, but those of one of its off-shoots, *Stella Matutina,* whose rituals differ considerably from the original ones. It was only in 1972 that R. G. Torrens published *The Secret Rituals of the Golden Dawn*, which contained rituals taken from manuscripts dated 1899, before the split of 1900. Unfortunately, Torrens only published the rituals of the outer order. In 1984 Regardie published his massive *The Complete Golden Dawn System of Magic*, which includes the rituals from Neophyte to Philosophus in volume six, and the Ritual of the Portal and the Adeptus Minor Grade ritual in volume seven. These rituals were issued to Leigh F. Gardner *c.* 1894–1896, and the original manuscripts are in the Gerald Yorke Collection, the Warburg Institute, University of London.

Description of the Neophyte Ritual

The rituals of the Golden Dawn follow the same basic pattern that can be found in virtually all Western rituals of initiation, and they show all characteristics of this type of rituals. The Grade Names primarily derive from the ones used by the SRIA, who in its turn borrowed them from *Der Orden des Gold- und Rosenkreuzes*, a masonic order active in the latter half of the eighteenth century in Germany. The officers in the rituals of the Golden Dawn, whose titles are taken from the Eleusinian mysteries, correspond directly to officers in masonic rituals:

Golden Dawn	Freemasonry
Hierophant	Worshipful Master
Hiereus	Senior Warden
Hegemon	Junior Warden
Kerux	Inner Guard
Stolistes	Senior Deacon
Dadouches	Junior Deacon
Sentinel	Tyler

The Neophyte Ritual can be divided into six parts, namely Opening, Admission into the Temple, Obligation, Admission into the order, Instruction, and Closing.

Opening

As in any opening of a masonic ritual, it starts with the usual assurance that the temple is properly guarded by posting a Sentinel (in masonry Tyler) outside the doors. The members present, who wear the proper regalia, give proof of being initiated members by giving the signs of a Neophyte. It is stated that the names of the three chief officers all commence with the letter H, for example, Hierophant, Hiereus, and Hegemon. This letter is a symbol of "life, because the character H is one mode of representing the ancient Greek aspirate; and Breathing, and Breath, are evidence of life."[22] Then follows a description of the three assistant officers (i.e., Dadouches, Stolistes, and Kerux) and the Sentinel. The object of the Sentinel is to guard the door, to keep out any intruders, and to prepare the candidate. The Dadouches, who is placed in the south, symbolizes heat and dryness. His duty is to "attend the censer, and the incense, and [to] assist in the purification and consecration by Fire of the Hall, of the Members, and of the Candidate." The Stolistes, placed in the north, symbolizes cold and moisture. His duty is to check that the regalia of the officers is properly worn, to "attend to the cup of lustral water," and to purify and consecrate the Hall, members, and candidate with water. The Kerux is placed within the portal of the Temple, which he protects. He further leads the mystic circumambulation and carries a lamp and a wand, which symbolizes "the Light of Occult Science and directing power."

Then follows the questioning of the Hegemon and Hiereus: the Hegemon is placed between the pillars of Hermes and Solomon and faces the cubical altar of the Universe. When asked by the Hierophant what his duties are, he gives the following reply:

> I preside over the symbolized gateway of Occult Science. I am the reconciler between light and darkness. I immediately follow the Kerux in the mystic circumambulations. I superintend the preparation of the Candidate; lead him through the path of darkness into light and assist in his reception, and I aid the other officers in the execution of their duties.[23]

The white color of his robe symbolizes purity, and his peculiar ensign of office is a mitre-headed scepter, which symbolizes "religion, to guide and regulate life." His office symbolizes "those higher aspirations of the soul, which should guide its actions."

The Hiereus is placed on a throne in the west, which symbolizes "increase of darkness; decrease of light." He wears a black robe, symbol of darkness, and carries a sword (severity and judgment) and a so-called Banner of the West, symbol of twilight. His office symbolizes fortitude, and his duty is thus described:

> I preside over the twilight and darkness, which encompass us in the absence of the Sun of Life and Light. I guard the gate of the West. I assist in the reception of the Candidate and I superintend the inferior officers in the execution of their duties.[24]

Finally, the Hierophant, the chief officer, describes his office:

> My place is on the Throne of the East, which symbolizes the rise
> of the Sun of Life and Light—my duty is to rule and govern this
> Hall in accordance with the laws of the Order: the red colour of
> my robe symbolizes Light: my insignia are the Sceptre and the
> Banner of the East, which signify power and light, mercy and
> wisdom, and my office is that of expounder of the mysteries.[25]

The Hall, or temple, and the members are then purified with water by
the Stolistes, and with fire by the Dadouches. A procession is then made
round the temple, called the mystic circumambulation. It is "symbolic of
the rise of the light," and it is done in due form: "Kerux first, then
Hegemon, Hiereus, other members and Stolistes and Daduouches last.
They pass three times around from East by South to West. After first
round Hiereus returns to his place, after second round Hegemon, after
third remaining members, each as he passes the throne of the East
salutes and lowers insignia, except Hierophant." After the completion of
the circumambulation the Hierophant adores the Lord of the Universe:

> Holy art Thou, Lord of the Universe.
> Holy art Thou, whom nature hath not formed.
> Holy art Thou, The Vast and Mighty One.
> Lord of the Light and of the Darkness.[26]

The Kerux is commanded by the Hierophant, "in the name of the Lord
of the Universe," to declare that the Hall of the Neophytes has been
opened, which he does by proclaiming:

> In the name of the Lord of the Universe, I declare that the Sun
> hath arisen, and that the Light shineth in the Darkness.[27]

The Opening ends with the three chief officers uttering the following
words, alternating the uttering starting with the Hierophant and ending
with the Hiereus:

> Khabs Am Pekht
> Konx Om Pax
> Light in Extension[28]

Admission into the Temple

The Hierophant states that he has received a dispensation from the
Greatly Honoured Chiefs of the Second (i.e., Inner) Order to admit the

candidate, to the Neophyte degree. The Hegemon is ordered to prepare the candidate, which he does by leaving the temple and hoodwinking the Candidate and tying a rope thrice round his waist. The Candidate is then addressed by the Hegemon:

Child of Earth, arise and enter the Path of Darkness.[29]

Prompted by the Kerux, the Hierophant affirms that he gives his consent to the candidate to be admitted, and that the candidate from now on is to be known by a certain motto. The candidate is led by the Hegemon into the Temple, but the Kerux informs the candidate that he cannot enter the Sacred Hall since he is unpurified and unconsecrated. The Stolistes purifies the candidate (who is addressed as "Child of Earth" throughout this part of the ritual) by making a cross on his forehead with water. The Dadouches purifies the candidate in his turn with fire. The Hierophant asks the candidate why he requests admission into the order, to which he answers, prompted by the Hegemon:[30]

My soul is wandering in darkness, seeking for the Light of Occult Knowledge, and I believe that in this Order the knowledge of that Light may be obtained.[31]

The Hierophant proceeds by asking the candidate to take an obligation to "keep inviolate the secrets and mysteries of our Order." He is assured that there is nothing in the obligation that might be incompatible with his civil, moral, or religious duties.

Obligation

The candidate kneels on both knees in front of the altar. His right hand is placed in the center of a triangle and the left is held by the Hierophant. The Hiereus stands on the candidate's left side, the Hegemon on the candidate's right. The Hierophant stands behind the altar in the east. With bowed head, the candidate repeats his full name at length and says after the Hierophant the obligation. The obligation, which is rather lengthy, can be summarized as follows:

The Candidate affirms that he, by his own free will and accord:

1. Will not divulge anything whatsoever concerning the order, its members or its teachings.

2. Will maintain a kind and benevolent relation with all the members of the order.

3. Will not seek to obtain any ritual or instruction which he is not entitled to, and that he will guard any documents pertaining to the order carefully.

4. Will "undertake to prosecute with zeal the study of Occult Sciences, seeing that this Order is not established for the benefit of those who desire only a superficial knowledge thereof."

5. Will not be hypnotized or mesmerized, or place himself in such a condition that he loses the control of his thoughts, words or actions.

6. Will not use his occult powers in any evil purposes.

7. Will persevere throughout his ceremony of admission.

8. Will observe his obligation, under the penalty of:

[. . .] being expelled from this Order, as a wilfully perjured wretch, void of all moral worth, and unfit for the society of all right and true persons, and in addition under the awful penalty of voluntarily submitting myself to a deadly and hostile current of will set in motion by the chiefs of the Order, by which I should fall slain and paralysed without visible weapon as if slain by the lightning flash. So help me the Lord of the Universe and my own higher soul.[32]

At the moment when the candidate has said (. . .) "by which I should fall slain by the lightning flash," the Hiereus suddenly lays the blade of his sword on the nape of the candidate's neck and withdraws it again.

Admission into the Order

The candidate, addressed as Neophyte for the first time, is urged to rise up by the Hierophant, and directed to the north, the place of the greatest symbolic darkness. The Hierophant recites the following:

The voice of my higher soul said unto me, 'Let me enter the Path of Darkness, peradventure thus shall I obtain Light. I am the only being in an abyss of darkness. From the darkness came I forth ere my birth, from the silence of a primeval sleep, and the voice of ages answered unto my soul, "I am he that formulates in darkness, Child of Earth; the Light shineth in the darkness, but the darkness comprehendeth it not."[33]

A mystic circumambulation takes "place in the path of darkness with the symbolic Light of Occult Science to guide the way." The Kerux leads the procession with Light and Wand, the Hegemon guides the candidate, the Stolistes and the Dadouches follow, thrice round. They halt in the south. The candidate is halted by the Kerux who informs him that he cannot enter the "path of the West" since he is unpurified and unconsecrated. The Stolistes duly consecrates him with water, and the Dadouches with fire. The Hegemon allows the candidate, twice consecrated, to approach the "gate of the West." Being conducted to the west, the candidate's hoodwink is slipped up for the first time. Prompted by the Hiereus, the Hegemon declares that the name of the Guardian of the West is Darkness, "the Great One of the Paths of the Shades." The Hiereus addresses the candidate:

> Child of Earth, fear is failure. Therefore be without fear, for in the heart of the coward virtue abideth not. Thou hast known me, so pass thou on.[34]

The hoodwink is slipped down again, and the candidate informed that he cannot enter the "Path of the East" since he is unpurified and unconsecrated. Once again he is purified with water and fire, and accordingly admitted to approach the "gate of the East." When arrived at the throne in the east, the Hierophant rises with the banner in his left hand, and raises the scepter with his right hand as to strike the candidate. The Hegemon slips up the candidate's hoodwink. The Hierophant says "Thou canst not pass by me, saith the Guardian of the East, unless thou canst tell me my name." The Hegemon answers "Light dawning in darkness is thy name, the light of a golden day." As the Hierophant lowers the scepter, he says to the candidate:

> Child of Earth, remember that unbalanced force is evil, unbalanced mercy is but weakness, unbalanced severity is but oppression. Thou hast known me, so pass thou unto the Cubical Altar of the Universe.[35]

The hoodwink is slipped back again, and the candidate is led to the west of the altar. Surrounded by the officers, the candidate is ordered to kneel as the Hierophant invokes the Lord of the Universe.

> Lord of the Universe, the Vast and the Mighty One, Ruler of Light and of Darkness, we adore thee and invoke thee. Look with favour upon this Neophyte, who now kneeleth before Thee

and grant Thine aid unto the higher aspirations of his soul, so that he may prove true and faithful Frater among us unto the Glory of Thy Ineffable Name. Amen. Let the Candidate rise. Child of Earth, long hast thou dwelt in darkness. Quit the night and seek the day.[36]

The hoodwink is finally removed, and all officers and members clap their hands. The three chief officers join the points of their scepters and swords over the candidate's head, and say together: "Frater X.Y.Z. we receive thee into this the Order of the Golden Dawn." As in the opening, Khabs Am Pekht, etc., is recited.

Instruction

The candidate is informed that before him, during his wanderings in darkness, the Kerux had carried a lamp, which is a symbol of the Hidden Light of Occult Science. Conducted east of the altar, the candidate is instructed in the secrets of the Neophyte degree, which consists of two signs, a grip or token, a grand word, and a password, the latter being changed at each equinox. The candidate receives a final consecration by water and fire. The rope is removed from his waist, "the last remaining symbol of the path of darkness," and he is then invested with the badge of the grade by the Hegemon, which symbolizes "Light dawning in darkness." A final circumambulation follows, after which there is a lengthy address by the Hierophant. This address is important since it explains many of the symbols encountered by the Neophyte in the ritual.

(. . .) I now direct your attention to a brief explanation of the principal symbols of this grade. Let me first premise that the hoodwink placed over your eyes at your preparation represented the darkness of ignorance, while the rope round your waist showed those earthly inclinations which ever endeavour to drag down and fetter the soul. The central object of the Hall, the Cubical Altar, is emblematic of the material universe which is described in the Sepher Yetzirah, or Book of Formation, as being an Abyss of Height, an Abyss of Depth, an Abyss of the East, an Abyss of the West, an Abyss of the North and an Abyss of the South. The Altar is represented black to show the darkness and obscurity of nature in her workings. The White Triangle is the symbol of the Divine Light and Creative Spirit, which formed the universe in darkness, and it therefore represents Light dawning in darkness. The red Calvary Cross that surmounts it symbolizes Life. At its East, South, West and North Angles are a Rose, Fire, a Cup of Wine, Bread and Salt. These allude to the four elements of Air, Fire, Water and Earth. The mystic words KHABS AM PEKHT, KONX OM PAX are ancient Egyptian and Greek, which were repeated in the Eleusinian Mysteries.

Their literal translation is 'Light in Extension' and their import is 'May light be extended in abundance upon you.' East of the Cubical Altar of the universe are the two pillars alike of Seth, of Hermes and of Solomon. They represent eternal equilibrium, Severity and Mercy, Active and Passive, Fixed and Volative, and the phenomena of the dual polarity of the magnet. The designs painted upon them in black and white are taken from certain chapters of the Egyptian Ritual of the Dead. The twin lamps which burn on their summits shine upon you, though their light is partly veiled, yet that through the knowledge of their equilibrium lies the pathway to occult science. Therefore stood I between them when you were restored to light, and therefore were you placed between them to receive the signs of these grades and the final consecration. Two contending forces and one which unites them eternally are represented by the two basal angles of the Triangle and one which forms the apex. Such is the origin of all creation; it is the Triad of Life. My Throne in the East represents the rise of the Sun of Life and Light. The Throne of the Hiereus facing me in the West represents increase of darkness and decrease of light. The Hegemon seated between the columns is the synthesis of our equilibrium and the reconciler between Light and Darkness. These symbolical meanings are further enlarged by the colours of our robes and by our insignia. The Wand and Lamp of the Kerux are the Magic Light and Staff of Occult Science to guide us in darkness.

The seat of the Stolistes in the North represents the powers of Cold and Moisture, as that of the Dadouches in the South does those of Heat and Dryness. (. . .)[37]

The Hierophant ends his address by ordering the Kerux to declare that the candidate has been duly admitted as a member, which he does, followed by everyone clapping hands. The Hiereus further instructs the Neophyte in a short address, which can be summarized as follows:

(1) Do not forget to give due honor and reverence to the Lord of the Universe.

(2) Do not ridicule the form of religion professed by another.

(3) Do not forget to keep everything pertaining to the order secret.

4) Study the "Great Arcanum," that is, the proper equilibrium of mercy and severity.

5) Don't be daunted by the difficulties of Occult Study.

The Hierophant informs the Neophyte what he needs to do before being eligible to proceed to the next grade, which consist of becoming thoroughly acquainted with certain occult knowledge. The Neophyte is then led to a table where he pours a few drops of a solution on a plate, which turns red in the semblance of blood, which is a final warning to heed his oath of secrecy. Lastly, the Hierophant reminds the Neophyte that his admission does not entitle him to initiate any person into the order without "dispensation from the Grand High Chiefs of the Second Order."

Closing

The Kerux proclaims "Ekas, Ekas, Este, Bebeloi," after which the Hierophant bids the members to assist him in closing the Hall in the Neophyte Grade. The three chief officers knock three times each, and the Kerux checks that the Hall is properly guarded. All members are ordered to give the signs of a Neophyte, which is followed by the Stolistes and the Dadouches purifying the Hall and the members by water and fire, respectively. The mystic circumambulation takes place as in the opening, save that the procession forms in the south and goes the reverse way. The Hierophant states that the circumambulation is symbolic of the fading light, and adores the Lord of the Universe as in the opening. The Hierophant urges the members to remember the pledge of secrecy and instructs them in partaking of the four elements.

> I invite you to inhale with me the perfume of this Rose; eat with me this bread and this salt as types of earth, and finally drink with me this wine, the consecrated emblem of Elemental Water.[38]

All members receive this in silence, each from his immediate predecessor in rank and seniority. The last one to partake is the Kerux, who inverts the cup and says "It is finished." The Hierophant exclaims "Tetelestai," and the chief officers knock once. Then follows Khabs Am Pekht, etc., as in the opening. The Closing is rounded off by the words of the Hierophant:

May what we have partaken of sustain us in our search for the Quintessence; The Stone of the Philosophers and Perfect Happiness and the Summum Bonum.[39]

Analysis of the Neophyte Ritual

Opening

The ritual of initiation for the Neophyte grade is quite lengthy compared to the subsequent rituals of the Golden Dawn. It is, to a certain degree, the foundation of all subsequent rituals because it not only contains fundamental phenomena that will be present throughout the initiatory system, but it was considered to be the most important ritual, perhaps only equaled by the ritual for the Adeptus Minor grade of the Inner Order. The structure of the ritual closely follows that of Craft Freemasonry, especially that of the Entered Apprentice degree, and the officers correspond directly to masonry. The Hierophant has his seat in the east, as does the Worshipful Master in those in masonry, in order to illuminate the temple in likeness of the sun. The two pillars are present within masonic lodges as well, where they are referred to as Jachin and Boaz. In fact, a large part of the items used in the ritual can be derived from masonic rituals, but their *import* does not necessarily correspond with one another. The symbols used by the Golden Dawn were interpreted from an esoteric perspective, or more properly from an Occultist perspective. Fortunately, we are able know at some depth how the symbols were interpreted by the originators of the rituals because some documents describing them have survived. Chief among these are Documents Z.1 "Symbolism of the Temple" and Z.3 "On the Grade of Neophyte."[40] I will thus avail myself of these documents in analyzing the ritual of the Neophyte grade.

The officers, even though they derive from masonry, differ in their import compared to Freemasonry. The Dadouches and Stolistes symbolize Fire and Water, and they have their seats in the south and north. In Western esotericism the four elements correspond to the four points of the compass: Fire to South, Water to North, Air to West, and Earth to East. In Document Z.1 it is stated that the Neophyte grade is connected to the Tree of Life, and that the Temple is arranged in accordance with its symbolism:

The Temple as arranged in the 0 = 0 Grade of Neophyte of the Order of the Golden Dawn in the Outer is placed looking towards the Yod He of Yod He Vau He in the Malkuth of Assiah, that is, that as Yod and He answer unto the Sephiroth Chokmah and Binah in the Tree, unto Abba and Aima, through whose knowledge that of Kether may be obtained, Vau for the rest, except Malkuth, which is the He final: even so, the sacred rites of the Temple may gradually, and as it were in spite of themselves, raise the Neophyte unto the Knowledge of his Higher Self.[41]

The name of the Lord, Yod He Vau He (יהוה), has many meanings within esotericism: for instance, the four letters refer to the four elements: or the four so-called mother letters: in this case they represent a formula of creation, or rather emanation, since in kabbalah the world is considered to have emanated from God, and thus they are attributed to the Tree of Life and the four kabbalistic worlds, *Atziluth*, the Archetypal World, *Briah*, the creative world, *Yetzirah*, the world of formation and *Assiah*, the material world.[42] The last part, referring to the Neophyte reaching Knowledge of his higher self, is an intimation of the prime objective of the Inner Order.

The initiation is considered to take place in Malkuth, the Kingdom, which usually is considered as the Material World. The Sephiroth Yesod, Hod, and Netzach are also symbolically present in the temple, but the Neophyte does not venture to these higher spheres. In the east, there is a veil, which symbolizes the Veil of Paroketh, which separates the lower Sephiroth from Tiphareth, which in the system of the Golden Dawn marked the separation between the Outer and Inner orders. Behind the veil, unknown by the candidate, the three ruling chiefs of the order had their seats.

The two pillars of the temple are painted in white and black, respectively, just as in some masonic lodges, but in the Golden Dawn they are attributed with kabbalistic significance:

> They represent Mercy and Severity, the former being white and in Netzach, the latter black and in Hod. Their bases are cubical and black to represent the Earth Element in Malkuth, the columns are respectively white and black to manifest eternal balance of the Scales of Justice. Upon them should be represented in counterchanged colours any appropriate Egyptian design emblematic of the soul. The scarlet tetrahedronal capitals represent the Fire of Test and Trial and between the Balance is the Porchway of the Immeasurable Region.[43]

The kabbalistic columns referred to run along the "outer" Sephiroth of the Tree of Life—the white: Netzach, Chesed, and Chokmah; and the black: Hod, Geburah and Binah. The Egyptian designs are taken from the Vignettes to chapter 17 of the *Book of the Dead* (White Pillar) and from the Vignette to chapter 125 of the same work (Black Pillar). The design on the white pillar is intended to accompany the Hymn to the Rising Sun, and the one on the black represents the deceased, passing by the forty-two assessors to the Hall of Judgment, where the soul is weighed, previous to being conducted into the presence of Osiris.

> The Black Pillar symbolizes the pathway of darkness, the Negative Confession, as the White Pillar represents the Hymn to the Rising Sun, the Pathway of Light, and the Positive Confession. Between the two is the straight and narrow path that must be trodden by the initiate.[43]

The use of Egyptian symbolism was very much in vogue during the last decades of the nineteenth century, especially in occultist circles, since ancient Egypt was considered to be the birthplace of not only alchemy and magic, but of "true initiation" as well. Mathers staged what he termed the Rites of Isis in Paris and he was a great admirer of Egyptology, which is evidenced in the rituals of the Golden Dawn. The officers in the Neophyte grade were considered to be symbolic of certain Egyptian gods:

> *Hierophant*: Osiris in the Netherland. Expounder of the Mysteries in the Hall of the Dual Manifestation of the Goddess of Truth.
>
> *Hierus*: Horus in the Abode of the Blindness unto Ignorance of the Higher. Avenger of the Gods.
>
> *Hegemon*: Thmaa-Est "Before the Face of the Gods in the Place of the Threshold."
>
> *Kerux*: Anubis of the East. Watcher of the Gods.
>
> *Stolistes*: Auramo-ooth.
>
> *Dadouchos*: Thaum-Aesh-Niaeth.
>
> *Sentinel*: Anubis in the West.[45]

The pathway leading between the two pillars is conceived of as the gateway of Occult Science, and the Hegemon who presides over this position carries a mitre-headed scepter, symbol of "religion, to guide and regulate life." The notion of "Occult Science" reoccurs throughout the ritual and is of prime importance for a proper understanding of the Golden Dawn's initiatory system. By looking at the prescribed courses of study for each degree, the vast area of knowledge intended under the heading "Occult Science" is easily discerned.[46] Another reoccurring notion is "Light," which, as far as I can see, is used in two manners. First, there is the Light of Occult Science, which aims at awakening the "hidden" properties in man, and thus to render him "more than human," or super-human. Second, the Light is considered in general terms as the spiritual light as opposed to the material darkness, but more specifically as the limitless light (Ain Soph Aur), which spreads downward through the Tree of Life, that is, the emanations of the godhead. The mystic circumambulation, which is symbolic of the rise of the light, should be interpreted in accordance with these notions of light.

The adoration of the Lord, which concludes the opening is interesting because it clearly states that the Lord is one, that despite the frequent allusions and uses of a wide range of gods, the concept of the Lord is monotheistic. All the various gods, angels, and demons encountered in the system of the Golden Dawn are, in the end, nothing but various aspects of the One God, since they are all attributable to the Tree of Life, which is the emanations of the godhead.

Admission into the Temple

The purifications by water and fire do not necessarily reflect esoteric connotations since such purifications are common in nonesoteric masonic rituals as well. However, to the members of the Golden Dawn they certainly had their esoteric meaning. The most important aspect of this part is the candidate's answer to the question why he seeks admission into the order:

> My soul is wandering in darkness, seeking for the Light of Occult Knowledge, and I believe that in this Order the knowledge of that Light may be obtained.[47]

This answer adequately summarizes the main object of the Golden Dawn—to teach its members Occultism, which will render their soul free from the material darkness. In this sense the Golden Dawn can be seen not only as an initiatory society, but also as an esoteric school. The members of the Golden Dawn did not only encounter esoteric teachings through the rituals, but they were also required to follow detailed courses of study of esoteric doctrines in order to advance through the degrees.

Daniël van Egmond has defined what he terms an esoteric school, under which heading he discusses the Golden Dawn, the *Esoteric Section* of the *Theosophical Society*, and the *Mysteria Mystica Aeterna*, allegedly founded by Rudolf Steiner (1861–1925):

> I define an esoteric school as an institution that teaches its students particular theories and practices that may enable them to transform themselves into human beings who are aware of, and are guided by, their "souls," "higher selves," or "holy guardian angels."[48]

The definition points toward the object of the teachings, namely to transform the members. This transformation can be seen as an intrinsic part of the initiatory system of the Golden Dawn whose stated object was to render the members "more than human."

Obligation

From an esoteric perspective there are a number of interesting aspects to the obligation that the candidate takes. First, he promises that he will "undertake to prosecute with zeal the study of Occult Sciences, seeing that this Order is not established for the benefit of those who desire only a superficial knowledge thereof." Indeed, if he had the desire to proceed within the initiatory system of the Golden Dawn, he could not do so if he did not "prosecute with zeal the study of Occult Sciences" since vigorous examinations awaited him before he could become eligible to proceed. Second, he swore that he would not let himself be "hypnotized or mesmerized, or place himself in such a condition that he loses the control of his thoughts, words or actions." This might seem contradictory to the common notion of the occultist as someone who willingly submits himself to the influence of foreign dominion, but the occultism of the Golden Dawn had a rational and "scientific" approach to occult phenomena, and a strong personal will was a prime requisite in order to become an efficient magician.[49] The third aspect of the obligation that needs to be examined is the penalty, which includes the part that states that the candidate "voluntarily submitting [himself] to a deadly and hostile current of will set in motion by the chiefs of the order, by which I should fall slain by the lightning flash." There has been much speculation as to the nature of the "current of will" set in motion by the chiefs, but it appears that the chiefs of the order claimed to posses the ability to eliminate people through supernatural means. It is thus an intimation of the possible power of occult science to which Adepts can attain.

Admission into the Order

This part is marked by the purification and consecration of the candidate, which in a mystical manner exalts his nature to such an extent that he becomes worthy of the order. The part that states "Child of Earth, remember that unbalanced force is evil, unbalanced mercy is but weakness, unbalanced severity is but oppression" is a further reference to the two pillars of the Tree of Life in the sense that the initiates of the Golden Dawn strived for spiritual balance, symbolized by the two pillars of the Tree of Life. The Hierophant ends his invocation of the Lord and urges the candidate: "Child of Earth, long hast thou dwelt in darkness. Quit the night and seek the day." This is a further prompting of the candidate to turn his back to the material darkness and to seek the spiritual Light.

Instruction

This is the most crucial part of the initiation as it instructs the candidate in the symbolism of the degree and for the first time discloses the order's guarded secrets. "Candidate is informed that before him during his wanderings in darkness, the Kerux had carried a lamp, which is a symbol of the Hidden Light of Occult Science." This can be interpreted as the way of the material darkness, that is, by studying the occult science of the Golden Dawn the candidate will find a path in the darkness. The reference to *Sepher Yetzirah*, or *Book of Formation* is important as it gives a direct reference to a kabbalistic text. The *Sepher Yetzirah* is one of the oldest kabbalistic texts and is especially devoted to the emanations of God, that is, the ten Sephiroth. The book was translated into Latin by Guillaume Postel (1510–1581), "that strangely stubborn French Hebraizing Christian mystic and Cabalist,"[50] in the middle of the sixteenth century, and it was a well-known work among Christian Kabbalists. The *Sepher Yetzirah* was available to the members of the Golden Dawn in a translation by Westcott, first published in 1890 in a private edition limited to a hundred copies.[51]

The Rose, Fire, Cup of Wine, Bread, and Salt allude, as stated in the ritual, to the four elements (air, fire, water, and earth). In the concluding address of the Hiereus, there are two points that directly refer to occultism, namely to "Study the 'Great Arcanum,' i.e. the proper equilibrium of mercy and severity" and "Don't be daunted by the difficulties of Occult Study." The reference to proper equilibrium between mercy and severity is a final reference to the Adept's path between the two kabbalistic pillars, which will lead to light. The encouragement not to be daunted by the apparent difficulties of Occult study is probably well founded since it was not a small task to become a bona fide student of the Golden Dawn's Occult Science.

Closing

The closing follows the procedure of the opening, with the important exception of the partaking of the elements. This can be regarded as an extended form of communion: the members inhale the perfume of a Rose (air); feel the warmth of the sacred Fire by spreading hands over it (fire);[52] eat bread and salt (earth); and finally drink wine (water).

The concluding address to the members is full of references to the classical goals of alchemy: "May what we have partaken of sustain us in our search for the Quintessence; The Stone of the Philosophers and Perfect Happiness and the Summum Bonum." Traditionally the goal of the alchemist was eternal life and the ability to transmute base metals into gold, the latter often conceived of in a spiritual manner in which the transmutation was seen as a spiritual purification of the alchemist's soul.

What conclusions are to be drawn from this analysis of the Golden Dawn's first ritual of initiation? In my opinion, the foremost characteristic of the ritual is the marked kabbalistic influence. It is stressed on a number of occasions throughout the ritual that the path to occult illumination leads between the kabbalistic pillars of Mercy and Severity, and that the candidate should strive for balance between these two forces. In the subsequent rituals the kabbalistic influence becomes even more tangible and apparent as the candidate symbolically journeys upward along the paths and the *Sephiroth*. Another characteristic are the frequent allusions to the Occult Science and the Occult Light. The quest for light runs as a red thread throughout the rituals of the Golden Dawn, and it is the ultimate goal of the members to become illuminated with this Occult Light.

Concluding Remarks

The *Hermetic Order of the Golden Dawn* is one of the most important and influential English masonic initiatory societies of the late nineteenth century. The originators of the order, Westcott, Mathers, and Woodman, were masons with a particular interest in the more esoteric and obscure masonic systems of the day. Given the fact the order, in its original form, was active for only twelve years, from 1888 to 1900, its legacy to later esoteric societies is remarkable. The initiatory system of the Golden Dawn, based on the linear scheme of the kabbalistic Tree of Life, has been adopted by innumerable later societies. This initiatory system was, furthermore, connected to a very specific spiritual "enlightenment" that the members were expected to reach as Adeptus Minor, an enlightenment that later has become known as the Knowledge of and Conversation with the Holy Guardian Angel. Although this particular spiritual state, or enlightenment, was not unique to the Golden Dawn, the Golden Dawn was nonetheless instrumental in defining it and placing it in the context of an initiatory system.

Another significant part of the legacy of the Golden Dawn to later initiatory societies was that men and women were admitted on an equal basis. Even though women could become members of certain masonic initiatory societies already during the eighteenth century, it was still an uncommon practice during the end of the nineteenth century to allow women to join initiatory societies. *The Hermetic Order of the Golden Dawn* challenged the existing circumstances of the day and opened— definitely—the world of Western esoteric rituals of initiation for women in an unprecedented way. In that sense, at least, the Golden Dawn can be seen as a forerunner to such initiatory societies as the *Ordo Templi Orientis* and the witchcraft movement of the 1950s.

Chapter 7

Modern Pagan Witchcraft or Wicca

Gerald Gardner and the Birth of Wicca

In the mid-1950s British media reported that witchcraft was by no means an extinct tradition, but a living and flourishing form of religion practiced in modern Britain. Most of the reports centered on the author and self-styled witch, Gerald B. Gardner (1884–1964), who had caught the attention of the public through his book *Witchcraft Today*, published in 1954. The book was followed by *The Meaning of Witchcraft* in 1959. In these two books Gardner claimed that witchcraft actually was a pagan, pre-Christian religion that had survived through the centuries as a secret tradition, despite efforts of the church to destroy it during the witch trials in the sixteenth and seventeenth centuries. According to Gardner, the religious tradition of witchcraft centered on the worship of two deities, a goddess and a horned god, often called Aradia and Cernunnos. The religious practices described were essentially those of fertility worship and magical rituals.[1]

Furthermore, the witches were organized in small groups, called covens, into which new members were admitted through rituals of initiation. Gardner himself claimed to have been initiated into such a coven in New Forest, 1939.[2] Gardner's description of witchcraft was not presented from the standpoint of a modern witch, but as that of an anthropologist who had stumbled across a hitherto unknown tradition. Unknown, that is, as a *still living* tradition, for the idea that the victims of the witch-persecutions were adherents of a survival of a pagan fertility cult had been suggested earlier by the scholar Margaret A. Murray (1862–1963) in *The Witch Cult in Western Europe* (1921), and *The God of the Witches* (1933). Many of the witchcraft practices described by Murray, such as the worship of a goddess and a horned god, the organization of members in covens, the use of initiation rituals and ritualized

145

sex, were later included in Gardner's concept of modern witchcraft. Murray's theory was, however, heavily criticized by her fellow scholars, and in the 1950s when Gardner's two books were published, the theory of a surviving pagan fertility cult was sharply repudiated by the academic world. But this did not deter Gardner from basing his books to a large extent on Murray's work—in fact, she even wrote the preface to *Witchcraft Today*.

Gardner began to initiate members into his coven, and soon enough some of these set up covens of their own all over Britain. With Gardner dead by 1964, some of the witches initiated by Gardner assumed leading positions in the witchcraft movement, but the perhaps most influential, and certainly the most public relations–minded, witch of the 1960s and early 1970s, was not initiated by Gardner. Alex Sanders (1926–1988), who called himself the King of the Witches, claimed that he had been initiated by his grandmother into witchcraft at an early age, and that the tradition he represented was far more genuine than the one deriving from Gardner.[3] Together with Maxine Morris, with whom he married in 1965, Alex Sanders figured prominently in media as a self-appointed representative for the witchcraft movement. Sanders' flirtation with the media, and some of his more flamboyant claims, resulted in a rift with the Gardnerians.[4] It is now, however, generally accepted that much of Sanders' knowledge of witchcraft derived from Gardner via one of Gardner's High Priestesses, and that his *Book of Shadows* actually was a Gardnerian one. The differences between Gardnerian and Alexandrian witchcraft are minor, especially those in the rituals of initiation.[5]

Both the Gardnerian and Alexandrian traditions spread to the United States in the 1960s and 1970s. Here witchcraft became a much larger movement than in Britain. The decidedly most characteristic form of witchcraft that developed in the United States was connected to radical feminism. Feminists, such as Mary Daly, criticized Christianity for being an upholder of patriarchal oppression, and many feminists turned to alternative religious traditions. A large number of them were attracted by the importance given to the Goddess in the witchcraft movement, and a feminist form of witchcraft gradually evolved, with such authors as Starhawk and Zsuzsanna Budapest as front figures. One branch of this feminist form of witchcraft did away with the horned God entirely, and became known as the Goddess movement.[6]

Witchcraft, or Wicca, is by many scholars seen as a new religious movement that is today an established part of Western religiosity— showing no tendencies of fading away. One author estimated in 1991 the number of adherents to the neopagan movement in the U.S. and Canada at around 200,000, and the number of covens at around 5,000 in the U.S.

alone.[7] It is, however, important to distinguish witchcraft from neopaganism in general, since the witchcraft movement is only one of many new religious movements that can be classified as neopagan. Hanegraaff, in his discussion of the term neopaganism, points out that the term is not a modern one, but can be found in "connection with certain religious and philosophical developments in prewar Germany."[8] He suggests the following broad definition of neopaganism:

> As a general term, "neopaganism" covers all those modern movements which are, firstly, based on the conviction that what Christianity has traditionally denounced as idolatry and superstition actually represents / represented a profound and meaningful religious worldview and, secondly, that a religious practice based on this worldview can and should be revitalized in our modern world.[9]

This actually fits very well with what Gardner aimed to accomplish with his witchcraft movement. Hanegraaff raises the question of the relationship between Wicca and New Age. According to Hanegraaff, Wicca is a "neopagan development of traditional occultistic magic," which, he maintains, is not in itself a pagan movement.[10] This assertion can, however, be questioned. In my opinion, the British Occultistic movement from which Gardner's Wicca originates is tightly connected to neopaganism, if not from an emic perspective, then most definitely from an etic one.[11] For instance, the rituals of the Hermetic Order of the Golden Dawn (see chapter 6), can, at least to a certain extent, be seen as an attempt to re-create the initiatic rituals of pre-Christian, pagan Greece and Egypt.[12] This can also be seen from the writings of some of its members, such as *Egyptian Magic* (1896) by Florence Farr. Further, the new religious movement promulgated by Aleister Crowley, Thelema, was considered, at least to a certain extent, to be a reconstruction of the old Sumerian religion.[13] The writings of Dion Fortune (1891–1946), another influential author of the Occultistic genre, also show clear traces of neopaganism in the form of what she considered to be pagan Celtic practices.[14]

According to Hanegraaff, Gardner's Wicca was a "relatively self-contained, England-based occultist religion," but when it spread to the United States in the 1960s it was "interpreted and developed in increasingly unorthodox and syncretistic directions."[15] It was especially with the movement known as "women's spirituality" that Wicca intermingled, which gave birth to the Goddess Movement mentioned above. This syncretistic form of Wicca has adopted many of the beliefs, practices and to a certain extent the vocabulary of the New Age movement.

For many witches, both in the United States and Europe, the use of rituals of initiation is an intrinsic part of the craft: for some self-initiation is a valid option,[16] whereas for others the strict adherence to an initiatic tradition is of crucial importance, usually going back to either Gerald Gardner (Gardnerian witchcraft) or Alex Sanders (Alexandrian witchcraft). Rituals of initiation are thus an important aspect of the modern witchcraft movement—a fact that warrants a closer look into the nature of these rituals.

The Crowley Connection

The relationship between Gerald Gardner and Aleister Crowley has been the source of much speculation, and to a certain extent controversy, among authors writing about the witchcraft movement. The influence of Crowley on the early versions of the rituals of initiations in the Gardnerian *Book of Shadows* is apparent to anyone familiar with Crowley's published writings.[17] It is therefore understandable that many witches accepted the claim made by Francis King in 1970, that Crowley had written the rituals of initiation for Gardner's movement. In discussing the relationship between Gardner and Crowley, King wrote:

> He [Gerald Gardner] had known Aleister Crowley for some time, for he was not only a VII° initiate of the O.T.O. but actually held a Charter authorising him to operate some sort of O.T.O. Lodge—although, in fact, he never seems to have done this. He accordingly hired Crowley, at a generous fee, to write elaborate rituals for the new 'Gardnerian' witch-cult and, at about the same time, either forged, or procured to be forged, the so-called Book of Shadows, allegedly a sixteenth-century witches rulebook, but betraying its modern origins in every line of its unsatisfactory pastiche of Elizabethan English.[18]

While King was correct in stating that Gardner had been a member of the Ordo Templi Orientis (O.T.O.)., he mistook his degree in the or-der—Gardner had the IV° (Perfect Initiate), not the VII° (Sovereign Grand Inspector General). The reason for King's mistake can possibly be attributed to the fact that Gardner himself seems to have had prob-lems with the degree system of the O.T.O.[19] Furthermore, Gardner did in fact receive a charter from Crowley to operate a Camp (not a Lodge) of the order in London, working the Minerval degree only.[20] It appears that Gardner tried to set up a camp in London before Crowley's death in 1947, and that some of Crowley's followers actually believed that

Gardner was the head of O.T.O. in England after Crowley's death. Gardner, however, seems to have lost his interest in the O.T.O. and instead focused his attention on the development of the Witchcraft movement as evidenced by the publishing of *High Magic's Aid* in 1949. That Gardner lost interest in the O.T.O. is also demonstrated by the fact that his name is not even mentioned in the *Manifesto of the British Branch of the Ordo Templi Orientis* published in 1948 by Kenneth Grant (b. 1924).[21] Grant was Crowley's secretary in the early 1940s, and he was also personally acquainted with Gardner in the 1950s.[22] As Grant knew both Crowley and Gardner, and was also actively involved with the O.T.O., his testimony on the relationship between the two men is important as a first-hand witness:

> There have always been doubts about the claims made by some writers concerning the production by Aleister Crowley of rituals for Dr. Gardner's witch-cult. Both men were worlds apart in their intellectual and occult pursuits. Although they met, nothing substantial transpired between them. It is true that A. C. admitted Dr. G. to the O.T.O. (Outer Court) in 1947, but it is evident from Dr. G's novel, 'High Magic's Aid' that he confused, on the title page, the two Orders O.T.O. and A∴A∴, and mistook the IV°, O.T.O.,—which A. C. had conferred upon him— for 4° = 7□ of the other Order! It is also true that Dr. G. appropriated and paraphrased particular passages of A.C.'s writings ('Book of the Law,' in particular), but this does not amount to A.C.'s having written rituals for the witch-cult. However, please do not gather from these remarks that I have no regard for Dr. G's achievements. I knew him and liked him; he was a fascinating character, and I believe that he would have repudiated a lot of the nonsense that some of his followers have lain at his door à propos of his dealings with A.C.[23]

The *Ordo Templi Orientis,* or the *Order of the Oriental Templars,* was founded in Germany around 1912 by Theodore Reuss (1855–1923)[24] on the basis of a charter issued by John Yarker (1833–1913)[25] on September 24, 1902. The Charter was for an irregular masonic Rite called "Antient and Primitive Rite of Freemasonry," consisting of 33 degrees.[26] The transformation of this Rite in Germany into O.T.O. seems to have been a gradual affair, probably prompted by the fact that Reuss wanted to allow women into the order, something that would have been unthinkable to Yarker. One of the reasons for Reuss to allow women into the order might have been the fact that to him the central secret of Freemasonry was sexual magic. This secret was kept closely hidden from the public in the early years of the O.T.O., but in 1912 the nature of the central secret of the order was announced to the public:

> Our Order possess the Key which opens up all Masonic and Hermetic secrets, namely, the teaching of sexual magic, and this teaching explains, without exception, all the secrets of Nature, all the symbolism of Freemasonry and all systems of religion.[27]

Reuss had heard about Crowley in 1910 in connection with a much-publicized trial. Crowley was printing the rituals of the Hermetic Order of the Golden Dawn in his bi-annual publication, *The Equinox*, and he had announced that the March 1910 issue would include the Second Order rituals. MacGregor Mathers tried to restrain the publication by suing Crowley, to no avail. According to Crowley's autobiography he received letters from all over Europe as a result of this trial, and many honorary degrees from a number of esoteric organizations.[28] One of the people who contacted Crowley was Reuss, who called on him in London and conferred upon him the VII° of the O.T.O. Crowley was apparently not overly impressed with Reuss, and thought little of this degree. However, later Reuss reappeared at Crowley's door and accused him of exposing the secrets of the order in one of his published books, *The Book of Lies*.[29] Crowley denied that he had done so, with the argument that he was not informed of the secrets that he was supposed to have revealed. Reuss then promptly elevated Crowley to the IX° and thereby swore him to secrecy regarding the central secret of the O.T.O.

> This Art was communicated to me in June, An. VIII [1912], ☿ in ♊ by the O.H.O.[30] It was practised by me in a desultory way until An. IX ☿ in 10° ♑ [1 January 1914] when I made the Experiments recorded elsewhere of the Art derived from and parallel to this. The Knowledge thus gained enabled me to make further research with more acumen and directness, so that I was able definitely to assert that I had produced certain results at will. For example, my bronchitis, which had been most intractable was cured in a single day. I obtained money when needed. I obtained 'sex-force and sex-attraction' so strongly that for months after I was never at a loss. Better than all, I was able to excite my art-creative power and my magical intuition so that much of the very great work done by me all this summer may be considered due entirely to this Art.[31]

From that year on, Crowley experimented with sexual magic and his diaries, both published and unpublished, show that he kept a careful record of all "operations," stating the object; partner(s); quality of the "elixir"; and the apparent results. In 1923 Crowley assumed the office as the worldwide chief of the O.T.O., or Outer Head of the Order as the office was officially known. The use of sex in magical and religious rituals fitted well with the principles of Thelema, a new religious movement of which Crowley was the prophet. In 1904 Crowley had "channeled" a text known as *The Book of the Law*, which he later technically labeled *Liber AL vel Legis*.[32] According to Crowley, this text proved to be the foundation of a new religion and it identified Crowley as its prophet, the Beast 666. Thelemic doctrines were incorporated in the revised rituals of the O.T.O. that Crowley wrote at the request of Reuss during his stay in the U.S. during WWI.

Gerald Gardner had been working for the commercial branch of the British Service in the Far East, and for a period he had been stationed in Malaysia where he worked as an overseer of a rubber plantation. During his time in the East, Gardner had joined Co-Masonry and been "exalted" to its Royal Arch degree.[33] Co-Masonry is a version of masonry that admits both men and women on an equal basis. In most English-speaking countries its rituals are infused with theosophical ideas,[34] since Annie Besant (1847–1933), who was (since 1907) President of the Theosophical Society, was also—since 1909—Lieutenant Grand Commander (= Deputy Grand Master) of the "Ordre Maçonnique Mixte International 'Le Droit Humain,' " as well as Grand Commander (= Grand Master) of the British Federation of that Order. Upon Gardner's return to England in 1936 he moved in theosophical and co-masonic circles, and subsequently got involved with the "Rosicrucian Theatre," which was directed by Annie Besant's daughter. Gardner's familiarity with the rituals of Co-Masonry, and theosophy in general, might explain his later interest in the O.T.O. and Thelema. As Martin P. Starr has pointed out, there were many similarities between the pre-WWII theosophical and thelemic movements:

> Despite all the one-sided invective, the parallels between Theosophy and Thelema as developed in Crowley's O.T.O. were numerous. In keeping with the First Object of the T.S. [Theosophical Society], its Lodges and allied orders of the Third Section, such as the Co-Masonic Order, admitted men and women on an equal basis, as did the O.T.O. They both had connections to John Yarker, the Grand Hierophant of the Antient

& Primitive Rite and a perennial thorn in the side of the Ancient and Accepted Rite. Blavatsky had been made a member of Yarker's Rite of Adoption in 1877. The Co-Masons attempted to seize control of the Sovereign Sanctuary of the Antient & Primitive Rite in England after Yarker's death in March 1913, but they were thwarted by Crowley and Reuss as detailed in the September issue of *The Equinox*. Both the Co-Masonic Order and the O.T.O. used rituals adopted from Regular Freemasonry while believing themselves to be more spiritual in aim than their source. They each had their own church, the Liberal Catholic (founded 1916) and the Gnostic Catholic (of uncertain foundation). Post-Blavatsky Theosophists like Leadbeater saw the degrees of their fraternal society to be parallels to the orders in their church. And behind both the Co-Masonic Order and the O.T.O. were oath-bound bodies devoted to "the investigation the unexplained laws of Nature and the psychical powers latent in man," the E.S., the Second Section of the movement, and the Order of the A∴A∴[35] [...] Although their oaths were quite disparate in nature, the first level in both the E.S. [Esoteric Section] and the A∴A∴ was that of a Probationer. Perhaps most significantly, they each fostered the belief in a World Teacher, embodied in Krishnamurti (Alcyone) and Crowley (Therion), and in a World Religion (despite disclaimers), Theosophy and Thelema. The movements were ultimately led by invisible superiors. The Theosophists had their Mahatmas who communicated regularly via their precipitated letters to the T.S. elite. The Thelemites had their Secret Chiefs, some discarnate like Aiwass, to whom Crowley attributed the authorship of *The Book of the Law*, and some seemingly present in the flesh; they too spoke through their sole authorized messenger, Aleister Crowley.[36]

To what extent was Gardner influenced by Crowley when he decided to include a sexual union between the initiator and the initiate in the Third Degree of the witchcraft rituals? It is obvious that both men shared the idea that sex could be seen as a sacred act, but it is questionable whether Gardner shared Crowley's conviction that sex could be used in a willed act of magic, or indeed if Gardner ever had access to the secrets of the Sanctuary of the Gnosis of the O.T.O. As a Fourth degree member of the O.T.O. Gardner was not formally entitled to knowledge of the supreme secrets of the O.T.O., but that does not necessarily mean that Crowley did not entrust him with documents of instruction in sexual magic. It is known that Crowley did not put too much emphasis on degrees toward the end of his life. However, the textual analysis of Gardner's different versions of the *Book of Shadows* made by Kelly[37] shows that all the borrowings from Crowley are taken from published sources—most notably *The Book of the Law* and *Ecclesiae Gnosticae Catholicae Canon Missae*. Significantly enough, there are no references to, or quotations from, the instructional papers in sexual magic that Crowley wrote, such as *De Arte Magica, Agape vel Liber C vel Azoth* and *Emblems and Mode of Use*.[38] Furthermore, it needs to be emphasized that use of sex is not to be found in the rituals of the O.T.O.—in fact, there are no rituals of initiation for the highest degrees where sexual magic is being taught: only documents of instruction. The sexual magic of the O.T.O. was initially confined to the Eighth and Ninth degrees. In the Eight degree, Perfect Pontiff of the Illuminati, the initiate was instructed in the practice of auto-sexual magic, or masturbation. In the Ninth degree, Initiate of the Sanctuary of the Gnosis, the initiate was taught a particular form of magic, which involved sexual intercourse. Crowley would later include an Eleventh degree concerned with anal intercourse. One significant characteristic of the O.T.O. version of sexual magic is the sacramental consumption of the so-called elixir (in the Ninth degree the elixir consists of a mixture of male and female sexual fluids, gathered from the vagina). In Gardner's witchcraft rituals there are no references to masturbation or anal intercourse, and, as Valiente has observed, Gardner did not include the sacramental consumption of the elixir.[39] If anything, it appears that Gardner's use of sex in the Third Degree had a different purpose and had more to do with his attempt to re-create a fertility cult, rather than the performing of an act of sexual magic in Crowley's sense.

Gardner and the Witchcraft Rituals of Initiation

Various authors have made a detailed analysis of the origins of the neopagan witchcraft movement: with special attention to the sources from which Gerald Gardner drew the information, which he later incorporated in the so-called *Book of Shadows*.[40] According to Gardner, the *Book of Shadows* was an ancient *grimoire*, or collection of rituals that he had received from the coven into which he claimed to have been initiated in 1939. The text was supposed to be secret, and each coven should copy out by hand its own copy, adding pertinent material on their own. Parts of Gardner's *Book of Shadows*, or versions of it, have been published several times, and accurate versions of it can now even be found on the Internet.[41] It includes sabbatic rituals for the vernal and autumnal equinoxes, the summer and winter solstices, rituals for consecration of magical weapons, various instructions, and so on. But the most important rituals, for this thesis, are the three rituals of initiation of neopagan witchcraft.

Gardner had described the first two rituals in a fictional form in his novel *High Magic's Aid*, published in 1949. He claimed that he had received permission from his coven to publish these rituals, but that not all witches were pleased with it. In this book Gardner describes the first two rituals only; the third one is only hinted at.[42]

Doreen Valiente (1922–1999), a High Priestess and close collaborator of Gerald Gardner, and Stewart and Janet Farrar, both whom were initiated by Alex Sanders, have published the Gardnerian rituals of initiation based on three different versions.[43] The three different versions are called *Text A, B,* and *C.* The first version, *Text A,* is supposed to be the oldest version, and it consists of "Gardner's original rituals as copied down from the New Forest coven which had initiated him, and amended, expanded or annotated by himself."[44] The Farrars state that Gardner's amendments were very much influenced by the O.T.O. of which Gardner had been a member. *Text B* is a later version used by Gardner in 1953. The last version, *Text C,* is the final version, which Gardner and Doreen Valiente composed together, in which much of the Crowley and O.T.O.–related material was eliminated. Many new passages were included, most of which were written by Valiente. In my analysis of the rituals I have to a large extent availed myself of the rituals as described by the Farrars, but as far as possible tried to focus on *Texts A* and *B* as these versions can be considered to be the "original" ones, as far as it is possible to call any of the Gardnerian texts original. Gardner seems to have revised the *Book of Shadows* as an ongoing process, adding new material without indicating when this was done.

Aidan A. Kelly has made the most thorough textual analysis of Gardner's *Book of Shadows* so far, and established that the text went through several revisions.[45] According to Kelly, the three versions he published in *Crafting the Art of Magic* correspond to the three text versions of the Farrars: *The Book of Shadows* of 1949 to *Text A, The Book of Shadows* of 1953 to *Text B,* and finally *The Book of Shadows* of 1957 to *Text C.*[46]

Kelly has managed to locate and analyze what can be called the "proto-type" of the *Book of Shadows,* a handwritten manuscript entitled "Ye Bok of ye Art Magical." In this manuscript Gardner copied down portions from published occultistic books, most notably from Crowley's *Magick in Theory and Practice* (1930) and the medieval grimoire *The Greater Key of Solomon* (1907 2nd ed.), which was translated into English from French and Latin sources and published by MacGregor Mathers.

The reader is referred to Kelly's indispensable work for a concise textual analysis of Gardner's three rituals of initiation in which he identifies the precise passages from works used by Gardner in creating the rituals.[47]

First Degree: Witch and Priestess/Priest

Just as all other Western esoteric rituals of initiation, the three Gardnerian Wicca rituals of initiation begin with a formalized opening. The opening is identical for all the three rituals, and it consists of a so-called "Casting of the Circle." The Casting of the Circle is actually a ritual in itself, which is used not only in connection with the rituals of initiation, but in connection with all other important Wicca rituals as well.

The three major aspects of the Casting of the Circle are the "Summoning of the Watchtowers," "Calling down the Moon," and the "Charge." The ritual is performed by the High Priest and High Priestess, while the other members of the coven initially wait outside the circle, on its northeast side. After a ritual exorcism and blessing in the names of Cernunnos and Aradia, performed by the High Priestess and High Priest, the High Priest leaves the circle to join the other members. The High Priestess then "casts" the circle by pointing the sword at the perimeter and proceeding clockwise from north to north, saying:

> *I conjure thee, O Circle of Power, that thou beest a meeting-place of love and joy and truth; a shield against all wickedness and evil; a boundary between the world of men and the realms of the Mighty Ones; a rampart and protection that shall preserve and contain the power that we shall raise within thee. Wherefore I bless thee and consecrate thee, in the names of Cernunnos and Aradia.*[48]

At the northeast she lets the members enter the circle, beginning with the High Priest. Men and women admit women and men with a kiss, respectively. When all have entered the circle, the High Priestess closes it with the sword. Then three witches, named by the High Priestess in turn, carry a bowl of water, a smoking incense burner, and a lighted candle from the altar round the circle. The High Priestess draws the invoking Pentagram of Earth in the air with the so-called athame, that is, a dagger for ritual use. This is a standard feature of banishing/invoking rituals of the Golden Dawn, which Gerald Gardner most likely encountered in the writings of Aleister Crowley, or Israel Regardie.[49] The High Priestess goes on to call the Watchtowers in the four directions of the compass, which she "summons, stirs and calls" "to witness our rites

and to guard the circle." The Watchtowers correspond to the four elements: east to air, south to fire, west to water, and north to earth. The
Watchtowers also derive from the magical system of the Golden Dawn.

The second part of the opening consists of the "Drawing Down of
the Moon," which can be interpreted as an empowerment of the High
Priestess with cosmic energy. The High Priest gives the High Priestess
the "Fivefold Kiss," which is done in the following manner:

> *'Blessed be thy feet, that have brought thee in these ways'* (kissing
> the right foot and then the left foot).

> *'Blessed be thy knees, that shall kneel at the sacred altar'* (kissing
> the right knee and then the left knee).

> *'Blessed be they* [sic!] *phallus [womb],' without which we would
> not be'* (kissing just above the pubic hair).

> *'Blessed be thy breast, formed in strength [breasts, formed in beauty]'*
> (kissing the right breast and then the left breast).

> *'Blessed be thy lips, that shall utter the Sacred Names'* (embracing
> him and kissing him on the lips).[50]

The Fivefold Kiss correlates with the Masonic Five Points of Fellowship,
which Gardner undoubtedly had encountered as a Co-Mason in the
Master Mason's degree,[51] but also in the Master Magician Degree of
O.T.O. in which the "Seven Bonds of Brotherhood" are to be found as
an elaborated version of the Five Points of Fellowship.[52] The High Priest
then touches the High Priestess two times each on the breasts and
womb, and finally one more time on the right breast, and calls out:

> *I invoke thee and call upon thee, Mighty Mother of us all, bringer
> of all fruitfulness; by seed and root, by stem and bud, by leaf and
> flower and fruit do I invoke thee to descend upon the body of this
> thy servant and priestess.*[53]

After an adoration of the High Priestess, as Aradia, by the High Priest,
the High Priestess draws the Invoking Pentagram of Earth, and says:

> *Of the Mother darksome and divine*
> *Mine the scourge, and mine the kiss;*
> *The five-point star of love and bliss—*
> *Here I charge you, in this sign.*[54]

The third part of the opening, the delivery of the Charge, begins with a quite lengthy charge by the Great Mother, or Star Goddess, to her worshippers, pronounced by the High Priestess. Part of the charge is a paraphrase of the first chapter of Crowley's *Liber AL vel Legis*. The High Priest calls upon the "Great God Cernunnos," the male principle. The Charge finishes with the whole coven, circling clockwise, while chanting a hymn called the "Witches' Rune."

The First Degree Initiation

In all three degrees of Wicca, the candidate is initiated by a person of the opposite sex.[55] The blindfolded candidate is prepared outside the circle, where he[56] waits at the northeast, by having his wrists tied together behind his back, a cord tied around the right ankle, and another above the right knee. The initiator then says, "Feet neither bond nor free." This preparation of the candidate bears close resemblance to the preparation of the candidate in the masonic Entered Apprentice Degree, where he is prepared in the following manner:

> His shirt is unbuttoned and opened to expose the left breast, and the right sleeve is rolled up above the elbow. His left trouser leg is rolled up above the knee [. . .]. The right shoe is taken off and replaced by a slipper (slipshod) of the "mule" type. A rope noose (cable-tow) usually of craft-blue silk is placed about his neck, the end hanging down his back. The Candidate is blindfolded with a 'hoodwink' which may be of black velvet or of craft-blue.[57]

The words of the initiator, "Feet neither bond nor free," are probably an allusion to masonic catechisms in which the Entered Apprentice answers the question what the circumstances were at his entrance. For instance, *La Reception Mysterieuse*, published in 1738, gives the following answer to the question: "This entrance was made neither naked nor clothed, neither shod nor bare-foot, without any metal in a strolling & not ungainly posture."[58]

The candidate waits outside the circle until the Drawing Down of the Moon. The initiator then gives the "Cabalistic Cross," a short ritual, which derives from the Golden Dawn, after which the Witches' Rune, and the Charge are declaimed.[59] After the initiator has asked the candidate whether he has the courage to make the assay, as he is standing on "the threshold between the pleasant world of men and the dread domains of the Lords of the Outer Spaces," she places the tip of the sword or the athame against the heart of the candidate, and says: "For

I say verily, it were better to rush on my blade and perish, than make the attempt with fear in thy heart." Again, this is a feature to be found in the Entered Apprentice ritual where the candidate is met by the Inner Guard at the door of the Lodge, who applies the point of a poignard to his bared left breast.[60]

The candidate gives the two passwords "Perfect love" and "Perfect trust," and the initiator welcomes him inside the circle by first giving him a kiss, and then embracing him from behind, in order to push him forward with her body into the circle. As in masonry, the candidate is led around the circle, and at each cardinal point the initiator says, "Take heed, ye Lords of the East [South, West, North] that [name] is properly prepared to be initiated a priest [priestess] and witch." The candidate is then brought to the centre, and the members move round him clockwise while chanting:

> *Eko, Eko, Azarak,*
> *Eko, Eko, Zomelak,*
> *Eko, Eko, Cernunnos,*
> *Eko, Eko, Aradia.*[61]

The chanting goes on for a while, and the candidate is pushed back and forth between the members, until the initiator tells them to stop. This is a common feature in many non-Western rituals of initiation, but it is also evident that the effect of disorienting and scaring the candidate was strived at in masonic rituals during the eighteenth century to a much larger extent than in later ones. The candidate is then directed to face the altar, and the initiator kneels and gives the Fivefold Kiss. After this has been done, the initiator takes the candidate's "measure":

> The Initiator, with the help of another witch of the same sex, stretches the twine from the ground at the Postulant's feet to the crown of his head, and cuts this length off with the white-handled knife (which her Partner brings her). She then measures him once round the forehead and tied [sic!] a knot to mark the measurements; once (from the same end) round the heart, and ties a knot; and once round the hips across the genitals, and ties a knot. She winds up the measure and lays it on the altar.[62]

The ordeal consists of a ritual whipping with a scourge, performed by the initiator. The candidate is instructed to kneel, with head bowed and shoulders forward. His ankles and knees are bound together. A total amount of forty strokes are given. It is explicitly stated that the purpose of the ordeal is to purify the candidate.

After the ordeal follows the Oath, which closely resembles the masonic Oaths. The candidate is first asked if he is ready to swear that he will "always be true to the Art," and that he will protect and defend his "bothers and sisters of the Art." Giving an affirmative answer to these questions, he then repeats the Oath, which the initiator spells out for him, phrase by phrase:

> *I, [name], in the presence of the Mighty Ones, do of my own free will and accord most solemnly swear that I will keep secret and never reveal the secrets of the Art, except it be to a proper person, properly prepared within a Circle such as I am now in; and that I will never deny the secrets to such a person if he or she be properly vouched for by a brother or sister of the Art. All this I swear by my hopes of a future life, mindful that my measure has been taken; and may my weapons turn against me if I break this my solemn oath.*[63]

The candidate then receives the Triple Sign, which is given by the Initiator in three parts. First, the candidate is consecrated with oil by the initiator who touches him with oil just above the pubic hair, on the right and left breasts, and above the pubic hair again. Second, he is anointed with wine on the same spots. Third, he is consecrated with kisses in the same places. This so-called Triple Sign is connected to the special emblem of this degree, the inverted triangle. When the Triple Sign has been given, the blindfold is removed and the candidate is untied. The candidate is now an initiated witch and the members of the coven welcome him with either kisses or handshakes.

The ritual then proceeds with the instruction of the secrets of the degree, which consists of the working tools. This practice is a common feature in masonic rituals of initiation, and it is interesting to note that the ritual paraphernalia of Freemasonry is also called "working tools." The tools are presented to the newly made witch, one by one, with a kiss.

> *Now I present to thee the Working Tools. First, the Magic Sword. With this, as with the Athame, thou canst form all Magic Circles, dominate, subdue and punish all rebellious spirits and demons, and even persuade angels and good spirits. With this in thy hand, thou art the ruler of the Circle.*
>
> *Next I present the Athame. This is the true witch's weapon, and has all the powers of the Magic Sword.*

Next I present the White-hilted Knife. Its use is to form all instruments used in the Art. It can only be used in a Magic Circle.

Next I present the Wand. Its use is to call up and control certain angels and genii to whom it would not be meet to use the Magic Sword.

Next I present the Cup. This is the vessel of the Goddess, the Cauldron of Cerridwen, the Holy Grail of Immortality. From this we drink in comradeship, and in honour of the Goddess.

Next I present the Pentacle. This is for the purpose of calling up appropriate spirits.

Next I present the Censer of Incense. This is used to encourage and welcome good spirits and to banish evil spirits.

Next I present the Scourge. This is the sign of power and domination. It is also to cause purification and enlightenment. [. . .]

Next and lastly I present the Cords. They are of use to bind the sigils in the Art; also the material basis; also they are necessary in the Oath.[64]

The initiator then gives the candidate one final kiss, and says "I now salute thee in the name of Aradia, newly made priest[ess] and witch." The ritual ends with a formal proclamation of the new witch, which is done at each of the cardinal points in the circle:

Hear ye Mighty Ones of the East [South, West, North]; [name] has been consecrated priest[ess], witch and hidden child of the Goddess.[65]

Second Degree: High Priestess/High Priest

The ritual of the second degree closely follows the one of the first degree, in both structure and content. After the usual opening (Casting of the Circle, etc.), the candidate stands bound and blindfolded in the center of the circle. The initiator takes him around the circle, and at each cardinal point proclaims: "Hear, ye Mighty Ones of the East [etc.] [ordinary name], a duly consecrated Priest[ess] and Witch, is now properly prepared to be made a High Priest and Magus [High Priestess and Witch Queen]."[66] The candidate is then led back to the middle of the circle, after which the coven links hands and circles around him three times. With the consent of the initiate, he then undergoes the ordeal of being whipped by the initiator with a scourge of forty strokes.

After the ordeal, the initiate is given a new name that he or she has chosen beforehand, a so-called witch name. According to Janet and

Stewart Farrar the name should be chosen with thoughtful consideration, and it can be either a God- or Goddess-name, the name of a historical or mythical person, or even a "synthetic name made up of the initial letters of aspects which create a balance desirable to the initiate (a process drawn from a certain kind of ritual magic)."[67] The use of a special name or motto is a common feature in British occultism, and it was for instance a standard practice in the Golden Dawn. Gardner was undoubtedly familiar with this practice, as is demonstrated by the title page of his novel *High Magic's Aid*, published in 1949, where he prints his magical name as a member of the O.T.O.—Scire.[68] The new name is imprinted on the mind of the candidate as each member of the coven gives him a light smack or push while asking what his name is.

The name-giving rite is followed by the taking of the oath:

> *Repeat thy new name after me, saying: "I [name], swear upon my mother's womb, and mine honour among men and my Brothers and Sisters of the Art, that I will never reveal, to any at all, any of the secrets of the Art, except it be to a worthy person, properly prepared, in the centre of a Magic Circle such as I am now in. This I swear by my hopes of salvation, my past lives, and my hopes of future ones to come; and I devote myself and my measure to utter destruction if I break this my solemn oath."*[69]

After the Oath follows a peculiar practice in which the initiator "wills all her or his power into the initiate."

> The Initiator kneels beside the Initiate and places her left hand under his knee and her right hand on his head, to form the Magic Link.
> She Says:
> *'I will all my power into thee.'*
> Keeping her hands in the Magical Link position, she concentrates for as long as she feels necessary on willing all her power into the Initiate.[70]

As in the first degree ritual, the initiator then consecrates the initiate with oil, wine, and kisses. But this time on the spots that correspond to the inverted pentagram of the second degree: just above the pubic hair, on the right breast, on the left hip, on the right hip, on the left breast, and finally just above the pubic hair again. The initiate is untied and the blindfold is removed. The members of the coven congratulate him in turn, either with a kiss or a handshake. The nine tools of witchcraft are then presented as in the first degree, but this time the initiate is instructed to perform a short ritual act with each of the tools in turn. For instance, when he is presented with the magic sword, he "re-casts" the circle. The last item to be presented, the scourge, is followed by the words:

> *Ninth, the Scourge. For learn, in Witchcraft you must ever give as you receive, but ever triple. So where I gave thee three, return nine; where I gave seven, return twenty-one; where I gave nine, return twenty-seven; where I gave twenty-one, return sixty-three.*[71]

The candidate gives the initiator a total amount of one hundred twenty strokes with the scourge. Finally, the candidate is being led round the circle by the initiator, who proclaims at each cardinal point: "Hear, ye Mighty Ones of the East [etc.]: [witch name] has been duly consecrated High Priest and Magus [High Priestess and Witch Queen]."

The second degree ritual ends with the narration of "The Legend of the Descent of the Goddess," which can be ritually enacted. If the legend is enacted, the part of the Goddess, the Lord of the Underworld, and the Guardian of the Portals are acted out by members of the coven— usually the initiate acts either as the Goddess (if female) or the Lord of the Underworld (if male). In brief, the legend consists of a story in which the Goddess descends to the Underworld, the realm of the dead, which is governed by the Lord of the Underworld. At the Portals to the underworld the Guardians challenge her, and order her to strip off her garments and lay aside her jewelry, since one is not allowed to bring anything to the underworld. The Lord of the Underworld, Death himself, fell in love with the Goddess, and asked her to stay with him in the underworld, but the Goddess answered that she did not love him and that she would rather receive Death's scourge. As the Lord of the Underworld scourged her tenderly, she cried out: "I feel the pangs of love!" Death answers, "Blessed be!" and gives her the Fivefold Kiss, and then teaches her all the mysteries, "and they loved and were one." The moral of the story is described at the end of the narration:

> For there are three great events in the life of man: Love, Death, and Resurrection in the new body; and Magic controls them all. For to fulfil love you must return again at the same time and place as the loved one, and you must remember and love them again. But to be reborn you must die and be ready for a new body; and to die you must be born; and without love you may not be born; and this is all the Magics [sic!].[72]

No explanations of the meaning of the legend are given in the three versions of the *Book of Shadows*, but the legend resembles many antique myths, such as those of Inanna and Demeter. There are numerous myths associated with the Sumerian deity Inanna, later known as Ishtar by the Akkadians and the Assyro-Babylonians. The myths, which resemble "The Legend of the Descent of the Goddess," can be found in the Sumerian *Innana's Descent to the Netherworld* and the Akkadian *Ishtar's Descent*. These myths centers around the theme of love and death, and the lovers of Innana and Ishtar, that is, Dumuzi and Tammuz, represent the annual dying and regenerated vegetative cycle. The goddesses, in their turn, represent the embodiment of the generative force in nature. Furthermore, the intercourse of the gods was ritually enacted in an annual rite in which "the king, representing Dumuzi-Tammuz, entered into a *hieros gamos*, a sacred marriage, with a sacred temple prostitute, representing Innana-Ishtar, and thus sympathetically brought regeneration to the land."[73] It seems to me likely that Gardner was influenced by this alleged practice when he composed the Third Degree ritual, which includes sexual intercourse between the initiator and the candidate. The Greek myth of Demeter and Persephone (Kore) has a similar theme in which Persephone's annual stay (for four months) in the underworld together with Hades symbolizes the unfertile winter. The cult of Demeter has its most famous expression in the Eleusinian Mysteries.

Another possible parallel is to be found in "the dying and resurrecting gods" of Frazer's *The Golden Bough*. According to Frazer, a large portion of the Mediterranean gods of antiquity was modeled on the theme of death and resurrection. He offered two explanations to this theme; the euhemeristic and the natural theory, respectively. The euhemeristic theory offers the explanation that the gods actually have their origin in one or more powerful kings that were killed by their subjects when their potency dwindled due to old age. The natural theory takes a different approach and explains the dying and resurrecting gods as personifications of the yearly cycle of vegetation. The two possibilities of interpretation that Frazer offers are connected to the idea that death follows when fertility wanes, and that the period of sterility is followed by rejuvenation. Gardner, who was familiar with *The Golden Bough*, probably considered these explanations as strengthening his own arguments of witchcraft as a pagan fertility religion with its roots in remotest antiquity.

Mention should also be made to the parallel of "The Legend of the Descent of the Goddess" to the masonic legend of the Third Degree, that is, the Hiramic legend. Gardner was familiar with the legend of Hiram both as a member of Co-Masonry, and of the O.T.O. In the revised

1917 O.T.O. rituals of Crowley, Hiram is exchanged for Mansur el-Hallaj, in full Abū al-Mughīth al-Ḥusayn ibn Manṣ ūr al-Ḥallāj (858–922), the Sufi mystic.[74] The legend of Hiram, discussed in chapter 4, deals with the theme of death and resurrection, which is a common feature in rituals of initiation. The chief difference between the masonic legend, and that of the witchcraft second degree, is that Hiram (and Mansur el-Hallaj in the case of the O.T.O.) is slain, whereas the Goddess in the witchcraft legend embraces death out of love for the "Lord of the Underworld."

Third Degree: High Priestess/High Priest

The third degree ritual differs, both in structure and content, from the two previous rituals, and thus also from Western esoteric rituals in general.[75] Standard features such as the taking of an obligation, circumambulations round the circle/temple, and instructions in the secrets of the degree, are marked by their absence. On the other hand, the ritual includes a feature that, to my knowledge, was new in the whole corpus of Western esoteric rituals of initiation in the 1950s when the ritual was composed by Gerald Gardner. This unique feature is called the Great Rite and consists of a sexual union of the candidate and the initiator. The candidate, if female, assumes the role of the Priestess, or, if male, that of the Priest.

Following the customary opening, the Priestess seats herself on the altar, or if the altar is too small, on a throne. She sits in the characteristic position of Osiris with wrists crossed in front of her chest, holding the athame in her right hand, and the scourge in her left. The Priest kneels before her in the same manner as the Priest kneels before the Priestess in Crowley's Gnostic Mass, that is, with his arms along her thighs and head bowed to her knees. After a short period of adoration, the Priest rises and brings the filled chalice, which he hands to the Priestess, and then resumes his kneeling position. She lowers the point of the athame into the wine,[76] and says: "As the athame is [to] the male, so is the cup [to] the female; and conjoined, they bring blessedness."[77] She kisses the Priest, drinks from the chalice, and with a kiss passes the chalice to him. The Priest drinks, and gives the chalice to a female member of the coven with a kiss, who drinks, and then passes it on to a male member with a kiss. This is repeated until all members have partaken of the chalice. This part of the ritual clearly inspired by Crowley's Gnostic Mass.[78]

The Priest offers a paten with cakes, and the Priestess touches each cake with the moistened tip of her athame, as the Priest says:

*O Queen most secret, bless this food unto our bodies, bestowing
health, wealth, strength, joy and peace, and that fulfilment of Will,
and Love under Will, which is perpetual happiness.*[79]

The Priestess, Priest and members of the coven each take a cake in the
same manner as the chalice. The Priest then adores the Priestess as
before, by kissing her knees, folding his arms along her thighs, and
bowing down his head. The Priest and Priestess then proceed to purify
each other by scourging. The Priest is the first to receive the strokes,
then the Priestess, and then finally the Priest receives yet another round
of strokes.[80]

After the scourging session, the Priest says, "Now I must reveal a
great mystery" and gives the Priestess the Fivefold Kiss. The Priestess
lies down in the center of the circle, on the altar or a couch, face upward.
She is positioned so as to have her vagina in the center of the circle, the
symbolic point within the circle. The Priest kneels by her side, facing
north across her body, and says:

*Assist me to erect the ancient altar, at which in days past all
    worshipped,*
The Great Altar of all things;
For in old times, Woman was the altar.
Thus was the altar made and placed;
*And the sacred point was the point within the centre of the
    circle.*
*As we have of old been taught that the point within the centre
    is the origin of all things,*
Therefore should we adore it. [kiss]
*Therefore whom we adore we also invoke, by the power of the
    Lifted Lance*
(he touches his own phallus and continues:)
O Circle of Stars [kiss]
Whereof our father is but the younger brother [kiss]
Marvel beyond imagination, soul of infinite space,
Before whom time is bewildered and understanding dark,
Not unto thee may we attain unless thine image be love. [kiss]
*Therefore by seed and root, by stem and bud, by leaf and flower
    and fruit,*
Do we invoke thee,
O Queen of Space, O dew of light,
Continuous one of the heavens [kiss],
Let it be ever thus, that men speak not of thee as one, but as none;

And let them not speak of thee at all, since thou art continuous.
For thou art the point within the circle [kiss] *which we adore*
    [kiss],
The fount of life without which we would not be [kiss],
And in this way are erected the Holy Twin Pillars, B. and J.
(He kisses her left breast, and then her right breast.)
In beauty and in strength were they erected,
To the wonder and glory of all men.[81]

At this stage all the members of the coven leave the circle if the Great Rite is performed "in reality."[82] (The ritual does not state how the Great Rite is supposed to be enacted in a symbolic form, but it seems likely that it would include the use of the athame and the chalice.) The Priest continues:

O Secret of Secrets,
That art hidden in the being of all lives,
Not thee do we adore,
For that which adoreth is also thou.
Thou art That, and That am I. [kiss]
I am the flame that burns in the heart of every man,
And in the core of every star.
I am life, and the giver of life.
Yet therefore is the knowledge of me the knowledge of death.
I am alone, the Lord within ourselves,
Whose name is Mystery of Mysteries.[83]

As in the two previous degrees, the Priest kisses the Priestess in the particular pattern of the Sigil of the degree—which in the Third degree is the upright triangle above the upright pentagram. It is given in the following manner: "above the pubic hair, on the right foot, on the left knee, on the right knee, on the left foot, and above the pubic hair again; then on the lips, the left breast, the right breast and finally the lips again."[84] The Priest lays his body over the Priestess's and says:

Make open the path of intelligence between us;
For these truly are the Five Points of Fellowship—
Foot to foot,
Knee to knee,
Lance to Grail,[85]
Breast to breast,
Lips to lips.

By the great and holy name Cernunnos;
In the name of Aradia;
Encourage our hearts,
Let the light crystallize itself in our blood,
Fulfilling of us resurrection.
For there is no part of us that is not part of the Gods.[86]

The Priest then rises, while the Priestess remains laying down, and goes to each of the cardinal points and proclaims: "Ye Lords of the Watchtowers of the East [South, West, North]; the thrice consecrated High Priestess greets you and thanks you."[87]

Concluding Remarks

The three Gardnerian rituals of initiation are not ancient rituals preserved in secrecy from a pagan prehistory—despite claims to the contrary—but modern compilations made by Gerald Gardner in the late 1940s and 1950s. Large portions of these rituals have been identified as taken from previously published works, such as Mathers's edition of *The Greater Key of Solomon*. The first two rituals closely follow traditional masonic rituals of initiation, and include standard features such as a formalized opening, the swearing of oaths, circumambulations, hoodwinks, trials, etc. The legend of the second degree, "The Legend of the Descent of the Goddess," can be seen as a typical legend of masonic rituals, of which there is such abundance. The theme of death and resurrection is a standard feature in most masonic systems of initiation, perhaps most famously expressed in the Hiramic legend of the Master Mason's degree in Craft masonry.

Gardner's third degree differs, however, significantly from other masonic rituals of initiation, most notably by the fact that it includes a sexual union between the initiator and the initiate. This is, to my knowledge, the first example of a Western esoteric ritual of initiation, which includes ritualized sex, at least in an actual sense. The use of sex in the initiation to High Priest(ess) should be understood out of Gardner's aim at (re-)creating a pagan fertility cult, and not as an act of sexual magic as practiced by Crowley and the highest initiates of the O.T.O.

The legacy of Gerald Gardner to the modern witchcraft movement is decisive, but at the same time the movement is in constant change and evolution. This is especially true regarding the rituals of initiation of which there are today an incalculable number of versions. Each and every coven active today probably has its own peculiar way of performing the rituals. Some covens are more conservative, while others emphasize the need for change and innovation. Today, the witchcraft movement is larger than ever before and this popularity shows that rituals of initiation have a place in our postmodern Western society. What began as a small-scale attempt by Gardner to set up his own coven of witches eventually developed into the first large-scale *initiatic* Western esoteric new religious movement, in the true sense of the word.[88]

Chapter 8

Conclusions

Conclusions

This study has endeavored to present masonic rituals of initiation as a phenomenon that has been present in our culture at least since the end of the seventeenth century. Furthermore, focus has been directed toward those masonic rituals of initiation through which Western esotericism has been transmitted. The admittedly wide historical scope of the thesis, spanning over three centuries, asks whether it is legitimate to treat such rituals of initiation as one phenomenon. After all, what has a modern witch to do with a mason of the eighteenth century? Actually, quite a lot.

The basic components of a masonic ritual of initiation, which can be traced even in the earliest masonic manuscript catechism, *The Edinburgh Register House MS* from 1696, are constant throughout the history of these rituals. In other words, both a mason and a witch would recognize themselves if a ritual of initiation would be described to them as consisting of (a) a formal opening of the ritual work during which the candidate is not present; (b) the admission of the initiate into the lodge (or circle in the case of witchcraft) at which the initiate answers a number of questions, often including why he or she wants to be admitted; (c) circumambulations around the lodge room during which the initiate is led by an initiator, at which point there often occurs some form of ordeal; (d) the swearing of an oath never to divulge the traditional secrets of the degree (such as a sign, grip, word), and to follow certain ethical rules; (e) the formal admission into the degree, often proclaimed by the chief initiator in the name of the order; (f) instruction in the traditional secrets and in the particular teachings connected to the degree; (g) the receiving of one or more visible tokens connected to the degree (such as gloves, an apron, a sash), sometimes also a name or

169

motto; (h) finally, a formal closing of the lodge during which the initiate is present.

These components constitute the skeleton, as it were, of all Western esoteric rituals of initiation (there are always, of course, exceptions to a rule), and with this skeleton as a starting point, each ritual takes its individual form and content. As evidenced by the example of the Neophyte ritual of the Golden Dawn, some rituals are highly elaborate and rich in symbolical contents, while other rituals, such as the True Mason of the *Rite Ecossais philosophique*, are less elaborate from a ritual perspective. Radical innovations, such as the inclusion of the practice of sex in the Gardnerian third-degree ritual, are on the whole quite rare. However, once a significant innovation has been made within a particular system, it is likely that it will be taken over by later societies. For instance, the attribution of the degrees of the Golden Dawn with the *Sephiroth* of the Kabbalistic Tree of Life is today a common feature among occultist initiatory societies. An illustrative example of how the use of the Tree of Life as a structural component has been adopted by a modern occultist organization, is the initiatory system of the Swedish organization *Ordo Draconis et Atri Adamantis*, more commonly known as the *Dragon Rouge*. The initiatory system of the *Dragon Rouge*, however, differs from the Golden Dawn's in that the degrees are not attributed to the *Sephiroth*, but to the spheres of the so-called dark side of the Tree of Life, the *Klippoth*.[1] The development of new forms of Western esoteric rituals of initiation is an ongoing process, which as yet has not received any academic attention.

In my introduction I stated that the present study actually consists of two fields of research: rituals of initiation and Western esotericism. What conclusions, then, can be drawn about these two fields of research from the examples of Western esoteric rituals of initiation discussed? The easiest way to answer this question is to address the two questions posed at the outset of this study; namely, how is Western esotericism transmitted through the esoteric rituals of initiation? And further, what "kind" of esotericism is transmitted?

Esoteric discourses, including rituals, are essentially symbolic in nature. This means that each ritual has to be interpreted as a whole, and it must be understood that the symbols encountered in a ritual can have different meanings. To a certain extent, it is the interpreter who "decides" if a symbol is to be regarded as esoteric or not. For instance, a grail in a ritual can be interpreted from a traditionally Christian perspective, but it can also have a wide variety of esoteric meanings to an esotericist. This problem is especially apparent in rituals connected specifically to Freemasonry since Freemasonry is not dogmatic in the sense that the symbols used in the rituals have an official meaning. On the contrary, most of the symbols used in Freemasonry have different meanings, and it is up to the individual mason to form his own interpretation of the rituals that he is undergoing.[2] Nevertheless, explicit references to esotericism are easily detectable in the rituals that have been analyzed in this study, especially if the Craft degrees are left out. It is particularly during the part of the ritual in which the initiate is instructed in the special teachings of the degree, that Western esotericism is explicitly transmitted to the initiate. The instruction can be either in the form of a direct explanation of a certain part or aspect of the ritual, such as the explanation of the principal symbols of the Golden Dawn Neophyte ritual by the Hierophant, or as a separate instruction in one or more esoteric topics, such as the alchemical catechism at the end of the True Mason ritual, and the explanation of the working tools of the Gardnerian witchcraft rituals.

Western esoteric rituals of initiation can be regarded as mirrors of contemporary esotericism as they reflect the esoteric currents and notions, which are in vogue at the time when the rituals were written. The rituals analyzed in this study are examples of how contemporary esotericism has been integrated with masonic rituals of initiation. For instance, the rituals of the Golden Dawn epitomize the occultist teachings and traditions, which were current at the turn of the twentieth century. It is further significant to note that most of the esoteric teachings that were transmitted through the rituals, and consequently were considered to be secret, were not confined to the initiatory societies as such. On the contrary, most of the teachings were readily available to the public in printed books, of which, for instance, the alchemical doctrines transmitted in the True Mason ritual are clear example. There are some significant exceptions to this rule, such as the teachings of the inner order of the Golden Dawn (e.g., the orders instructions in Enochian magic), and the ones of the original Gardnerian rituals of initiation (e.g., the use of sex in the third-degree initiation).

Many of the esoteric symbols encountered in the rituals are of a religious or philosophical nature in the sense that they are concerned with an "esoteric worldview"—or more correctly, a number of esoteric worldviews as formulated by Christian Kabbalah, Rosicrucianism, Theosophy, Occultism, Wicca, etc. Through the rituals the initiates are thus able to reach a knowledge concerning the relationship among God, nature, and man. Scholars such as Snoek have emphasized the importance placed on the *experience* of undergoing the rituals, and this experience, connected to the knowledge of an esoteric worldview, in one form or another, has in my opinion a direct relation to Hanegraaff's definition of esotericism as *gnosis*, a revelatory knowledge. One further significant aspect of masonic rituals of initiation in this context is the importance placed on the individual interpretation of the ritual, not only during the ritual, but also afterward. The initiates often return to the ritual, not only in the capacity of officiating initiators, but as spectators of the ritual.

The esoteric teachings are, however, not only of a religious or philosophical nature, but also of a specifically practical nature. These teachings are often concentrated in the instructional part of the rituals, and can consist of such topics as alchemy, astrology, and magic. These instructions can be of a general and introductory level, such as the instruction in the witchcraft working tools of the Gardnerian first-degree ritual, or more elaborate and advanced as in the alchemical instructions of the True Mason ritual.

Masonic rituals of initiation in general, and Western esoteric rituals of initiation in particular, have suffered from academic neglect far too long, and it is hoped that this study will do something to bring this fascinating field of research to the attention of a wider public. It seems appropriate to close this book with the closing words from a Western esoteric ritual of initiation. I choose those from the twenty-sixth degree of the *Egyptian Masonic Rite of Memphis*:

> Remember this—never condemn unheard.
> EXAMINE, REFLECT,
> and
> TOLERATE!

Appendix

The usage of the term ritual and related terms

[**bold**: the preferred term.
<u>underscored</u>: the dominant use of the term]

Before c. 1900:
— **ritual**: the prescription (book or otherwise)
— **ceremony**: ritual behavior
— **rite**: a building block of a ceremony (e.g., changing rings as part of a wedding ceremony)

c. 1900–c. 1960:
— **ritual** (1): the prescription (book or otherwise)
— ceremony or **ritual** (2): ritual behavior
— **rite**: a building block of a ceremony

c. 1960–c. 1980:
— **ritual** (1): the prescription (book or otherwise)
— ceremony (1), **ritual** (2); or **rite** (2): religious ritual behavior
— <u>**ceremony**</u> (2): secular ritual behavior
— **rite** (1): a building block of a ritual or ceremony

Since c. 1980:
— **ritual** (1): the prescription (book or otherwise)
— ceremony, **ritual** (2), or **rite** (2): ritual behavior
— **rite** (1): a building block of a ceremony

After Grimes 2000:
— **ritual** (1): the prescription (book or otherwise)
— <u>**rite**</u> (2): traditional religious ritual behavior
— **ritualization**: ritual-like behavior
— **rite** (1): a building block of a rite (2) (sic!)

J.A.M. Snoek 1987 (2003)
— **ritual** (1): the prescription (book or otherwise)
— **rite** (1): smallest building block of a ceremony (e.g., changing rings at a wedding)
— **ceremony** (1): a group of rites (e.g., church wedding)
— **ceremonial**: a group of ceremonies (all of the wedding, including reception and dinner)
— **Rite**: the total cult (the Russian Orthodox Rite)
— **ritual**: a "role" or "part" played in a ceremonial[1]

Notes

Chapter 1

1. For an account of the emergence of Western esotericism as an academic field of research see Hanegraaff, "Introduction: the birth of a discipline" in Faivre and Hanegraff (eds.) *Western Esotericism and the Science of Religion* (1998).

2. In particular, certain sections of the conferences organized by the International Association for the History of Religions (IAHR), and American Academy of Religions (AAR). Academic organizations devoted to the study of Western esotericism include the Association for Research and Information on Esotericism (ARIES), the Hermetic Academy, the Association for the Study of Esotericism (ASE), and the newly created European Society for the Study of Western Esotericism (ESSWE).

3. There are a number of journals devoted to Western esotericism (or specific aspects of esotericism), of which *Aries: Journal for the Study of Western Esotericism* (E. J. Brill academic publishers) is of special importance. The electronic journal *Esoterica* (www.esoteric.msu.edu) can be accessed through the Internet, and it maintains a high scholarly standard. Concerning book series mention should be made of State University of New York Press (SUNY), "SUNY series in Western Esoteric Traditions," in which no less than 39 titles have been issued so far. The Aries Book Series: Texts and Studies in Western Esotericism is a new monograph series devoted to publication of textual editions and scholarly studies in the domain of Western esotericism, published by Brill Academic Publishers. Gnostica, published by Equinox Publ., is devoted to various aspects of the study of Western esotericism.

4. In 1965 a chair in "History of Christian Esotericism" was established at the École Pratique des Hautes Études (Sorbonne). Francois Secret held this chair from 1965 to 1979, when he was succeeded by Antoine Faivre, who held the chair from 1979 to 2002. Faivre was, in his turn, succeeded by Jean-Pierre Brach in 2002. From 1979 the academic chair was entitled "History of Esoteric and Mystical Currents in Modern and Contemporary Europe." In 1999 a chair was established at the University of Amsterdam, devoted to the "History of Hermetic Philosophy and Related Currents," which is held by Wouter J. Hanegraaff.

5. A good example of this is the monumental eight-volume work by Thorndike, *History of Magic and Experimental Science* (1923–1958).

6. Hanegraaff, "The Study of Western Esotericism" (2004), 496.

7. Van den Broek and Hanegraaff, "Preface" to *Gnosis and Hermeticism from Antiquity to Modern Times* (1998), vii.

8. Van den Broek and Hanegraaff, "Preface" to *Gnosis and Hermeticism from Antiquity to Modern Times* (1998), vii.

9. An often referred to example of a modern scientist who simultaneously was an esotericist (in this case alchemist) is Sir Isaac Newton (1643–1727). See Dobbs, *The Janus faces of genius: The role of alchemy in Newton's thought* (1991). See also Linden, *The Alchemy Reader* (2003), 243–247, which includes a short alchemical tract by Newton entitled "The Key" (Keynes MS 18), and a commentary by Newton on the *Emerald Tablet* (Keynes MS 28).

10. Hanegraaff, "The Study of Western Esotericism" (2004), 500.

11. Hanegraaff, "The Study of Western Esotericism" (2004), 500–501. For a detailed study of Traditionalism, see Sedgwick, *Against the Modern World* (2004).

12. For example, Pierre Riffard's methodology, which, according to Hanegraaff, can be characterized as "universalist, religionistic, and trans-historical." Hanegraaff, "On the Construction of 'Esoteric Traditions'" (1998), 24. See also Riffard, *L'Ésotérisme: Qu'est-ce que l'ésoterisme? Anthologie de l'ésotérisme occidental* (1990); Riffard, *Dictionnaire de l'ésoterisme* (1993), particularly "Introduction" (9–17) and the entries for *ésotéricisme, ésotérique* (adj.), *ésotérique* (subst.), and *ésotérisme*; Riffard,"The Esoteric Method" (1998).

13. For further information of the *Eranos* meetings, see Wasserstrom, *Religion After Religion* (1999); Hakl, *Der verborgene Geist von Eranos* (2001).

14. For the importance of Star Wars as a modern myth, see Brooker, *Using the Force: creativity, community, and Star Wars fans* (2002).

15. For instance, in *The Rosicrucian Enlightenment* (1972), Yates refers extensively to Waite's *Brotherhood of the Rosy Cross* (1924), and *The Real History of the Rosicrucians* (1887).

16. Hanegraaff, "The Study of Western Esotericism" (2004), 507.

17. For further information, see Hanegraaff, "Beyond the Yates Paradigm: The Study of Western Esotericism between Counterculture and New Complexity" (2001).

18. Faivre, "Renaissance Hermeticism and the concept of Western Esotericism" (1998); Faivre, *Access to Western Esotericism* (1994); Faivre, *Theosophy, Imagination, Tradition* (2000); Faivre and Voss, "Western Esotericism and the Science of Religions" (1995); Faivre, "Ancient and Medieval Sources of Modern Esoteric Movements" (1992).

19. Perennial philosophy, or the Ancient Wisdom Tradition, views esotericism as single tradition that can be found within all exoteric religions. For an account of this approach to esotericism see Quinn, *The Only Tradition* (1997); Faivre, "Histoire de la notion moderne de tradition dans ses rapports avec les courants ésotériques (XVe–XXe siècles)" (1999).

20. Faivre, *Theosophy, Imagination, Tradition* (2000), xxi–xxiv.

21. Faivre and Voss, "Western Esotericism and the Science of Religions" (1992), 49. Although Hanegraaff does not share Faivre's definition of esotericism as a "form of thought," he agrees with Faivre that the various esoteric currents

or traditions share a "family-resemblance": "Along the lines of a Wittgensteinian concept of family-resemblance, contemporary New Agers may have little or nothing in common with fifteenth-century Renaissance hermetists (not to mention the hermetists of late antiquity), and yet be historically connected to them by means of many intermediate links." Hanegraaff, "The Study of Western Esotericism" (2004), 510.

22. Faivre, *Access to Western Esotericism* (1994), 10.

23. Faivre, *Access to Western Esotericism* (1994), 10.

24. Coulinano, *Eros and Magic in the Renaissance* (1987).

25. Faivre, *Access to Western Esotericism* (1994), 14.

26. Hanegraaff, "The Study of Western Esotericism" (2004), 508.

27. Hanegraaff, "The Study of Western Esotericism" (2004), 497.

28. Bechert, "Buddhist Revival in East and West" (1991), 274.

29. Throughout his life, Crowley maintained his high regard for Bennett, whom he referred to as "the noblest and the gentlest soul" that he had ever known. Crowley, *Confessions* (1989), 234.

30. Vivekananda's teachings derived to a large extent from his spiritual teacher, the ecstatic mystic Ramakrishna (1834–1886). Ramakrishna emphasized the religious experience, as opposed to religious doctrines and rituals.

31. For discussions on New Age as a globalized, or Americanized, form of spirituality, see Rothstein (ed.), *New Age Religion and Globalization* (2001), in particular Hanegraaff, "Prospects for the Globalization of New Age: Spiritual Imperialism Versus Cultural Diversity"; Frisk, "Globalization or Westernization? New Age as a Contemporary Transnational Culture"; Hammer, "Same Message from Everywhere: The Sources of Modern Revelation."

32. See especially Hanegraaff, "How Magic Survived the Disenchantment of the World" (2003), 357–380.

33. The excessive commercialism and the failed "utopias" of New Age have provoked internal criticism among New Agers, expressed, for instance, by the development of a "Next Age" movement. For more information, see Introvigne, "After the New Age: Is There a Next Age?" (2001).

34. Hanegraaff, "The Study of Western Esotericism" (2004), 510.

35. It is clear from the writings of Hanegraaff that he is aware of the problems of defining gnosis in a satisfactory manner—he touched on this as early as 1990 in his article "The Problem of «Post-Gnostic» Gnosticism" (1994).

36. Lévi, *Transcendental Magic* (1896), 229.

37. It is significant to note that the will of the chiefs of the Golden Dawn was, in the Neophyte ritual, accredited with a supernatural and deadly potential. The penalty of breaking the obligation of the degree was: "(. . .) the awful penalty of voluntarily submitting myself to a deadly and hostile current of will set in motion by the chiefs of the Order, by which I should fall slain and paralysed without visible weapon as if slain by the lightning flash." Torrens, *The Secret Rituals of the Golden Dawn* (1973), 79.

38. Crowley, "The Method of Thelema" (1998), 177.

39. Faivre and Voss, "Western Esotericism and the Science of Religions" (1992), 62.

40. "Enfin, il faut toujours se souvenir qu'un document qualifié, avec les precautions méthodologiques necessaries, d'ésotérique, n'est jamais cela uniquement ou exclusivement." Faivre, "La Question d'un Ésotérisme Comparé des Religions du Livre" (2000), 115.

41. "[W]e observe indeed that the esoteric discourse might also bear on texts, works of art, and so on that neither at face value, nor following a nonesoteric form of scrutiny, would appear to the common reader as esoteric. It becomes a matter of making a text mean things that its author did not, one believes, think about, or did not want to say explicitly." Faivre, "The Notions of Concealment and Secrecy in Modern Esoteric Currents since the Renaissance" (1999), 166.

42. "(. . .) esotericism began to be a matter for specialists whose audience was likely to be comprised of those already 'in the know'; i.e., *of persons who shared the same basic worldviews as they did themselves, and for whom essentially the same body of reference functioned as the object of their inquiry.*" (My emphasis) Faivre & Voss, "Western Esotericism and the Science of Religions" (1992), 52.

43. In discussing the notions of explicit and implicit secrecy in relation to Western esotericism, Faivre states: "Many alchemists have interpreted the writings of their predecessors by demonstrating that underneath the manifest symbols, other symbols and layers of meaning lay hidden. *This is consistent with the fact that esoteric discourses are essentially interpretative.* The exegesis of texts that are already exegetic is supposed to be required." (My emphasis) Faivre, "The Notions of Concealment and Secrecy in Modern Esoteric Currents since the Renaissance" (1999), 165.

44. The interpretative nature of esoteric discourses (*vide supra*) requires that each text should be studied within its particular context. For instance, Aleister Crowley frequently employed alchemical and Rosicrucian symbols when writing instructions in "Sexual Magick." The Rose and the Cross should in this particular context be interpreted as the Yoni and Lingam of the practitioners. Further, Crowley would interpret earlier alchemical discourses as pertaining to Sexual Magick.

45. An illustrative example of this is Michael Maier's *The Laws of the Fraternity of the Rosie Crosse (Themis Aurea)* (1656).

46. The relationship between fantasy and esotericism is more complicated than what first meets the eye. The migration of esoteric elements is not only to be found in fantasy literature, but also in fantasy role-playing games such as Dungeons & Dragons. Based on my limited knowledge of modern practitioners of magic and Wicca it seems clear to me that many of them became interested in esotericism mainly through role-playing games. This can partly be explained through the emphasis on the imaginative faculty in both esotericism and role-playing games. It is an interesting subject that deserves to be studied more closely.

47. Hanegraaff suggests that the so-called "Yates paradigm" is characterized by two elements: the suggestion of a relatively unitary and self-sufficient "hermetic tradition," and an implicit dependence on modernist narratives of secular and scientific progress. Hanegraaff, "Introduction: The Birth of a Discipline" (1998); Hanegraaff, "Beyond the Yates Paradigm: The Study of Western Esotericism between Counterculture and New Complexity" (2001).

48. Hanegraaff, "Empirical Method in the Study of Esotericism" (1995), 118. For a discussion on motivations for constructing an "Esoteric Tradition" see Hanegraaff, "On the Construction of 'Esoteric Traditions' " (1998).

49. Or in the words of Faivre: "The question is not what esotericism would be "in itself." No doubt esotericism is not even a domain, in the sense in which one speaks of the domains of painting, or philosophy, or chemistry. It is, rather, a form of thought, and *the point is to identify its nature, on the basis of those currents or forms of spirituality which appear to illustrate it.*" (My emphasis) Faivre, "Introduction 1" in Faivre and Needleman, *Modern Esoteric Spirituality* (1992), xi.

50. Faivre, *Theosophy, Imagination, Tradition* (2000), xxviii.

51. Hanegraaff is critical to this aspect of Faivre's definition, and instead emphasis the changeable nature of esotericism.

52. For the impact of Western esotericism on NRMs, and especially New Age, see Hanegraaff, *New Age Religion and Western Culture* (1998); Hanegraaff, "La fin de l'ésotérisme? Le mouvement du Nouvel Age et la question du symbolisme religieux" (1999); Hammer, *Claiming Knowledge—Strategies of Epistemology from Theosophy to the New Age* (2001); Bogdan, "New Religious Movements and Western Esotericism" (2005).

53. Faivre, "Questions of terminology proper to the study of esoteric currents in modern and contemporary Europe" (1998).

54. Faivre, "Questions of terminology proper to the study of esoteric currents in modern and contemporary Europe" (1998), 3.

55. "Emphasis on transmission implies that an esoteric teaching can or must be transmitted from master to disciple following a preestablished channel, respecting a previously marked path." Faivre, *Access to Western Esotericism* (1994), 14.

56. Faivre stresses that the word theosophy has three different meanings. Faivre, "Questions of terminology proper to the study of esoteric currents in modern and contemporary Europe" (1998), 5–6.

57. Yates, *The Rosicrucian Enlightenment* (1996), 206.

58. Professor Andrew Prescott—Director of the "Centre for Research into Freemasonry," University of Sheffield (established 2000); Professor Anton van de Sande, "Vrijmetselarij als geestesstroming en sociaal-cultureel Europees verschijnsel," University of Leiden (established 2000); Professor Leon Zeldis "Chair of Philosophic and Masonic Studies," La Republica University, Santiago, Chile (established 1996). For an introduction to the academic study of Freemasonry, see Prescott, "The Study of Freemasonry as a New Academic Discipline" (2003), 5–31.

59. See Gilbert, "Quatuor Coronati Lodge No. 2076, The Premier Lodge of Research" (2003), and Starr, "Halls of Learning: American Masonic Research in Review" (2003).

60. Yates, *The Rosicrucian Enlightenment* (1996), 206–219. The so-called Rosicrucian furor was not confined to the German-speaking parts of Europe, but spread also quickly to France and England. For a discussion of the reactions to early Rosicrucianism in France, see Kahn, "The Rosicrucian Hoax in France (1623–24)" (2001), 235–344.

61. Faivre, *Access to Western Esotericism* (1994), 78; Hanegraaff, "The Study of Western Esotericism" (2004), 495.

62. Faivre, *Access to Western Esotericism* (1994), 78.

63. Faivre, *Access to Western Esotericism* (1994), 79. See also chapter 5 of the present book.

64. Hanegraaff, "The Study of Western Esotericism" (2004), 495.

Chapter 2

1. Asad, "Toward a Genealogy of the Concept of Ritual" (1993); Boudewijnse, "The Conceptualization of Ritual" (1995); "British roots of the concept of ritual" (1998); Bremmer, " 'Religion,' 'Ritual' and the Opposition 'Sacred vs. Profane' " (1998); Snoek, *Initiations* (1987).

2. Asad, "Toward a Genealogy of the Concept of Ritual" (1993), 57.

3. Boudewijnse, "British roots of the concept of ritual" (1998), 277.

4. "Belief in certain series of myths was neither obligatory as a part of true religion, nor was it supposed that, by believing, a man acquired religious merit and conciliated the favor of the gods. What was obligatory or meritorious was *the exact performance of certain sacred acts prescribed by religious tradition.*" [My emphasis] Robertson Smith, *Lectures on the Religion of the Semites* (1889), 19. The last part of the quotation illustrates what Robertson Smith considered to be a ritual.

5. Robertson Smith, *Lectures on the Religion of the Semites* (1889), 20.

6. Robertson Smith, *Lectures on the Religion of the Semites* (1889), 19–21.

7. Boudewijnse, "The Conceptualization of Ritual. A History of its Problematic Aspects" (1995), 52.

8. Moore and Myerhoff (eds.), *Secular Ritual* (1977).

9. Bell, *Ritual: perspectives and dimensions* (1997), 52.

10. Such as Gluckman (ed.), *Essays on the Ritual of Social Relations* (1962).

11. Snoek, *Initiations* (1987).

12. Grimes, *Deeply into the Bone* (2000).

13. See Appendix.

14. It is, however, important to note that earlier scholars such as Robertson Smith also discussed initiations. Regarding puberty rites Robertson Smith wrote in a characteristically Victorian manner: "Further, there is an extensive class of rites prevalent among savage and barbarous peoples in which blood-shedding forms part of an initiatory ceremony, by which youths, at or after the age of puberty, are admitted to the status of man, and to a full share in the social privileges and sacra of the community." Robertson Smith, *Lectures on the Religion of the Semites* (1889), 304. "Among rude nations the transition from civil and religious immaturity to maturity is frequently preceded by certain probationary tests of courage and endurance; for the full tribesman must above all things be a warrior. In any case the step from childhood to manhood is too important to take place without a formal ceremony, and public rites of initiation, importing the full and final incorporation of the neophyte into the civil and religious fellowship of his tribe or community" (p. 309). "Among wholly barbarous races these initiation

ceremonies have a very great importance, and are often extremely repulsive in character." Robertson Smith, *Lectures on the Religion of the Semites* (1889), 310.

15. Gluckman, "Les Rites de passage" in Gluckman (1962), 3.

16. Van Gennep, *Les Rites de Passage* (1909), 209–210.

17. For a discussion of Eliade, see Smith, *Map is not territory* (1993), chapter 4: "The Wobbling Pivot," 88–103.

18. Eliade, *Rites and Symbols of Initiation* (1995), xii.

19. For a discussion of the masonic legend of Hiram, see Covey-Crump, *The Hiramic Tradition* (n.d.). See also chapter 4 in the present book.

20. Turner, *The Ritual Process* (1995), 95.

21. Turner, *The Ritual Process* (1995), 95.

22. Turner, *The Ritual Process* (1995), 103.

23. Turner, *The Ritual Process* (1995), 125.

24. Turner, *The Ritual Process* (1995), 125.

25. Turner, *The Ritual Process* (1995), 167.

26. Turner, *The Ritual Process* (1995), 168.

27. In some masonic jurisdictions, particularly in the U.S.A., groups of candidates can be collectively initiated into certain degrees.

28. Turner, *The Ritual Process* (1995), 169.

29. For instance, *Collins English Dictionary* (1992), gives the following explanation of initiation: "1. the act of initiating or the condition of being initiated. 2. the often secret ceremony initiating new members into an organisation."

30. Quoted in La Fontaine, *Initiation* (1985), 20.

31. La Fontaine, *Initiation* (1985), 20–21.

32. La Fontaine, *Initiation* (1985), 23–24.

33. Eliade, *Rites and Symbols of Initiation* (1995), 69.

34. Eliade, *Rites and Symbols of Initiation* (1995), 74.

35. Eliade, *Rites and Symbols of Initiation* (1995), 84.

36. Eliade, *Rites and Symbols of Initiation* (1995), 87.

37. Certain occultistic initiatic orders do, however, emphasize specific mental states in connection to certain initiations. A good example is the A∴A∴ founded 1907 by Aleister Crowley.

38. Bleeker "Some introductory remarks on the significance of initiation" (1965), 18–19.

39. Bleeker, Preface to *Initiation* (1965).

40. Gist, *Secret Societies* (1940).

41. La Fontaine, *Initiation* (1985).

42. Heckethorn, *The Secret Societies of all Ages and Countries. Embracing the mysteries of ancient India, China, Japan, Egypt, Mexico, Peru, Greece, and Scandinavia, the Cabbalists, early Christians, Heretics, Assasins, Thugs, Templars, the Vehm and Inquisition, Mystics, Rosicrucians, Illuminati, Freemasons, Skopzi, Camorristi, Carbonari, Nihilists and other sects* (1966).

43. Weckham, "Secret Societies" (1987), 151–154.

44. One should in fact not refer to the "Rosicrucians" as one coherent society or movement, since there have existed, and still exist, various different societies of that name.

45. Heckethorn, *The Secret Societies of All Ages and Countries* (1966), 3.

46. Gist, *Secret Societies* (1940).

47. Gist, *Secret Societies* (1940), 20.

48. Gist, *Secret Societies* (1940), 24.

49. For a full discussion of the Ancient and Accepted Scottish Rite, see Naudon, *Histoire, rituels et tuileur des Hauts Grades Maçonniques* (1993). See also chapter 5.

50. Gist, *Secret Societies* (1940), 28.

51. Weckman, "Secret Societies" (1987), 151.

52. Weckman's five "distinguishing features" can be found, slightly rephrased, in a number of popular books on secret societies, such as Barrett, *Secret Societies* (1997), 16.

53. "It is a strange secret society that publishes it (sic) *Constitutions* and *Regulations*, which can be readily purchased over the counter at Freemasons' Hall. It is an equally strange secret society whose meeting places are easily identified, either by their exterior decoration or from having the words 'Masonic Hall' over their door or on a brass plate on the doorway, and which are listed in telephone and street directories. So secret is it that members of the public can walk into its London headquarters, visit its Library and Museum, and be taken on a conducted tour of the Grand Temple and Ceremonial Suite. Can one really call an organization which keeps minutes of its meeting at all levels, those of the Grand, Provincial and District Grand Lodges being printed by outside printers, and issued for circulation amongst members a *Grand Lodge Year Book* and Provincial *Year Books* listing lodges and Chapters with their meeting dates and places and lists of members, again printed by outside printers, a secret society?" Hamill, *The Craft—A History of English Freemasonry* (1986), 146.

54. Most important Masonic libraries are today open to the public, and scholars are given full access to their collections of manuscript rituals.

55. Snoek, "Oral and Written Transmission of the Masonic Tradition" (1998), 41.

56. Bolle, "Introduction" to *Secrecy in Religions* (1987).

57. Bolle, *Secrecy in Religions* (1987), 18.

58. Bolle, *Secrecy in Religions* (1987), 5.

59. "Three overlapping or complementary aspects can help us round off a presentation of the esoteric landscape from the perspective of concealment and secrecy: (A) many esoteric texts seem to be designed to mean something other than what they appear to mean at face value; (B) others, oftentimes the same texts described in "(A)," contain statements on secrecy as an essential element in traditions of the past; (C) contrariwise, others present themselves more as a pedagogical agenda than a praise of secrecy, and some in this category even undertake a systematic *desoccultation of the occult.*" Faivre, "The Notions of Concealment and Secrecy in Modern Esoteric Currents since the Renaissance" (1999), 167.

60. Faivre, "The Notions of Concealment and Secrecy in Modern Esoteric Currents since the Renaissance" (1999), 167.

61. Faivre, "The Notions of Concealment and Secrecy in Modern Esoteric Currents since the Renaissance" (1999), 167.

62. Snoek, "The Allusive Method" (1999), 51.

63. One of the concerns of psychologists of religion has been the effect of ritual experience on the personality of the performer of the ritual. *Vide* Heimbrock & Boudenwijnse (eds.), *Current Studies on Rituals* (1990).

64. Faivre, "The Notions of Concealment and Secrecy in Modern Esoteric Currents since the Renaissance" (1999), 170.

65. Snoek, "Oral and Written Transmission of the Masonic Tradition" (1998), 41.

66. Faivre, "The Notions of Concealment and Secrecy in Modern Esoteric Currents since the Renaissance" (1999), 165.

67. Faivre, "The Notions of Concealment and Secrecy in Modern Esoteric Currents since the Renaissance" (1999), 170.

68. Snoek, "Oral and Written Transmission of the Masonic Tradition," 41.

69. Snoek, "Oral and Written Transmission of the Masonic Tradition" (1998), 41. The idea of calling Freemasonry a "sacred game/play (Dutch: spel, German: Spiel) can probably be attributed to the Dutch Masonic scholar P. H. Pott. J.A.M. Snoek: personal communication dated June 13, 2002.

70. The English exposures mentioned in the text are to be found in Knoop, Jones, and Hamer, *The Early Masonic Catechisms* (1963) [hereafter referred to as *EMC*], and the French exposures in Carr, *The Early French Exposures* (1971) [hereafter referred to as *EFE*].

Chapter 3

1. Kieckhefer, *Magic in the Middle Ages* (1990), 133–134.

2. Kieckhefer, *Magic in the Middle Ages* (1990), 43–53.

3. Kieckhefer, *Magic in the Middle Ages* (1990), 158.

4. Kieckhefer, *Forbidden Rites* (1997).

5. Based on two texts by Ficino, the notion that Cosimo de' Medici founded a "New Platonic Academy" at Florence has long been generally accepted as an historical fact. This has, however, been contested by Hankins in "Cosimo de' Medici and the 'Platonic Academy' " (1990), 144–162. For a discussion about the intellectual milieu around the Platonic Academy, see Field, *The Origins of the Platonic Academy of Florence* (1988).

6. Hofmeier, "Philology versus imagination: Isaac Casaubon and the myth of Hermes Trismegistus" (2002), 569–572.

7. One of the most influential magical handbooks of the Renaissance, Cornelius Agrippa's *De Occulta Philosophia*, lists in detail objects that correspond to the seven planets. Agrippa, *Three Books of Occult Philosophy* (2003), 75–96.

8. For an example of how Ficino used Orphic Hymns together with music, see the letter by Ficino to Cosimo de' Medici from September 4, 1462, quoted by Hankins, "Cosimo de' Medici and the 'Platonic Academy' " (1990), 149–150.

9. In later esoteric traditions magic became less connected to the spirit, and more identified with the Neoplatonic idea of a "spiritual" or "astral" body. For further information on the division between the corporeal body and astral body, see Gibbons, *Spirituality and the Occult* (2001), 56–70.

10. The most important texts were Proclus' *De Sacrificiis et Magia*, Iamblichus' *De Mysteriis* and *Vita Pythagorae*, Porphyry's *De Abstinentia*, and finally the *Hermetica*, especially the *Asclepius*.

11. For a discussion of the early development of Christian Kabbalah, see Scholem, "The Beginnings of the Christian Kabbalah" (1997), 17–51.

12. Yates, *The Occult Philosophy in the Elizabethan Age* (1979), 20.

13. Yates, *The Occult Philosophy in the Elizabethan Age* (1979), 21.

14. Walker, *Spiritual and Demonic Magic from Ficino to Campanella* (1958), 83.

15. For the influence of Reuchlin on Christian Kabbalah, see Dan, "The Kabbalah of Johannes Reuchlin and its Historical Significance" (1997), 55–95.

16. Yates, *The Occult Philosophy in the Elizabethan Age* (1979), 24.

17. Basically, the kabbalistic proof consisted of adding the Hebrew letter Shin to the name of God, thus getting Yod He Shin Vau He, IHSV (i.e., U) H = Jeheshua.

18. Zika, "Reuchlin's *De verbo mirifico* and the magic debate of the late fifteenth century" (1976), 107.

19. For further information on Trithemius, see Brann, *Trithemius and Magical Theology* (1999); Hanegraaff (ed.) *Dictionary of Gnosis & Western Esotericism* [hereafter referred to as *DGWE*] (2005), 1135–1139.

20. For an account of Agrippa's life and thought, see the standard work of Charles G. Nauert, *Agrippa and the crisis of Renaissance thought* (1965); Zambelli, "Cornelius Agrippa, ein kritischer Magus" (1992); *DGWE* (2005), 4–8.

21. *De occulta philosophia* was written at a much earlier date than it was published. According to Thorndike a first draft of the work was given to Trithemius in 1510: Thorndike, *History of Magic and Experimental Science*, vol. V (1941), 130. See also the article by Paola Zambelli where she discusses the importance of the earlier manuscript edition of 1510: "Magic and radical reformation in Agrippa of Nettesheim" (1976), 69–103.

22. Yates, *The Occult Philosophy in the Elizabethan Age* (1979), 38.

23. Yates, *The Occult Philosophy in the Elizabethan Age* (1979), 37.

24. Yates, *Giordano Bruno and the Hermetic Tradition* (1964).

25. An English edition of the work has recently been published under the title *Three Books Occult Philosophy* (1993) (reprint of the 1651 translation by James Freake, ed. & annotated by Donald Tyson).

26. Yates, *The Occult Philosophy in the Elizabethan Age* (1979), 47.

27. Walker, *Spiritual and Demonic Magic from Ficino to Campanella* (1958), 96.

28. Yates, *The Occult Philosophy in the Elizabethan Age* (1979), 42.

29. Yates, *Giordano Bruno and the Hermetic Tradition* (1964).

30. Couliano, *Eros and the Magic in the Renaissance* (1987), xviii.

31. Couliano, *Eros and the Magic in the Renaissance* (1987), 87.

32. Couliano, *Eros and the Magic in the Renaissance* (1987), 93.

33. "In conclusion, the treatise 'De vinculis in genere' should be interpreted as a practical manual for the magician, teaching him to manipulate individuals according to their emotional natures and to keep himself at a distance

from the dangerous influence of Eros, to cure patients in the grip of a powerful erotic spell." Couliano, *Eros and the Magic in the Renaissance* (1987), 97. For further information on Bruno's system of magic, see *DGWE* (2005), 206–213.

34. It should be noted that Yates has been criticized for overemphasizing the importance of esotericism on the thought of Dee. For a discussion of the influence of hermetism on Dee, see Gilly, "Between Paracelsus, Pelagus and Ganellus: Hermetism in John Dee" (2002), 286–294.

35. The first English translation (by J. W. Hamilton Jones) was published in 1947: Dee, *The Hieroglyphic Monad* (1947).

36. Yates, *The Occult Philosophy in the Elizabethan Age* (1979), 83.

37. French, *John Dee. The World of an Elizabethan Magus* (1972), 65. For a thorough discussion of the symbolism and various interpretations of Dee's hieroglyphic monad, see Clulee, *"Astronomia inferior.* Legacies of Johannes Trithemius and John Dee" (2001), 173–233. See also Håkansson, *Seeing the Word* (2001), in particular 73–84.

38. *DGWE* (2005), 304–305.

39. For a thorough discussion of this particular form of Dee's esotericism, see Harkness, *John Dee's Conversations with Angels* (1999); Clulee, *John Dee's Natural Philosophy* (1988), 203–229; *DGWE* (2005), 306–308. An occultistic version of Enochian magic was taught in the Inner Order of the *Hermetic Order of the Golden Dawn* at the end of the nineteenth century. For further information see Regardie, *The Golden Dawn* (1940), Vol. 4, 260–368. For Aleister Crowley's exploration of the 30 so-called Æthyrs of the Enochian system, see Crowley, *The Vision & the Voice with Commentary and other papers* (1998). For an introduction to Dee's Enochian system, see James, *The Enochian Evocation of Dr. John Dee* (1984), and Skinner and Rankine, *Practical Angel Magic of Dr John Dee's Enochian Tables* (2004).

40. Clulee, *John Dee's Natural Philosophy* (1988), 214–215.

41. The text is in fact a German translation of an extract from Traiano Boccalini's *Ragguagli di Parnaso* (1612–1613).

42. For a bibliographical survey of the principal edition of the Rosicrucian manifestos, see Yates, *The Rosicrucian Enlightenment* (1972), 235–238.

43. It is only in *The Chemical Wedding of Christian Rosencreutz* that C. R. is spelled out as Christian Rosencreutz.

44. All quotations from *Fama* and *Confessio* are from the English translation in the Appendix of Yates, *The Rosicrucian Enlightenment* (1972), 238–260.

45. Yates, *The Rosicrucian Enlightenment* (1972), 243.

46. *Post 120 annos patebo.*

47. Yates, *The Rosicrucian Enlightenment* (1972), 44–45.

48. Faivre, *Access to Western Esotericism* (1994), 64.

49. Yates, *The Rosicrucian Enlightenment* (1972), 253.

50. Yates, *The Rosicrucian Enlightenment* (1972), 39.

51. Yates, *The Rosicrucian Enlightenment* (1972), 51.

52. For information on Andreae, see Montgomery, *Cross and Crucible* (1973); *DGWE* (2005), 72–75.

53. *DGWE* (2005), 74.

54. Yates, *The Rosicrucian Enlightenment* (1972), 65.

55. This has been pointed out among others by Faivre in *Access to Western Esotericism* (1994), 64.

Chapter 4

1. Anderson, *The CONSTITUTION, History, Laws, Charges, Orders, Regulations, and Usages, of the Right Worshipful FRATERNITY of Accepted Free Masons* (1723).

2. For more information on Anderson, see Stevenson, "James Anderson: Man & Mason" (2002).

3. Anderson, *The Constitution* (1723), 1. Anderson's constitution was, however, not the first masonic constitution to be published: in 1722 the so-called *The Old* [or *Robert's*] *Constitutions* was published. According to Piatigorsky, Robert's and Anderson's constitutions represent two streams of masonic opinion at the time: the Christian and the deistic, respectively. Piatigorsky, *Freemasonry* (1999), 45.

4. The term "Accepted" probably derives from the London "Company of ffreemasons" who had an additional category of membership, referred to as the "Acception." It is now generally assumed among scholars that the term "freemason" is an abbreviated form of "free-stone mason," that is, a mason working with "freestone." The latter is a form of stone (both limestone and sandstone), which is free from natural faults. For a detailed discussion of the terms "Acception" and "freemason," see Scanlan, "Freemasonry and the Mystery of the Acception, 1630–1723—A fatal Flaw" (2002).

5. Stevenson, "James Anderson: Man & Mason" (2002), 114.

6. According to Faivre the expression *Philosophia perennis* was proposed by Augustino Steuco in 1540. Faivre, *Acccess to Western Esotericism* (1994), 35.

7. Faivre, *Acccess to Western Esotericism* (1994), 35.

8. In early masonic literature geometry and masonry were sometimes seen as one and the same, but most often masonry was considered to be the practical aspect of geometry. The two were furthermore often referred to as the Royal Art.

9. Knoop, Jones, and Hamer, *The Early Masonic Catechisms* (1963), 189. [Hereafter referred to as *EMC*.]

10. Hamill, *The Craft* (1986), 29.

11. It should be noted, however, that it is doubtful if this distinction is made in the Old Charges. It is more likely that Masters and Fellows formed one group.

12. Hamill, *The Craft* (1986), 29.

13. I prefer to use the terms "operative" and "nonoperative" masonry in favor of the often-used terms "operative" and "speculative" masonry. According to Hamill, the "terms *Operative* and *Speculative* are used to differentiate between the old operative stonemasons and the newer free and accepted or speculative masons. Speculative is used in its original sense of one who engages in thought or reflection upon and meditation on or inquiries into a particular subject."

Hamill, *The Craft* (1986), 13. However, the usage of the latter differentiation is problematic, as the speculative element appears to have been important in operative masonry. Stevenson comments: "The stonemasons in their 'operative' lodges were doing 'speculative' things long before gentlemen non-stonemasons came on the scene, so a terminology which insists that lodges of operatives must be largely concerned with operative functions forces distortion on the facts." Stevenson, *The Origins of Freemasonry* (2001), 10.

14. Hamill states, "With others, I firmly believe that Free and Accepted or speculative Masonry had its origins in England." Hamill, *The Craft* (1986), 27.

15. Stevenson, *The Origins of Freemasonry* ([1988] reprinted 2001).

16. Stevenson, *The Origins of Freemasonry* (2001), 7.

17. Stevenson, *The Origins of Freemasonry* (2001), 6.

18. Stevenson, *The Origins of Freemasonry* (2001), 32

19. Stevenson, *The Origins of Freemasonry* (2001), 36.

20. Knoop, Jones, and Hamer, *Early Masonic Pamphlets* (1945) [hereafter referred to as *EMP*], 31. It should be noted that this is not merely the first printed reference to the Mason Word, but also the first printed reference to the Rosy Cross in the English language. Significantly, the text was printed in Scotland.

21. *EMP* (1945), 31.

22. I am indebted to Matthew Scanlan for sharing his notes on the "Green Ribbon Club."

23. For more information on Fludd, see Debus, *Robert Fludd and His Philosophical Key* (1979), 1–49; Huffman, *Robert Fludd and the End of the Renaissance* (1988).

24. *The Fame and Confession of the Fraternity of the R∴C∴* (1652) by Eugenius Philalethes [Thomas Vaughan]. For Vaughan's preface to the *Fame* and *Confession*, see Rudrum (ed.), *The Works of Thomas Vaughan* (1984), 477–510. There exists a manuscript translation into Scots of the *Fama* and the *Confessio* by Lord Balcarres, dated 1633. Stevenson, *The Origins of Freemasonry* (2001), 101.

25. Waite, *The Brotherhood of the Rosy Cross* (1924), 373. It has been argued that Fludd was a member of a masonic lodge, but the evidence for this assumption is merely circumstantial. Waite states: "We know that at Mason's Hall, a few yards from his house, a Lodge of non-operative Masons was meeting in the year 1620 and thence onward. We know that among its records was a BOOK OF CONSTITUTIONS, 'which Mr. Fflood gave.' It is idle to assume that this donor was Robertus de Fluctibus or to affirm that he was therefore a member; but again the facts offer an attractive field of speculation." Waite, *The Brotherhood of the Rosy Cross* (1924), 364. The "Book of Constitutions" referred to probably consisted of the type of texts called "Old Charges."

26. Stevenson, *The Origins of Freemasonry* (2001), 101. It should be noted, however, that even if there are apparent similarities among *New Atlantis* and the *Fama* and *Confessio* (and Andreae's utopian *Christianopolis*), the influence of Rosicrucianism on Bacon's work is a matter of speculation. For further information, see *DGWE* (2005), 154–156.

27. *EMP* (1945), 110.

28. *EMP* (1945), 156.

29. *EMP* (1945), 235–236.

30. For instance, Tobias Churton stresses the importance of Rosicrucianism to the origins of Freemasonry in his book, *The Golden Builders. Alchemists, Rosicrucians and the first Free Masons* (2002).

31. Ashmole noted in his diary, on October 16, 1646: "I was made a Free Mason at Warrington in Lancashire, with Coll: Henry Mainwaring of Karingcham in Cheshire." Ashmole, *Texts 1617–1692* (1966), vol. II, 395. Ashmole's "making" as a Mason is important as it is the earliest-known private account of a person becoming a Mason.

32. Yates, *The Rosicrucian Enlightenment* (1972), 194.

33. 1 Petr. 2: 4–7

34. Waite, *The Brotherhood of the Rosy Cross* (1924), 296–297. Eph. 2: 19–22.

35. *EMP* (1945), 44. Besides references to alchemy, *Long Livers* also includes detailed references to astrology (52, 53) and Neoplatonism (63). For "a royal Priesthood" see 1 Petr. 2: 4–7.

36. Math. 5: 13.

37. Math. 5: 14.

38. Compare Math. 3: 11–Luke 3: 16.

39. *EMP* (1945), 65–66.

40. For the development of the trigradal system, see Vibert "The Development of the Trigradal System" and "The Evolution of the Second Degree," both articles published in Carr, *The Collected "Prestonian Lectures" 1925–1960* (1967).

41. *EMC* (1963), 31–34.

42. Carr, *The Early French Exposures* (1971) [hereafter referred to as *EFE*].

43. Jackson, *English Masonic Exposures* (1986), [hereafter cited as *EME*].

44. *EMC* (1963), 19–20.

45. *EMC* (1963), 31.

46. In the *Chetwood Crawley MS* (*c.* 1700) it is stated: "Then he makes the Sign again, which is by drawing his hand under his Chin, alongst his throat; which denotes that it is to be cutt out, in case he shall break his word." *EMC* (1963), 36.

47. *EMC* (1963), 33.

48. *EMC* (1963), 32.

49. *EMC* (1963), 32.

50. *EMC* (1963), 32.

51. The same emphasis on the giving of the Mason Word is also found in the second oldest manuscript catechism, *The Chetwode Crawley MS*, *c.* 1700, in which the text begins with the following headline "The Grand Secret or the Forme of Giving the Mason-Word."

52. *EMC* (1963), 33.

53. *EMC* (1963), 34.

54. *EMC* (1963), 37.

55. *EMC* (1963), 72.

56. *EMC* (1963), 73. Read from right to left, the Hebrew letters form the word RóSHeM, which means "a symbol or token." The wrong form of S was

apparently used by the writer, Samech instead of Shin. See *EMC* (1963), note 1, 240. In *The Perjur'd Free Mason Detected*, published in 1730, Hebrew letters are used again in order to write the Mason Word [*EMC* (1963), 190], but with the Hebrew words printed the wrong way round. For a discussion of these words, see note 1 of *EMC* (1963) referred to above.

> *Mast.* Come hither, *young* Man, pray what do you wear that Apron, and these white Gloves for? Are you a *Free Mason?*

> *Jun.* N.B. [*Here instead of an Answer he pronounces* (as he thinks) דקפ the Secret Word, *by which he supposes he should pass for a Member.*]

> *Mast.* N.B. [*Here the Master pronounces* another Word, *which the Junior does not at all understand.*] דדצ

57. *EMC* (1963), 130.
58. *EMC* (1963), 63.
59. *EMC* (1963), 64.
60. See Joh. 2:19–21.
61. *EMC* (1963), 85.
62. *EMC* (1963), 70.
63. *EMC* (1963), 48.
64. *EMC* (1963), 72–73.
65. It has been suggested the *Dialogue Between Simon and Philip* was written as early as *c.* 1725, and not in 1740 as is usually assumed. This text includes another early reference to the murder of Hiram: "The reason of those three Knocks is not known to Prentices but to the Master which is from Hiram the Grand Master in Solomon's Temple. Being murdered by his three Prentices and was dispatched by the third Blow the last Prentice gave him and this because he would not discover the Secrets to them." *EMC* (1963), 179. See also Bernheim, "Did Early "High" or Écossais Degrees Originate in France?" (1996), 22–23.
66. *EMC* (1963), 93.
67. *EMC* (1963), 97.
68. *EMC* (1963), 98.
69. *EMC* (1963), 229–239.
70. *EMC* (1963), 235.
71. The Art of Memory is a technique of mnemonics, which to a certain extent has been connected to Western esotericism. For more information on this technique, see Yates, *The Art of Memory* (1967) and Rossi, *Logic and the Art of Memory* (2000).
72. *EMC* (1963), 171.
73. *EMC* (1963), 171.
74. Snoek, "Printing Masonic Secrets: Oral and Written Transmission of the Masonic Tradition" (2003).
75. *EMC* (1963), 166–167.
76. It is not immediately clear what the answer "Three" actually refers to in response to the question "What makes a Perfect Lodge of Masters," but a

comparison with earlier catechisms with the same type of question, that is, what a lodge is made up of, shows that the answer means three Masters.

77. For information on the square and compasses in masonic symbolism, see Jones, *Freemason's Guide and Compendium* (1994), 431–437.

78. In later versions of the myth Cassia was replaced by Acacia. The Acacia is a symbol of immortality and, according to Jones, "legend connects the acacia with the wood of the cross of Christ, and His crown of thorns." It has also been suggested that the Acacia is a symbol of initiation, "in the sense that initiation itself is symbolic of resurrection." For further information, see Jones, *Freemason's Guide and Compendium* (1994), 486–492.

79. *EMC* (1963), 169–170.

80. Perhaps the fiercest attack on Prichard's character is found in *The Perjur'd Free Mason Detected* published in 1730. It includes a fictitious interview with Prichard in the form of a catechism, in which Prichard is denounced in no uncertain words.

81. It is noteworthy that the Egyptian deity Harpocrates is especially mentioned. In certain later masonic rituals this deity will figure prominently. *EMC* (1963), 216.

82. *EMC* (1963), 219.

83. *EMC* (1963), 218.

84. "The pronunciation of *yhwh* as Yahweh is a scholarly guess. Hebrew biblical mss were principally consonantal in spelling until well into the current era. The pronunciation of words was transmitted in a separate oral tradition. The Tetragrammaton was not pronounced at all, the word *adonay*, "my Lord," being pronounced in its place; elohim, "God," was substituted in cases of combination *adonay yhwh* (305 times; e.g. Gen 15:2). Though the consonants remained, the original pronunciation was eventually lost." *The Anchor Bible Dictionary* (1992) Vol. VI, 1011.

85. Gilbert, *A. E. Waite—Magician of many parts* (1987), 12.

86. Waite, *The Secret Tradition in Freemasonry* (1911), Vol. 1, 39–40.

87. Indeed, for Waite, this did not only apply to the masonic tradition, for he firmly believed "that all mystical and hermetic traditions, from alchemy and the Hebrew Kabbalah to the quest for the Holy Grail, contained true paths to be followed in the quest for Mystical Union with God; and God, for Waite, is immanent rather than transcendent" Gilbert, *A. E. Waite—A Bibliography* (1983), 14.

88. "It is obvious therefore that the Word in Masonry is Christ, and again that the finding of the Word is the finding also of Christ. In its preliminary meaning, the loss of the Word signifies the death of Christ. The three assassins are the world, the flesh, and the devil—to make use of familiar technical and conventional terms. The Master-Builder who erected the House of Christian Doctrine is Christ Himself. From another point of view the malefactors were Pilate, Herod, and Caiaphas." Waite, *The Secret Tradition in Freemasonry* (1911), 424.

89. Derives from the Hebrew yĕhošua, which means "YHWH is salvation" or "YHWH saves/has saved." *The Anchor Bible Dictionary* (1992) vol. III, 773. See also the Adeptus Minor ritual of Waite's off-shot of the Golden Dawn, *The Fellowship of the Rosy Cross*, in which the name is ritually uttered by the three

chief officers. *The Pontifical Ceremony of the Admission to the Grade of Adeptus Minor* (1917), 11.

90. Snoek, "The Evolution of the Hiramic Legend from Prichard's *Masonry Dissected* to the *Emulation Ritual*, in England and France" (1999); Snoek, "On the Creation of Masonic Degrees: a Method and its Fruits" (1998).

91. Snoek, "The Evolution of the Hiramic Legend" (1999), 62.

92. "The form 'Jehovah' results from reading the consonants of the Tetragrammaton with the vowels of the surrogate word *Adonai*. The dissemination of this form is usually traced to Petrus Galatinus, confessor to Pope Leo X, who in 1518 A.D. transliterated the four Hebrew letters with the Latin letters jhvh together with the vowels of Adonai, producing the artificial form 'Jehovah.'" *The Anchor Bible Dictionary* (1992), Vol. VI, 1011.

93. Snoek, "The Evolution of the Hiramic Legend" (1999), 72, 85.

94. By using the allusive method, Snoek has shown that for a Christian mason, the lost Word of a Master Mason may be interpreted as referring to Jesus Christ. Snoek, "The Allusive Method" (1999), 57–58.

95. Snoek, "The Evolution of the Hiramic Legend" (1999), 79. The burying of Hiram in the *Sanctum Sanctorum* can, however, be interpreted in various ways. For instance, as early 1730 there is an allegorical interpretation of this part of the ritual:

Mast. Yes; and don't they tell you *Hiram* was buried in the *Sanctum Sanctorum*?

Jun. Yes, and he was buried there too to be sure.

Mast. Yes, allegorically; but not really; the Meaning of the Figure is this: That his Art sunk with him, was buried in the exquisite Workmanship which he perform'd for the Temple, and was never recover'd since. For that no such Things were ever done after it, in or for any Building in the World.

Jun. Was that the Meaning of it?

Mast. Yes; for you might easily know, a dead Body to have been buried in the Temple, would have polluted the Place, and the Jews would never have come into it again. [EMC, 192]

96. Moshe Idel has shown that mystical union with God is an intrinsic part of Kabbalah, contrary to what Gershom Scholem argued. "(. . .) I shall propose an alternative view on expressions of *unio mystica* in Kabbalah: far from being absent, unitive descriptions recur in Kabbalistic literature no less frequently than in non-Jewish mystical writings, and the images used by the Kabbalists do not fall short of the most extreme forms of other types of mysticism." Idel, *Kabbalah. New Perspectives* (1988), 60.

97. According to Snoek, initiations can be subdivided into initiations *sensu stricto* and *sensu lato*, reflecting whether they culminate into a confrontation and/or identification with a divine being or not. Snoek *Initiations* (1987), viii.

98. Carr (ed.), *The Early French Exposures* (1971).
99. Jackson, *English Masonic Exposures 1760–1769* (1986).

Chapter 5

1. In masonic literature Rite is often used synonymously with system, and the French regime. For a good overview of the large number of Masonic Rites, see Ligiou, *Dictionnaire de la Franc-Maçonnerie* (1987), 1021–1035. For modern British High degrees, see Jackson, *Beyond the craft* (1980).

2. The history of High degrees and Rites of the eighteenth century is a notoriously difficult subject, so I will limit this introduction to a mere historical outline. It should, however, be noted that a large part of the literature dealing with this subject is outdated due to recent research. Examples of such outdated literature are Smith, *The Rise of the Ecossais Degrees* (1965); Waite, *Templar Orders in Freemasonry* (1991); and, to a lesser extent, Forestier, *La Franc-Maçonnerie Templière et Occultiste aux XVIIIe et XIXe Siècles* (1970).

3. Mollier, "L'«Ordre Écossais» à Berlin de 1742 à 1751" (2002). See also Bernheim, "Did Early "High" or Écossais Degrees Originate in France" (1996).

4. Kervella and Lestienne, "Un haut-grade templier dans les milieux jacobites en 1750: L'Ordre Sublime des Chevaliers Elus" (1997), 229 ff.

5. For a representative collection of chivalric and Templar rituals, see Girard-Augry, *Rituels Secrets de la Franc-Maçonnerie Templière et Chevaleresque* (1996).

6. "Lodge of Antiquity (then No 1) made 9 Brn into Scots Masters"; "5 MMs were 'Rais'd Scots Masters' in No 137, Bristol"; "5 Brn made Scots Masters at Salisbury." Jackson, *Rose Croix* (1993), 219.

7. Bernheim, "Did Early "High" or Écossais Degrees Originate in France" (1996), 31–32. The first reference to Ecossais masonry found in French exposures is in *Les Francs-Maçons Ecrasés* (1746/47), *EFE* (1971), 292, 307–314.

8. The Oration was published a number of times and it was sent to Cardinal de Fleury on March 20, 1737. Two of Ramsay's letters to Fleury are reproduced in Lantoine, *La Franc-Maçonnerie Ecossaise en France* (1930). On Ramsay, see in particular "Le Pseudo-Créateur des Hauts Grades: Le Chevalier de Ramsay" (17–49) in the above mentioned work by Lantoine; and Lantoine, *Histoire de la La Franc-Maçonnerie Française* (1927), 113–124.

9. Mollier, "Des Francs-Maçons aux Templiers: Aperçus sur la constitution d'une légende au Siècle des Lumières" (1999), 97.

10. Snoek, "A Manuscript Version of Hérault's Ritual" (2001), 516.

11. Until the late 1990s, it was assumed that the claim that von Hund had been initiated into a Templar degree in France was a fabrication. However, new findings have shown that there actually existed a Templar degree in France prior to the formation of the Rite of the Strict Observance. For information on this ritual, see Kervella and Lestienne, "Un haut-grade templier dans les milieux jacobites en 1750: L'Ordre Sublime des Chevaliers Elus" (1997). See also Snoek, "A Manuscript Version of Hérault's Ritual" (2001).

12. Bernheim, "Johann August Starck: The Templar Legend and the Clerics" (2001), 252.

13. The inclusion of Unknown Superiors is a recurrent feature in many later Western esoteric societies and orders. For instance, the Mahatmas of the Theosophical Society; the Secret Chiefs of orders such as the Hermetic Order of the Golden Dawn, the A∴A∴, and the Order of the Solar Temple.

14. The Jacobite interest in Freemasonry did not prevent the Catholic Church from taking a negative position against Freemasonry. In 1738 and 1751 two papal bulls were issued against Freemasonry: "In Eminenti Apostolatus Specula" of Clemens XII, and "Providas Romanorum Pontificum" of Benedict XIV. For the text of "In Eminenti" in Latin and English see Mellor, *Our Separated Brethren the Freemasons* (1964), 156–160.

15. See Voorhis, *The Story of the Scottish Rite of Freemasonry* (1980); Naudon, *Histoire, Rituels et Tuileur des Hauts Grades Maçonniques* (1993); Lantoine, *La Franc-Maçonnerie Ecossaise en France* (1930); Blanchard, *Scotch Rite Masonry Illustrated. The Complete Ritual of the Ancient and Accepted Scottish Rite* (1950). The latter work is an anti-Masonic exposure, which nonetheless contains accurate accounts of the rituals of the AASR. It should, however, be noted that the rituals in this work actually describe the Cerneau version of the AASR.

16. The AASR contains more Ecossais degrees than Templar ones: only the 30th and 32nd degrees are Templar.

17. Chivalric themes can be found in the 15th degree, Knight of the East or Sword, and in the 21st degree, Noachite or Prussian Knight. For an emic interpretation of the rituals of the AASR, see Pike, *Morals and Dogma of the Ancient and Accepted Scottish Rite of Freemasonry* (1871), and Clausen, *Clausen's Commentaries on Morals and Dogma* (1974).

18. For more information on the Knight of the Sun degree, see Mollier, "Le Chevalier du Soleil: Contribution à l'étude d'un haut-grade maçonnique en France au XVIIIe siècle" (1992).

19. On the Rectified Scottish Rite, see Noël, "De la Stricte Observance au Rite Ecossais Rectifié" (1995).

20. "Les rituels du Rite Ecossais Rectifié furent élaborés en quelques vingt-quatre années, de 1775 à 1809, qui virent un travail intense et une mise en place laborieuse. On peut y distinguer quatre étapes essentielles: les rituels de Lyon [1778], ceaux de Wilhelmsbad [1782], la version "courte" de 1785, la version "longue" de 1788, cette dernière caractérisée par une imprégnation martinéziste qui devait culminer dans le rituel de 1809. Rien n'empêcherait, aujourd'hui, les loges rectifiées de choisir l'un ou l'autre de ces rituels successifs, tous conformes à un moment de la pensée du fondateur!" Noël, "De la Stricte Observance au Rite Ecossais Rectifié" (1995), 112.

21. Noël, "De la Stricte Observance au Rite Ecossais Rectifié" (1995), 120.

22. *DGWE* (2005), 1170–1173.

23. In Sweden, this Rite is referred to as "det Svenska Systemet," the Swedish System.

24. For a recent exposure of the rituals of the Swedish Rite, see Mogstad, *Frimureri: mysterier, fellesskap, personlighetsdannelse* (1994).

25. For Freeemasonry in Sweden, see in particular Thulstrup, *Anteckningar till Svenska Frimureriets Historia*, in two volumes, (1892, 1898); Kinnander, *Svenska Frimureriets Historia* (1943); Dahlgren, *Frimureriet med tillämpning på Sverige* (1925); Lenhammar, *Med murslev och svärd: Svenska frimurarorden under 250 år* (1985); Snoek, "Swedenborg, Freemasonry, and Swedenborgian Freemasonry: An Overview" (2001), 38–47.

26. For more information on Eckleff, see Berg, "Carl Friedrich Eckleff som människa och frimurare" (1998).

27. The fourth degree was later split into two degrees—Apprentice of St. Andrew (IV) and Companion of St. Andrew (V)—which makes a total of ten degrees.

28. That the origins of Freemasonry might be found in ancient Egypt was hinted at before Egyptian masonry as such appeared on the scene. See, for instance, *Le Sceau Rompu* (1745), *EFE* (1971), 208.

29. See Assman, *Moses the Egyptian. The Memory of Egypt in Western Monotheism* (1997); Hornung, *The Secret Lore of Egypt* (2001); Rich and Merchant, "The Egyptian Influence on Nineteenth-Century Freemasonry" (2001).

30. Faivre, *Access to Western Esotericism* (1994), 80.

31. Caillet, *Arcanes & Ritueles de la Maçonnerie Égyptienne* (1994), 17.

32. Köppen and Hymmen, *Crata Repoa. Oder Einweyhungen in der alten geheimen Gesellschaft der Egyptischen Preister*, [Berlin] (1770). Even though the text was not published until 1770, it was circulated in manuscript form prior to its publication. An English translation of the text was serialized in *The Kneph—Official Journal of the Antient and Primitive Rite of Masonry* Vol. II, No. 15–No. 22 (1882).

33. *DGWE* (2005), 225. For an English translation of these rituals, see "Cagliostro's Egyptian Rite" *Collectanea* Vol. 5, Part 2, (1954), 165–215.

34. McIntosh, *Eliphas Lévi and the French Occult Revival* (1975), 30–31.

35. Caillet, *Arcanes & Ritueles de la Maçonnerie Égyptienne* (1994), 19; *DGWE* (2005), 225–227. The term "theurgy" often refers to a blending of magical and philosophical traditions as expressed in the late second-century *Chaldean Oracles* and its later developments. Theurgy can be described as an ascent toward the supreme God, whose ultimate goal is spiritual salvation. *DGWE* (2005), 725–726.

36. "The Rite of Mizraim" *Collectanea* Vol. 6, Part 1 (1955), 17.

37. Lennhoff and Posner, *Internationales Freimaurerlexikon* (1932), 1044–1045. *Collectanea* Vol. 6, Part 1 p. 17 gives another explanation of the name of the Rite: "the Rite of Misraim, so called because its legend goes back to the ancient Egyptian King, Menes, who was also known as Mizraim."

38. *Collectanea* Vol. 6, Part 1 (1955), 18.

39. For an English translation of the rituals of the Rite of Misraim, see "The Rite of Mizraim" *Collectanea*. Vol. 6, Part 1 (1955); "The Rite of Mizraim" *Collectanea*. Vol. 7, Part 2 (1961), 120–164.

40. For more information on the chequered history of the *Rite of Memphis*, see Pike and Cummings, "The Spurious Rites of Memphis and Misraim" (2001).

41. For an English translation of the rituals of the Rite of Memphis, see "The Rite of Memphis" *Collectanea* Vol. 6, Part 2 (1956); *Collectanea* Vol. 7, Part 1 (1958), 69–95.

42. Rich and Merchant, "The Egyptian Influence on Nineteenth-Century Freemasonry" (2001), 34.

43. For more information, see the indispensable work by Le Forestier, *La Franc-Maçonnerie Occultiste au XVIIe Siècle & L'Ordre des Élus Coens* (1987) [1923]. See also *DGWE* (2005), 332–334.

44. *DGWE* (2005), 935.

45. *DGWE* (2005), 332–334, 931–935.

46. It is often stated that Dom Antoine Joseph Pernety (1716–1796) was the founder of not only the *Rite Hermétique d'Avignon*, but also of the *Rite Ecossais philosophique*. Modern scholarship, however, contest this assumption. See Snoek, "Swedenborg, Freemasonry, and Swedenborgian Freemasonry: An Overview" (2003), 28–32.

47. Snoek, "Swedenborg, Freemasonry, and Swedenborgian Freemasonry: An Overview" (2003), 32.

48. According to *Collectanea*, the original six degrees of the Rite were (1) The True Mason; (2) The True Mason in the Right Way; (3) The Knight of the Golden Key; (4) The Knight of the Rainbow; (5) The Knight of the Argonauts, and; (6) The Knight of the Golden Fleece. For a translation of these rituals into English, see *Collectanea* Vol. 6, Part 3 (1957).

49. Snoek, "Swedenborg, Freemasonry, and Swedenborgian Freemasonry: An Overview" (2003), 68.

50. For a detailed account of the development of the degree system of the *Rite Ecossais philosophique* see Snoek, "Swedenborg, Freemasonry, and Swedenborgian Freemasonry: An Overview" (2003), Appendix II.

51. Snoek, "Swedenborg, Freemasonry, and Swedenborgian Freemasonry: An Overview" (2003), 70.

52. For more information on *Der Orden des Gülden und Rosenkreutzes* see chapter six of McIntosh, *The Rosicrucians* (1997).

53. For an introduction to the alchemy of *Der Orden des Gold- und Rosenkreuzes* see McIntosh, "The Alchemy and the *Gold- und Rosenkreuz*" (1990), 237–244.

54. McIntosh has shown in *The Rose Cross and the Age of Reason* (1992) that the relationship of *Der Orden des Gold- und Rosenkreuzes* to the anti-*Aufklärung* movement is more complicated than first meets the eye.

55. McIntosh, *The Rosicrucians* (1997), 65–66.

56. McIntosh, *The Rosicrucians* (1997), 68.

57. McIntosh, *The Rosicrucians* (1997), 66.

58. For a description of the second degree ritual (Theoreticus), see McIntosh, *The Rosicrucians* (1997), 72–74.

59. Bernheim, "The Order of Kilwinning or Scotch Heredom, the Present Royal Order of Scotland" (1999/2000), 94.

60. For information on the history of ROS, see Lindsay, *The Royal Order of Scotland* (1971), and Draffen of Newington, *The Royal Order of Scotland—The Second Hundred Years* (1977). Bernheim, "The Order of Kilwinning or Scotch Heredom, the Present Royal Order of Scotland" (1999/2000).

61. The legendary history is mentioned in the Ritual of the Order. *The Royal Order of Scotland* (n.d.), 53.

62. For information on the history of the Rose-Croix of Heredom, Knight of the Pelican and Eagle degree, see Jackson, *Rose Croix* (1993), 24–30.

63. Jackson, *Rose Croix* (1993), 27.

64. The version Harodim is especially found in French versions of the ritual. It is a Hebrew word, the plural of Harod—one who rules or acts as an Overseer. Jackson, *Rose Croix* (1993), 6–7.

65. According to Jackson, the following suggestions have been offered to the meaning of the word Heredom: *Heres domus*, the Latin for house of the heir, or first-born. *Hieros domos*, the Greek for holy house. *Har Edom*, the Hebrew for (Holy) Mountain of the Earth. Jackson, *Rose Croix* (1993), 7.

66. *Collectanea* Vol. 6, Part 3 (1957), 207–226. I have checked the printed English translation against a French manuscript version of the ritual; Kloss XXVI.3, GON 193.C.68, Académie des Vrais Maçons. I am indebted to J.A.M. Snoek for a transcript of this manuscript.

67. Kloss XXVI.3, GON 193.C.68, states "Très Sage."

68. The English translation states "the apron should be embroidered, also in gold, the following three sets of letters, C.D., N.P., A.M." The French manuscript, however, state that the letters should be D C N P A M (Deus Creat Natura Producit Ars Multiplicat).

69. *Collectanea* Vol. 6, Part 3 (1957), 209.

70. The preparation room is usually called a Chamber of Reflection, which is often totally dark. In French rituals there are usually two rooms: the "Chambre de preparation," and the "Chambre obscure." After being prepared (i.e., addressed and properly clothed) in the first one, the candidate is placed in the second room in order to meditate. Usually there is a candle burning there.

71. *Collectanea* Vol. 6, Part 3 (1957), 210.

72. *Collectanea* Vol. 6, Part 3 (1957), 211.

73. According to Kloss XXVI.3, GON 193.C.68, the password is *Mitraton*. However, both Metralon and Mitraton are probably corruptions of Metraton or Metatron, the greatest of the angels in Jewish myths and legends. The function of Metatron differs in various stories, but the most important ones are as God's mediator with men and as a guardian of heavenly secrets.

74. *Collectanea* Vol. 6, Part 3 (1957), 213.

75. *Collectanea* Vol. 6, Part 3 (1957), 214.

76. *Collectanea* Vol. 6, Part 3 (1957), 214.

77. This theory was originally formulated by Empedokles (*c.* 492–*c.* 432 BC).

78. *Collectanea* Vol. 6, Part 3 (1957), 214.

79. *Collectanea* Vol. 6, Part 3 (1957), 214.

80. *Collectanea* Vol. 6, Part 3 (1957), 223.

81. Abraham writes: "The secret fire (the fiery water and the watery fire) lies hidden in the alchemist's raw matter ('gold') and is stirred into action by the application of the outer material fire." *A Dictionary of Alchemical Imagery* (2001), 76.

82. *Collectanea* Vol. 6, Part 3 (1957), 214–215.

83. Abraham, *A Dictionary of Alchemical Imagery* (2001), 137.

84. *Collectanea* Vol. 6, Part 3 (1957), 216.

85. For information on Hermes in Western esotericism, see Faivre, *The Eternal Hermes. From Greek God to Alchemical Magus* (1995).

86. *Collectanea* Vol. 6, Part 3 (1957), 216.

87. *Collectanea* Vol. 6, Part 3 (1957), 216–217.

88. For a modern translation of Pico's conclusions into English, see Farmer, *Syncretism in the West: Pico's 900 Theses* (1998).

89. *Collectanea* Vol. 6, Part 3 (1957), 217.

90. The three phases of the alchemical process, *Nigredo*, *Albedo*, and *Rubedo* are sometimes extended to include a fourth phase, *Citrinitas* or the yellow stage, considered to take place between *Albedo* and *Rubedo*. This was known already by the Greek alchemists. For instance, Maria the Jewess is attributed, by Zosimus of Panopolis (late third and early fourth centuries), to be familiar with the four phases of color transformation. Patai, "Maria the Jewess—Founding Mother of Alchemy" (1982), 181.

91. Abraham, *A Dictionary of Alchemical Imagery* (2001), 5.

92. It is tempting to draw a parallel between the three phases of alchemy and the three phases of Van Gennep's *Rites de Passage*: *Nigredo* corresponds to the first phase in which the candidate is separated from his or her previous state; *Albedo* to the marginal or liminal state; and finally, *Rubedo* to the aggregation phase, or the incorporation of the candidate into the new phase.

93. *Collectanea* Vol. 6, Part 3 (1957), 218.

94. Abraham, *A Dictionary of Alchemical Imagery* (2001), 68.

95. The *Prima Materia* presupposes a monistic theory of metals, in which all substances are believed to be basically one. The Greek alchemist Chymes is cited by Zosimus as having declared: "One is the All, and it is through it that the All is born. One is the All, and if the All does not contain all, the All will not be born." Patai, "Maria the Jewess—Founding Mother of Alchemy" (1982), 182.

96. These four qualities correspond to the theory of Galen (b.131) in which the human body is made up of four humors: blood (heat), bile (cold), black bile (dryness), and phlegm (moisture).

97. *Collectanea* Vol. 6, Part 3 (1957), 218–219.

98. On Paracelsus see Weeks, *Paracelsus—Speculative Theory and the Crisis of the Early Reformation* (1997); for his alchemical writings see *The Hermetic & Alchemical Writings of Paracelsus the Great* (1894). On the impact of Paracelsism on Eighteenth Century France, see Debus, *Chemistry, Alchemy and the New Philosophy, 1550–1700* (1987), 36–54. See also Debus, *The French Paracelsians* (1991).

99. Abraham, *A Dictionary of Alchemical Imagery* (2001), 176–177.

100. The theory of two principles of metals, is generally attributed to the Arab alchemist Geber, or pseudo-Jabir ibn Hayyan.

101. *Collectanea* Vol. 6, Part 3 (1957), 219.

102. *Collectanea* Vol. 6, Part 3 (1957), 221.

103. *Collectanea* Vol. 6, Part 3 (1957), 221–222.

104. In full, the passage reads: "What is above is like that which is below, and what is below is like that which is above." Or in Latin "Quod est Inferius est sicut quod est Superius, et quod est Superius est sicut quod est Inferius."

105. *DGWE* (2005), 102–103.

106. MS. Français 2018. Bibliothèque Nationale.

107. MS. Sloane 3778. British Library.

108. *DGWE* (2005), 694–696.

109. For an English translation of these works, see *The Alchemical Works of Geber* (1994).

110. *The Hermetic Museum* (1893), Vol. I, 311–357.

111. Reprinted in Linden, *The Alchemy Reader* (2003), 136–140.

112. *DGWE* (2005), 370–371.

113. See also Flamel, "A Short Tract, or Philosophical Summery" in *The Hermetic Museum* (1893), Vol. I, 141–147. *Livre des figures hiéroglyphiques* was first published in 1612 by Arnauld de la Chevalerie as a French translation of a presumably lost Latin original text. A Latin manuscript version exists, however, at the archives of the Swedish Grand Lodge of Freemasonry. A Swedish translation by Kjell Lekeby from the Latin manuscript was published in 1996, as Flamel, *Boken om de Hieroglyfiska Bilderna* (1996).

114. For more information on Thomas Vaughan, see the Biographical Introduction to Rudrum (ed.) *The Works of Thomas Vaughan* (1984), and *DGWE* (2005), 1157–1158.

115. These are included, together with "A Perfect and Full Discoverie of the True Cœlum Terræ, or The Magican's Heavenly Chaos, and First Matter of all Things," in *The Magical Writings of Thomas Vaughan (Eugenius Philalethes)* (1888). These are also included in Rudrum (ed.) *The Works of Thomas Vaughan* (1984).

116. Boyle was also deeply involved with alchemy. See Hunter (ed.), *Robert Boyle Reconsidered* (1994); *DGWE* (2005), 199–201; Linden, *The Alchemy Reader* (2003), 234–242.

117. Philalethes, Eirenæus "An Open Entrance to the Closed Palace of the King" in *The Hermetic Museum* (1893), Vol. II, 159–198; Eirenæus Philalethes "The Secret of the Immortal Liquor called Alkahest or Ignis-Aqua" in *Collectanea Chemica* (1963). See also *DGWE* (2005), 1082–1083, and Linden, *The Alchemy Reader* (2003), 211–221.

118. Manget, *Bibliotheca Chemica Curiosa* (1702).

119. Other alchemical works by Maier include *Arcana arcanissima* (1614); *Examen fucorum* (1617); *Tripus Aureus* (1618). His Rosicrucian apologetic works include *Silentium post clamores* (1617) and the celebrated *Themis aurea* (1618), translated into English as *Themis Aurea. The Laws of the Fraternity of the Rosie Crosse* (1656). For a thorough discussion of Maier's alchemical and Rosicrucian pursuits, see Tilton, *The Quest for the Phoenix* (2003).

120. *Collectanea* Vol. 6, Part 3 (1957), 222.

121. *Collectanea* Vol. 6, Part 3 (1957), 223.

122. For an overview of how alchemy of the sixteenth to eighteenth centuries differs from earlier forms of alchemy, see *DGWE* (2005), 42–50. For a good general introduction to alchemy, see Moran, *Distilling Knowledge* (2005).

Chapter 6

1. Occultism is defined as a "Current which also corresponds to Notions." "[Occultism] refers to the current which has appeared by the middle of the nineteenth century (notably under the influence of Éliphas Lévi), indirectly in the wake of the *philosophia occulta*, and which has remained very much alive up to the beginning of the 20th century. It is characterized by the attempt to reconcile modern science and gnosis, by drawing upon the occidental as well as oriental traditions of the past." Faivre, "Questions of Terminology proper to the Study of Esoteric Currents in Modern and Contemporary Europe" (1998), 8. See also Hanegraaff, *New Age Religion and Western Culture* (1998), 421–442.

2. "Correspondences" is one of the constitutive elements of Western esotericism, while "the Praxis of the Concordance" is one of the two "relative" elements. Vide Faivre, *Access to Western Esotericism* (1994), 10–14.

3. For the prescribed courses of study from the degree of Neophyte to that of Philosophus, see Gilbert, *The Golden Dawn Companion* (1986), 90–94.

4. Yorke, foreword to Howe, *The Magicians of the Golden Dawn* (1972), ix.

5. The degree system of the Golden Dawn was to a large extent taken from Kenneth Mackenzie's *The Royal Masonic Cyclopaedia*, issued in six parts from 1875 to 1877. Mackenzie had, in his turn, taken the degrees from Magister Pianco's *Der Rosenkreuzer in seiner Blösse* (1781). See Mackenzie, *The Royal Masonic Cyclopaedia* (1987), 616–617.

6. The English-speaking readers first came in contact with Lévi's writings primarily through the extensive quotations from his works in Blavatsky's *Isis Unveiled* (1877) and through Waite's *The Mysteries of Magic: A Digest of the Writings of Éliphas Lévi* (1886). Translations of Lévi's works include *The Paradoxes of the Highest Science* (1883); *Transcendental Magic* (1896), and *The History of Magic* (1913), the latter two translated by Waite; and *The Key to the Mysteries* (1913) translated by Aleister Crowley.

7. McIntosh, *Eliphas Lévi and the French Occult Revival* (1975), 148.

8. "Among the characteristics of secret societies are legendary accounts supporting the claims to antiquity of origin of the orders themselves. In some organizations the origin legends figure conspicuously in the structural framework; in others they play lesser roles. Some extravagantly assert a remote antiquity of origin. Others are more modest in their claims for an early beginning. But whatever may be the actual details of the origin legends or claims in any particular society, it seems reasonable to assume that these features furnish prestige and stability to the order as a whole and personal status to the individual members who are identified with the society." Gist, *Secret Societies* (1940), 70.

9. Anderson, *The Constitutions of the Free-Masons* (1723), 1.

10. Official in the sense that it was the story that was told its members, and legendary in the sense that the object was certainly not to convey factual circumstances, but rather to furnish a legitimate ground for the formation of the Golden Dawn. The story was given the members in a short work entitled "Historic Lecture for Neophytes" partly quoted by Howe, *The Magicians of the Golden Dawn* (1972), 23–25. For an introduction to the history of the Golden Dawn, see *DGWE* (2005), 544–550.

11. The SRIA was founded in 1866 and its membership limited to Master Masons. It was primarily focused on Rosicrucianism and remains active to this day.

12. According to a copy of a letter from Woodford in Westcott's hand, quoted by Howe, *The Magicians of the Golden Dawn* (1972), 9; Gilbert, *The Golden Dawn Scrapbook* (1997), 26.

13. Mackenzie was active in a number of occultist orders, and while his cyclopedia failed to attract the attention of masons in general, it is nonetheless important because it "distilled the essence of Victorian esoteric thought." For more information on the life and importance of Mackenzie, see the introduction by Hamill and Gilbert to Mackenzie's *The Royal Masonic Cyclopaedia* (1987).

14. Gilbert, "Provenance Unknown" (1996), 17–26.

15. Cf. Howe, *The Magicians of the Golden Dawn* (1972), 1–25; Gilbert, *The Golden Dawn Companion* (1986), 4–29.

16. Isis-Urania Temple was the third temple of the order after the alleged "Temple No. 1 of Licht, Liebe, Leben" [Germany] and "Hermanubis No. 2" [London]. The former consisted, according to Westcott, of a group of continental mystics, and the latter had ceased to exist because its chiefs had died. Gilbert, *The Golden Dawn Companion* (1986), 30–31.

17. For more information on the relationship between the Golden Dawn and the Esoteric Section, see Gilbert, *The Golden Dawn and the Esoteric Section* (1987).

18. For a discussion of the symbolism of the Inner Order Vault, see Grant, *Vault of the Adepts. The seven-pointed figure of its ceiling and floor with a study of doctrines enshrined in its symbols* (1963).

19. Quoted by Gilbert, *The Golden Dawn Scrapbook* (1997), 51.

20. The Golden Dawn broke into three main factions: (1) The Independent and Rectified Rite of the Golden Dawn under A. E. Waite; (2) Stella Matutina under R. W. Felkin and Brodie-Innes; (3) the Alpha and Omega which remained under Mathers, and later Mathers's wife Mina Mathers (1865–1928) after he died in 1918.

21. A large number of manuscripts pertaining to the Golden Dawn are in the Gerald Yorke Collection, Warburg Institute, University of London; and a collection of rituals of the *Stella Matutina* is in the library of Freemasons' Hall, United Grand Lodge of England, London.

22. Unless otherwise stated, all quotes in the description and analysis of the Neophyte ritual are taken from Torrens, *The Secret Rituals of the Golden Dawn* (1973), 71–89.

23. Torrens, *The Secret Rituals of the Golden Dawn* (1973), 73–74; Regardie, *The Complete Golden Dawn System of Magic* (1990), Vol. 6, 6.

24. Torrens, *The Secret Rituals of the Golden Dawn* (1973), 74; Regardie, *The Complete Golden Dawn System of Magic* (1990), Vol. 6, 7.

25. Torrens, *The Secret Rituals of the Golden Dawn* (1973), 74–75; Crowley, "The Temple of Solomon the King" (1909), 251; Regardie, *The Complete Golden Dawn System of Magic* (1990), Vol. 6, 8.

26. Torrens, *The Secret Rituals of the Golden Dawn* (1973), 75; Crowley, "The Temple of Solomon the King" (1909), 252; Regardie, *The Complete Golden Dawn System of Magic* (1990), Vol. 6, 9.

27. Torrens, *The Secret Rituals of the Golden Dawn* (1973), 75; Crowley, "The Temple of Solomon the King" (1909), 252; Regardie, *The Complete Golden Dawn System of Magic* (1990), Vol. 6, 9.

28. The words "Konx Om Pax" were taken from a "barbarous phrase" spoken at the Eleusinian mysteries, which, according to the originators of the Golden Dawn, were the Greek cognates of the Egyptian "Khabs Am Pekht," translated as "Light in Extension." According to Starr, this is "a bit of good mysticism but dubious etymology in keeping with the intellectual habits of the Golden Dawn's magical founder, S. L. Mathers, who, as Crowley twits, "will borrow any required properties." Starr, introduction to Crowley, *Konx Om Pax* (1990), v.

29. Torrens, *The Secret Rituals of the Golden Dawn* (1973), 76; according to Crowley, the text should read, "(. . .) arise and enter *into* the Path of Darkness." Crowley, "The Temple of Solomon the King" (1909), 253; Regardie, *The Complete Golden Dawn System of Magic* (1990), Vol. 6, 10.

30. According to Crowley, the Hegemon answers for the candidate. Crowley, "The Temple of Solomon the King" (1909), 254.

31. Torrens, *The Secret Rituals of the Golden Dawn* (1973), 77; Crowley, "The Temple of Solomon the King" (1909), 254; Regardie, *The Complete Golden Dawn System of Magic* (1990), Vol. 6, 11.

32. Torrens, *The Secret Rituals of the Golden Dawn* (1973), 79; Crowley only quotes this in part, but it has a slightly different rendering: "He then swears to observe the above under the awful penalty of submitting 'myself to a deadly and hostile current of will set in motion by the chiefs of the Order, by which I should fall slain *or* paralysed without visible weapon, as if *blasted* by the lightning flash.' " Crowley further notes that a later edition of the ritual, issued subsequent to the Horos scandals, reads "an awful and avenging punitive current etc." Crowley, "The Temple of Solomon the King" (1909), 255; Regardie, *The Complete Golden Dawn System of Magic* (1990), Vol. 6, 12.

33. Torrens, *The Secret Rituals of the Golden Dawn* (1973), 79; Crowley, "The Temple of Solomon the King" (1909), 254–255; Regardie, *The Complete Golden Dawn System of Magic* (1990), Vol. 6, 13.

34. Torrens, *The Secret Rituals of the Golden Dawn* (1973), 80; Crowley, "The Temple of Solomon the King" (1909), 254; Regardie, *The Complete Golden Dawn System of Magic* (1990), Vol. 6, 13.

35. Torrens, *The Secret Rituals of the Golden Dawn* (1973), 81; Crowley, "The Temple of Solomon the King" (1909), 257; Regardie, *The Complete Golden Dawn System of Magic* (1990), Vol. 6, 14.

36. Torrens, *The Secret Rituals of the Golden Dawn* (1973), 81; Crowley, "The Temple of Solomon the King" (1909), 257. Crowley omits the prayer, and only gives the last two sentences; Regardie, *The Complete Golden Dawn System of Magic* (1990), Vol. 6, 15.

37. Torrens, *The Secret Rituals of the Golden Dawn* (1973), 84–85; Regardie, *The Complete Golden Dawn System of Magic* (1990), Vol. 6, 18–19. The instruction is omitted by Crowley.

38. Torrens, *The Secret Rituals of the Golden Dawn* (1973), 89; Crowley, "The Temple of Solomon the King" (1909), 261. Torrens omits the element Fire, described by Crowley: "I invite you to inhale with me the perfume of this rose *as a symbol of Air (smelling rose): To feel with me the warmth of this sacred Fire (spreading hands over it): To* eat with me this Bread and Salt as types of earth *(eats):* and finally *to* drink with me this Wine, the consecrated emblem of Elemental Water *(drinks from Cup)*."; Regardie, *The Complete Golden Dawn System of Magic* (1990), Vol. 6, 22.

39. Torrens, *The Secret Rituals of the Golden Dawn* (1973), 89; Crowley, "The Temple of Solomon the King" (1909), 261. Crowley includes "the True Wisdom" before "Perfect Happiness." Regardie, *The Complete Golden Dawn System of Magic* (1990), Vol. 6, 23. Regardie also includes "True Wisdom."

40. Torrens, *The Secret Rituals of the Golden Dawn* (1973), 47–70. Regardie has different titles to the Z.1 and Z. 3 documents: "The Enterer of the Threshold" (Z-1) and "The Symbolism of the Admission of the Candidate" (Z-3). Regardie, *The Complete Golden Dawn System of Magic* (1990), Vol. 6, 53–83.

41. Torrens, *The Secret Rituals of the Golden Dawn* (1973), 49.

42. See the introduction by S. L. MacGregor Mathers to *The Kabbalah Unveiled* (1970), Plate VI (Plate illustrating the Analogy between the Soul, the Letters of the Tetragrammaton and the Four Worlds), facing page 35.

43. Torrens, *The Secret Rituals of the Golden Dawn* (1973), 50.

44. Westcott, "The Pillars IV" in Regardie, *The Complete Golden Dawn System of Magic* (1990), Vol. III, 14.

45. Regardie, *The Golden Dawn* (1939),Vol. III, 116–119.

46. Gilbert, *The Golden Dawn Companion* (1986), 90–94.

47. Torrens, *The Secret Rituals of the Golden Dawn* (1973), 77.

48. Egmond, "Western Esoteric Schools in the Late Nineteenth and Early Twentieth Centuries" (1998), 312.

49. The concept of Occultism as based on scientific premises and the importance of the will was later epitomized in the Law of Thelema, which Aleister Crowley championed.

50. Beitchman, *Alchemy of the Word* (1998), 101.

51. Westcott's translation of the *Sepher Yetzirah* is included in Westcott, *Collectanea Hermetica* (1998), as part 10. Later on, in 1923, A. E. Waite wrote an introduction to a Swedish author's English translation of the *Sepher Yetzirah*: Stenring, *The Book of Formation* (1923).

52. Torrens probably made a mistake when omitting this part of the ritual.

Chapter 7

1. According to Janet and Stewart Farrar, Aradia is the witches' teacher goddess, and daughter of Diana and Lucifer. Cernunnos is the name of a Celtic horned god. Farrar, *The Witches' God* (1989), 166–167 and 198.

2. The history of modern pagan witchcraft is expounded in the excellent study by Hutton, *The Triumph of the Moon* (1999). For a very good introduction to the beliefs and practices of modern Witchcraft and ritual magic, see Luhrmann, *Persuasions of the Witch's Craft* (1989).

3. For an account of Alex Sanders early activities, see Johns, *King of the Witches* (1969). This book includes the first printed version of the so-called "Charges" as appendix A, 'The Book of Shadows.' For more information on Sander's version of Wicca, see Sanders, *The Alex Sanders Lectures* (1984).

4. For the sake of simplicity, I use the standard terms Gardnerian and Alexandrian for the traditions stemming from Gerald Gardner and Alex Sanders, respectively.

5. The minor differences in the three rituals of initiation are discussed by the Farrars in *The Witches' Way* (1986).

6. See especially Hutton, *The Triumph of the Moon* (1999), 340–368; Hanegraaff, *New Age Religion and Western Culture* (1998), 85–86.

7. Kelly, *Crafting the Art of Magic* (1991), ix. For a discussion on the size of witchcraft movement in the United States, see Kelly, "An Update on Neopagan Witchcraft in America" (1992), 136–151.

8. Hanegraaff, *New Age Religion and Western Culture* (1998), 77.

9. Hanegraaff, *New Age Religion and Western Culture* (1998), 77.

10. Hanegraaff, *New Age Religion and Western Culture* (1998), 86.

11. For a thorough discussion of the neopagan roots of the modern Witchcraft movement, see Hutton, *The Triumph of the Moon* (1999), 3–171.

12. This does not, however, mean that the members of the Golden Dawn were neopagans. The Pledge Form of the order was soon after the founding in 1888 altered to include the following restriction: "Belief in a Supreme Being, or Beings, is indispensable. In addition, the Candidate, if not a Christian, should be at least prepared to take an interest in Christian symbolism." Quoted in Gilbert, *The Golden Dawn Scrapbook* (1997), 23.

13. "Aiwaz is not a mere formula, like many Angelic names, but it is the true, most ancient name of the God of the Yezidi, and thus returns to the highest antiquity. Our work is therefore historically authentic; the rediscovery of the Sumerian tradition." Quoted by Grant, *The Magical Revival* (1972), 52. This is from the "Note on Title" from the "long" versions of Crowley's *Commentaries on Liber AL vel Legis* (i.e., *The Book of the Law*), which has not been published as such. I am indebted to Martin P. Starr who identified this passage to me.

14. For information on Dion Fortune, the pen name of Violet Mary Firth, see Richardson, *Priestess—The Life and Magic of Dion Fortune* (1987).

15. Hanegraaff, *New Age Religion and Western Culture* (1998), 85.

16. In particular, witches belonging to what is sometimes called "Hedgewitchcraft." For a short description of this type of witchcraft, see Pearson,

""Going Native in Reverse": The Insider as Researcher in British Wicca" (2002), 100–101.

17. Even though no less than fifteen biographies of Crowley have been published, a scholarly work dealing with Crowley in relation with Western esotericism has yet to be written. The three latest biographies are Booth, *A Magick Life* (2000); Sutin, *Do What Thou Wilt* (2000); and Kaczynski, *Perdurabo* (2002). For a discussion of these biographies, see Pasi, "The Neverendingly Told Story: Recent Biographies of Aleister Crowley" (2003). Mention should also be made of Marco Pasi's *Aleister Crowley e la Tentazione della Politica* (1999), which focuses on the political aspects of Crowley's work. For a general introduction to the life and teachings of Crowley, see *DGWE* (2005), 281–287.

18. King, *Ritual Magic in England 1887 to the present day* (1970), 179–180.

19. See the title page of Gardner's *High Magic's Aid* (1949) where he confuses the degree systems of the O.T.O. with that of the A∴A∴, an order founded by Crowley in 1907.

20. Allen T. Greenfield possesses what purports to be the original charter from Crowley to Gardner. The authenticity of the document is, however, questioned.

21. Grant, *Manifesto of the British Branch of the Ordo Templi Orientis (O.T.O.)* (1948).

22. For Grant's reminiscence of Crowley, see Grant, *Remembering Aleister Crowley* (1991). Grant mentions his acquaintance with Gardner in *Nightside of Eden* (1977), 122–124.

23. Letter from Kenneth Grant to the author, dated June 17, 1999.

24. For Theodor Reuss (1855–1923), see Howe and Möller, "Theodor Reuss—Irregular Freemasonry in Germany, 1900–23" (1979).

25. For John Yarker (1833–1913), see "In Memoriam" in *The Co-Mason* Vol. V, April (1913), 65–71; Hamill, "The Seeker of Truth: John Yarker 1833–1913" (1993).

26. See chapter 5 above.

27. Quoted by King, *Ritual Magic in England* (1970), 119. Research is still wanting on the subject of Western esotericism and sex. It is, however, clear that the O.T.O. was not alone in combining magic with sex. For instance, the nineteenth-century American Rosicrucian Paschal Beverly Randolph (1825–1875) advocated a form of sexual magic. See Randolph, *Sexual Magic* (1988); Deveney, *Paschal Beverly Randolph* (1997). Another early protagonist of sexual magic was Ida Craddock (1857–1902). See Craddock, "Heavenly Bridegrooms" and "Psychic Wedlock" in Motta, (ed.) *The Equinox* Vol. V, No. 4 (1981). For a discussion of the apparent connections between the sexual magic of the O.T.O. with Tantra, see Urban, *Tantra* (2003), 215–223; Bogdan, "Challenging the Morals of Western Society" (2006).

28. Crowley, *Confessions* (1989), 628–629.

29. Crowley, *The Book of Lies* (1913). It has been suggested that the secrets of sexual magick was revealed by Crowley in Chapter 69: "The Way to Succeed—and the Way to Suck Eggs!" and/or Chapter 36: "The Star Sapphire."

30. O.H.O. = Outer Head of the Order, the technical name of the leader of the O.T.O.

31. Crowley, *The Magical Record of the Beast 666* (1993), 3.

32. For the circumstances of the reception of *The Book of the Law*, see Crowley, *The Equinox of the Gods* (1991, revised edition). For a collected edition of the canon of Thelema, see Crowley, *The Holy Books of Thelema* (1983).

33. The Royal Arch degree centers on the accidental discovery of a crypt under the Temple of Jerusalem. For more information on this degree, see Jones, *Freemason's Book of the Royal Arch* (1957). According to Gardner's biography, he was initiated into masonry when he was working in Ceylon, *c.* 1905 in the lodge the Sphinx, 113, I. C. in Colombo. Bracelin, *Gerald Gardner: Witch* (1999), 32.

34. For a thorough discussion of the historical roots of the *Theosophical Society*, see Godwin, *The Theosophical Enlightenment* (1994).

35. The A∴A∴ was founded by Crowley and George Cecil Jones (1873–1953) in 1907. It is often assumed that the letters stand for the Latin phrase of Silver Star, *Argentinum Astrum*. However, according to Eshelman the name is *Astron Argon* (ΑΣΤΡΟΝ ΑΡΓΟΝ), and it is alleged to be recorded twice in Crowley's handwriting. Another variant that Eshelman discusses is *Aster Argos* (ΑΣΤΗΡ ΑΡΓΟΣ), which is supposed to derive from one of Crowley's disciples—Charles Stansfeld Jones. Eshelman, *The Mystical & Magical System of the A∴A∴* (2000), 23.

36. Starr, *The Unknown God: W.T. Smith and the Thelemites* (2003), 45–46.

37. Kelly, *Crafting the Art of Magic* (1991), 45–167.

38. The only unpublished document on sexual magic written by Crowley that survived among Gardner's personal papers was a typescript copy of *Amrita*, in essence a prospectus for Crowley's course of treatment. Martin P. Starr, personal communication to the author, dated March 23, 2003. The text was, however, written for a general audience and does not include any technical information on the subject. See Crowley, *Amrita. Essays in Magical Rejuvenation*, edited by Martin P. Starr (1990).

39. Valiente, *Witchcraft for Tomorrow* (1987), 147.

40. In particular, see Valiente, *Witchcraft for tomorrow* (1987); Farrar, *The Witches' Way* (1986); Kelly, *Crafting the Art of Magic* (1991); Hutton, *The Triumph of the Moon* (1999).

41. http://www.sacred-texts.com/pag/gbos/index.htm (5/16/2003).

42. Gardner, *High Magic's Aid* (1949), 290–303.

43. Farrar, *The Witches' Way* (1986), 3.

44. Farrar, *The Witches' Way* (1986), 3.

45. Kelly, *Crafting the Art of Magic* (1991).

46. The *Book of Shadows* of 1949 was established from "Ye Bok of ye Art Magical" and *High Magic's Aid*; the 1953 version from *Witchcraft Today*, "Ye Bok of ye Art Magical" and *High Magic's Aid*, the Weschcke manuscripts, and *The Witches' Way*; the version of 1957 from *Witch*, the Weschcke manuscripts, *Witchcraft Today, Meaning of Witchcraft*, and *The Witches' Way*. Kelly, *Crafting the Art of Magic* (1991), 45, 109.

47. The first degree of 1949, pp. 54–58; the second degree of 1949, pp. 58–59; the third degree of 1949, pp. 60–61; the first degree of 1957, pp. 122–125; the second degree of 1957, pp. 125–128; the third degree of 1957, pp. 129–132. Kelly, *Crafting the Art of Magic* (1991).

48. Farrar, *The Witches' Way* (1986), 294.

49. The banishing/invoking rituals of the Golden Dawn were first published by Aleister Crowley in "Liber O vel Manus et Sagittae" in *The Equinox* Vol. I, No. 2 (1909) and *Magick: In Theory and Practice* (1930). Regardie's version was published in *The Golden Dawn* (1937), Vol. 1, 106–109.

50. Farrar, *The Witches' Way* (1986), 18.

51. Gardner appears to have been positive toward Freemasonry as late as 1960. "[Gardner] has always had a very soft spot for the Craft [i.e., Freemasonry], and nowadays feels that there are close similarities in the craft of the Witches; in fact he goes so far as to say that Witchcraft is the original lodge." Bracelin, *Gerald Gardner: Witch* (1999), 33.

52. For the Master Magician O.T.O. ritual, see Reuss and Crowley, *O.T.O. Rituals and Sex Magick* (1999), 207–219; King, *The Secret Rituals of the O.T.O.* (1973), 85–100.

53. Farrar, *The Witches' Way* (1986), 297.

54. Farrar, *The Witches' Way* (1986), 297.

55. "In Wiccan practice, a man is always initiated by a woman, and a woman by a man. And only a second- or third-degree witch may conduct an initiation. There is, however, a special exception to each of these rules. The first exception is that a woman may initiate her daughter, or a man his son[.] The other exception concerns the only time when a first-degree witch [. . .] may initiate another. Wicca lays great emphasis on male-female working partnerships, and most covens are delighted when a suitable couple come forward for initiation together." Farrar, *The Witches' Way* (1986), 11.

56. For the sake of simplicity, I have chosen, in accordance with the Farrars' edition of the rituals, to refer to the candidate as male, and the initiator as female.

57. Hannah, *Darkness Visible* (1952), 94–95. This describes the rituals in use in England.

58. *EFE* (1971), 19.

59. The Cabalistic Cross is part of the Lesser Banishing Ritual of the Pentagram.

60. Hannah, *Darkness Visible* (1952), 95.

61. Farrar, *The Witches' Way* (1986), 17.

62. Farrar, *The Witches' Way* (1986), 18.

63. Farrar, *The Witches' Way* (1986), 19. One author on witchcraft commented on the differences between oaths of masonry and witchcraft: "Though in this oath the blood-chilling visitations invoked by the Freemasons and other cults for apostasy are not mentioned—no talk of throats to be cut, tongues torn out burial up to the neck in sands where the tide will wash over the victim—for the witch its mild-sounding terms are as powerful a discouragement from oath-breaking as any of these. The witch is invoking the vengeance of elements on abjuration, for the weapons symbolise air, fire, earth and water. There is no hiding place for a traitor to the Craft." Glass, *Witchcraft, the Sixth Sense* (1974), 96.

64. Farrar, *The Witches' Way* (1986), 19–20.

65. Farrar, *The Witches' Way* (1986), 20.

66. Farrar, *The Witches' Way* (1986), 26.

67. Farrar, *The Witches' Way* (1986), 24.

68. The name was misspelled as Scrire. In occultistic lore, Scire is the first "power of the Sphinx" that the initiate needs to master. The four powers are Scire, Velle, Audere, and Tacere, or To Know, To Will, To Dare, and To Keep Silent. Eliphas Lévi wrote: "To attain to *Sanctum Regnum*, in other words, the knowledge and power of the magi, there are four indispensable conditions—an intelligence illuminated by study, an intrepidity which nothing can check, a will which cannot be broken, and a prudence which nothing can corrupt and nothing intoxicate. To KNOW, To DARE, To WILL, To KEEP SILENCE—such are the four words of the magus, inscribed upon the four symbolical forms of the sphinx." Lévi, *Transcendental Magic* (1896), 30.

69. Farrar, *The Witches' Way* (1986), 27.

70. Farrar, *The Witches' Way* (1986), 27.

71. Farrar, *The Witches' Way* (1986), 28.

72. Farrar, *The Witches' Way* (1986), 30.

73. Eliade (ed.), *The Encyclopedia of Religion* (1987), Vol. 7, 146.

74. For Crowley's revised version of the O.T.O. Third Degree, Master Magician, see Reuss and Crowley *O.T.O. Rituals and Sex Magick* (1999), 207–219; King (ed.) *The Secret Rituals of the O.T.O.* (1973), 85–100.

75. The third degree uses the same titles as in the second degree, that is, High Priestess and High Priest.

76. Cf. the sixth degree of O.T.O., Illustrious Knight Templar of the Order of Kadosh/Dame Companion of the Order of the Holy Grail. Reuss and Crowley, *O.T.O. Rituals and Sex Magick* (1999), 255; King (ed.) *The Secret Rituals of the O.T.O.* (1973), 162.

77. Farrar, *The Witches' Way* (1986), 35.

78. Crowley's Gnostic Mass, called "Liber XV; O.T.O. Ecclesiae Gnosticae Catholicae Canon Missae," written in 1913 in Moscow, was published three times during Crowley's lifetime: 1918, 1919, and 1929/30. For more information on the Gnostic Mass, see Apiryon and Helena, *Mystery of Mystery: A Primer of Thelemic Ecclesiastical Gnosticism* (1995).

79. Farrar, *The Witches' Way* (1986), 35.

80. Gardner does not state how many strokes are supposed to be given at this part, but the Farrars assume that Gardner had intended the traditional 3, 7, 9, 21 at each round. Farrar, *The Witches' Way* (1986), 304 (note 8 to page 36).

81. Farrar, *The Witches' Way* (1986), 36–37.

82. According to the Farrars the Great Rite is applied in practice to the third degree in the following manner: "There are only two active participants in the Rite; the rest of the coven merely support it by their silent presence, whether for the whole of a symbolic Rite or for the first part of an 'actual' one. These two may be either the man (already third degree) initiating the woman; or the woman (again, already third degree) initiating the man; or the man and woman may both be second degree, taking their third degree initiation together under the supervision of the High Priestess and/or High Priest." Farrar, *The Witches' Way* (1986), 33.

83. Farrar, *The Witches' Way* (1986), 37.

84. Farrar, *The Witches' Way* (1986), 37.

85. The Farrars state that the Text B version says Genitals to Genitals, but they find that "somewhat clinical in the poetic context of the rest, and prefer Text C's Lance-and-Grail metaphor." They further state that this is the "obviously intended moment of union" if the Great Rite is "actual." Farrar, *The Witches' Way* (1986), 305.

86. Farrar, *The Witches' Way* (1986), 38.

87. Farrar, *The Witches' Way* (1986), 38.

88. That is, the first large-scale esoteric new religious movement in which rituals of initiation is an integrated part of not only the organizational structure, but also the spiritual practices of the movement.

Chapter 8

1. For more information on the *Dragon Rouge*, see Bogdan, "Västerländsk esoterism i svensk ungdomskultur" (2003); Granholm, *Embracing the Dark* (2005).

2. This does not mean, however, that a symbol can be interpreted in any way possible. As Snoek has stated: "In true symbolism, the beholder is by no means free to interpret the symbols which are offered to him, on the basis of free association. On the contrary. Each symbol has a limited number of clear cut meanings, even though it is often difficult to describe them in words. Also, not always is every meaning a symbol has applicable. Which meaning or meanings are applicable, depends on both the context and the persons involved." Snoek, "The Allusive Method" (1999), 50.

Appendix

1 This list was presented by J.A.M. Snoek at a series of lectures entitled "Initiations: Concepts and Approaches" held at Göteborg University in 2001.

References

Year of publication is always that of the quoted edition, not necessarily that of the first edition.

Abraham, Lyndy. *A Dictionary of Alchemical Imagery*. Cambridge: Cambridge University Press, 2001.

Agrippa, H. Cornelius. *Three Books Occult Philosophy*. Reprint of the 1651 translation by James Freake, ed. and annotated by Donald Tyson. St. Paul, MN: Llewellyn Publications, (1993) 2003.

Åkermann, Susanna. *Rose-Cross Over the Baltic. The Spread of Rosicrucianism in Nothern Europe*. Leiden, Boston, Köln: E. J. Brill, 1998.

Allen, Paul M. (ed.). *A Christian Rosenkreutz Anthology*. Blauvelt, New York. Rudolf Steiner Publications, 1968.

The Anchor Bible Dictionary. New York: Doubleday, 1992.

Anderson, James. *The Constitutions of the Free-Masons. Containing the History, Charges, Regulations, &c. of that most Ancient and Right Worshipful FRATERNITY. For Use of the LODGES*. London: William Hunter, 1723.

Apiryon and Helena. "Mystery of Mystery: A Primer of Thelemic Ecclesiastical Gnosticism." *Red Flame: A Thelemic Research Journal*. Issue No. 2, Berkeley, CA 1996.

ARIES. Symboles et Mythes dans les mouvements initiatiques et ésotériques (XVIIe–Xxe siècles): Filiations et emprunts. Paris: Arché/La Table D'Émeraude, 1999.

Arnold, Paul. *Histoire des Rose-Croix et les Origines de la Franc-Maçonnerie*. Paris: Mercure de France, 1955.

———. *La Rose-Croix et ses Rapportes avec la Franc-Maçonnerie*. Editions G.-P. Paris: Maisonneuve & Larose, 1970.

Asad, Talal. "Toward a Genealogy of the Concept of Ritual" in Asad (ed.). *Genealogies of Religion: Discipline and Reasons of Power in Christianity and Islam*. Baltimore and London: Johns Hopkins University Press, 1993. 55–79.

Ashmole, Elias. *Texts 1617–1692*. London: Oxford University Press, 1966.

Assman, Jan. *Moses the Egyptian: The Memory of Egypt in Western Monotheism*. Cambridge Mass., London: Harvard University Press, 1997.

Barrett, David V. *Secret Societies: From the Ancient and Arcane to the Modern and Clandestine*. London: Blandford, 1997.

Bechert, Heinz. "Buddhist Revival in East and West" in Bechert, Heinz and Gombrich, Richard (eds.) *The World of Buddhism*. London: Thames and Hudson Ltd., (1984) 1991. 273–285.

Beitchman, Philip. *Alchemy of the Word. Cabala of the Renaissance*. Albany: State University of New York Press, 1998.

Bell, Catherine. *Ritual: Perspectives and Dimensions*. New York and Oxford: Oxford University Press, 1997.

Berg, Hans. "Carl Friedrich Eckleff som människa och frimurare" in *Acta Masonica Scandinavica* Vol. I. København & Uppsala, 1998. 118–135.

Bernheim, Alain. "Did Early "High" or Écossais Degrees Originate in France" in *Heredom* Vol. 5, 1996. 87–113.

———. "The Order of Kilwinning or Scotch Heredom, the Present Royal Order of Scotland" in *Heredom* Vol. 8, 1999/2000. 93–130.

———. "Johann August Starck: The Templar Legend and the Clerics" in *Heredom* Vol. 9, 2001. 251–296.

Blanchard, J. *The Complete Ritual of the Ancient and Accepted Scottish Rite*. Chicago: Ezra Cook, 1950.

Bleeker, C. J. "Some introductory remarks on the significance of initiation" in Bleeker (ed.) *Initiation: Contributions to the theme of the study-conference of the International Association for the History of Religions held at Strasburg, September 17th to 22nd 1964*. Leiden: E. J. Brill, 1965. 15–20.

Bogdan, Henrik. "Västerländsk esoterism i svensk ungdomskultur" in Larsson, Göran (ed.) *Talande tro. Ungdomar, religion och identitet*. Studentlitteratur, Lund 2003. 101–116.

Bogdan, Henrik. "Challenging the Morals of Western Society: The Use of Ritualised Sex in Contemporary Occultism" in *The Pomegranate: The International Journal of Pagan Studies* Vol. 8, No. 2 (2006), 211–246.

Bolle, Kees W. *Secrecy in Religions*. E. J. Brill, Leiden; New York; København; Köln, 1987.

Booth, Martin. *A Magick Life. A Biography of Aleister Crowley*. London: Hodder & Stoughton, 2000.

Boudewijnse, Barbara. "The Conceptualization of Ritual. A History of its Problematic Aspects" in *Jaarboek voor Liturgieonderzoek* 11, 1995. 31–56.

———. "British roots of the concept of ritual" in Molendijk and Pels (eds.) *Religion in the Making*. 1998. 277–295.

Bracelin, J. L. *Gerald Gardner: Witch*. I-H-O Books, Essex House, Thame [1960] 1999.

Brandon, S. G. F. "The Significance of Time in Some Ancient Initiatory Rituals" in Bleeker (ed.) *Initiation: Contributions to the theme of the study-conference of the International Association for the History of Religions held at Strasburg, September 17th to 22nd 1964*. Leiden: E. J. Brill, 1965. 40–48.

van den Broek, Roelef and Hanegraaff, Wouter J. *Gnosis and Hermeticism from Antiquity to Modern Times*. Albany: State University of New York Press, 1998.

Brooker, Will. *Using the Force: Creativity, Community, and Star Wars Fans*. New York: Continuum, 2002.

Caillet, Serge. *Arcanes & Ritueles de la Maçonnerie Égyptienne*. Paris: Trédaniel, 1994.

Carr, Harry. *The Collected "Prestonian Lectures" 1925–1960*. The Quatuor Coronati Lodge No. 2076, London 1967.

———. *The Early French Exposures*. The Quatuor Coronati Lodge No. 2076, London 1971.

Churton, Tobias. *The Golden Builders. Alchemists, Rosicrucians and the first Free Masons*. Lichfield, Staffordshire: Signal Publishing, 2002.

Clausen, Henry C. *Clausen's Commentaries on Morals and Dogma*. The Supreme Council, 33°, Ancient and Accepted Scottish Rite of Freemasonry. Southern Jurisdiction, U.S.A. 1974.

Clulee, Nicholas H. *John Dee's Natural Philosophy: Between Science and Religion*. London: Routledge, 1988.

———. *"Astronomia inferior.* Legacies of Johannes Trithemius and John Dee" in Newman and Grafton (eds.) *Secrets of Nature: Astrology and Alchemy in Early Modern Europe*. Cambridge, London: MIT Press, 2001. 173–234.

Collectanea. Published by the Grand College of Rites of the United States of America.

Collectanea Chemica. London: Vincent Stuart, 1963.

Collins English Dictionary. Glasgow: Harper Collins, 1992.

Colquhoun, Ithel. *Sword of Wisdom. Macgregor Mathers and the Golden Dawn*. New York: Putnam's Sons, 1975.

Combes, André. *Histoire de la Franc-Maçonnerie au XIXe siècle*. Monaco: Rocher, 1998.

Couliano, Ioan P. *Eros and Magic in the Renaissance*. Chicago: University of Chicago Press, 1987.

Covey-Crump W. W. *The Hiramic Tradition. A Survey of Hypotheses Concerning it*. London, no date.

Craddock, Ida. "Heavenly Bridegrooms" and "Psychic Wedlock" in Motta, M. (ed.) *The Equinox* Vol. V, No. 4. 1981. 439–591 and 597–618.

Crowley, Aleister. *The Temple of Solomon the King*, in *Equinox Vol. I, No. II*. London: Simpkin, Marshall, Hamilton, Kent & Co., 1909. 212–334.

———. "Liber O vel Manus et Sagittae" in *The Equinox Vol. I, No. II*. London: Simpkin, Marshall, Hamilton, Kent & Co., 1909. 11–30; and in *Magick: In Theory and Practice*. Paris: Lecram Press [1930]. 375–389.

———. *The Book of Lies*. London: Weiland & Co., 1913.

———. *777 Revised*. London: Neptune Press, 1955.

———. *The Holy Books of Thelema*. York Beach, Maine: Samuel Weiser, 1983.

———. *The Confessions—An Autohagiography*. Edited by John Symonds and Kenneth Grant. London: Arkana, 1989.

———. *Amrita. Essays in Magical Rejuvenation*. Edited by Martin P. Starr. Kings Beach, CA: Thelema Publications. 1990.

———. *The Equinox of the Gods*. New York: 93 Publishing, 1991.

———. *The Magical Record of the Beast 666*. London: Duckworth, 1993.

———. "The Method of Thelema" in *The Revival of Magick and Other Essays*. Tempe, AZ: New Falcon, 1998. 176–183.

————. *The Vision & the Voice with Commentary and other papers*. York Beach, Maine: Samuel Weiser, Inc., 1998.

Dahlgren, Carl. *Frimureriet med tillämpning på Sverige*. Stockholm: Aktiebolaget H. Klemmings Antikvariat, 1925.

Dan, Joseph. "The Kabbalah of Johannes Reuchlin and its Historical Significance" in Joseph Dan (ed.) *The Christian Kabbalah: Jewish Mystical Books and their Christian interpreters*. Cambridge, Mass.: Harvard College Library, 1997. 55–95.

Debus, Allen G. *Robert Fludd and His Philosophical Key*. New York: Science History Publications, 1979.

————. *Chemistry, Alchemy and the New Philosophy, 1550–1700. Studies in the History of Science and Medicine*. London: Variorum Reprints, 1987.

————. *The French Paracelsians. The Chemical Challenge to Medical and Scientific Tradition in Early Modern France*. Cambridge: Cambridge University Press, 1991.

Dee, John. *The Hieroglyphic Monad*. London: John M. Watkins, 1947.

Deveney, J. Patrick. *Paschal Beverly Randolph—A Nineteenth-Century Black American Spiritualist, Rosicrucian, and Sex Magician*. Albany: State University of New York Press, 1997.

Dobbs, Betty Jo Teeter. *The Janus faces of genius: The role of alchemy in Newton's thought*. Cambridge: Cambridge University Press, 1991.

Draffen of Newington, George. *The Royal Order of Scotland: The Second Hundred Years*. Edinburgh: ROS, 1977.

Egmond, Daniël van. "Western Esoteric Schools in the Late Nineteenth and Early Twentieth Centuries" in *Gnosis and Hermeticism from Antiquity to Modern Times*. Ed. by van den Broek and Hanegraaff. Albany: State University of New York Press, 1998. 311–346.

Eliade, Mircea. "L'Initiation et le monde moderne" in Bleeker (ed.) *Initiation: Contributions to the theme of the study-conference of the International Association for the History of Religions held at Strasburg, September 17th to 22nd 1964*. Leiden: E. J. Brill, 1965. 1–14.

————. *Rites and Symbols of Initiation: The Mysteries of Birth and Rebirth*. Dallas: Spring Publications, 1995.

————. (ed.) *Encyclopaedia of Religion*. Macmillan, New York 1987.

Encyclopaedia Britannica.

Eshelman, James A. *The Mystical & Magical System of the A∴A∴* Los Angeles: The College of Thelema, 2000.

Evola, Julius. *Revolt Against the Modern World*. Rochester: Inner Traditions, 1995.

Faivre, Antoine. *Access to Western Esotericism*. Albany: State University of New York Press, 1994.

————. *The Eternal Hermes. From Greek God to Alchemical Magus*. Grand Rapids: Phanes Press, 1995.

————. "Introduction 1" in Faivre & Needleman (eds.) *Modern Esoteric Spirituality*. New York: Crossroad, 1995.

————. "Ancient and Medieval Sources of Modern Esoteric Movements" in Faivre and Needleman (eds.) *Modern Esoteric Spirituality*. New York: Crossroad, 1995. 1–70.

—— and Voss, Karen-Claire "Western Esotericism and the Science of Religion" in *Numen International Review for the History of Religions*. Vol. XLII, No. I, January 1995. 48–77.

—— and Hanegraaff, Wouter J. *Western Esotericism and the Science of Religion*. Leuven: Peeters, 1998.

——. "Renaissance Hermeticism and the Concept of Western Esotericism," in van den Broek, and Hanegraaff (eds.) *Gnosis and Hermeticism from Antiquity to Modern Times*, Albany: State University of New York Press, 1998. 109–123.

——. "Questions of terminology proper to the study of esoteric currents in modern and contemporary Europe" in Faivre and Hanegraaff (eds.) *Western Esotericism and the Science of Religion*. Leuven: Peeters, 1998. 1–10.

——. "Histoire de la notion moderne de tradition dans ses rapports avec les courants ésotériques (XVe–XXe sècles)," in *Symboles at Mythes dans les mouvements initiatiques et ésotériques (XVIIe–XXe siècles): Filiations et emprunts*, Paris: Aries 1999. 7–48.

——. "The Notions of Concealment and Secrecy in Modern Esoteric Currents since the Renaissance" in Wolfson (ed.) *Rending the Veil: Concealment and Secrecy in the History of Religions*. New York and London: Seven Bridges Press, 1999. 155–176.

——. "La Question d'un Ésotérisme Comparé des Religions du Livre" in Cahiers du Groupe d'Études Spirituelles Comparées, *(Henry Corbin et le comparatisme spirituel)*, Paris: 2000. 89–120.

——. *Theosophy, Imagination, Tradition. Studies in Western Esotericism*. Albany: State University of New York Press, 2000.

—— and Needleman, Jacob (eds.). *Modern Esoteric Spirituality.* New York: Crossroad, 1992.

Farmer, S. A. *Syncretism in the West: Pico's 900 Theses (1486). The Evolution of Traditional Religious and Philosophical Systems*. Tempe, AZ: Medieval & Renaissance Texts & Studies, 1998.

Farrar, Janet and Stewart. *The Witches' Way. Principles, Rituals and Beliefs of Modern Witchcraft*. London: Robert Hale, (1984) 1986.

——. *The Witches' God. Lord of the Dance*. London; Robert Hale, 1989.

Field, Arthur. *The Origins of the Platonic Academy of Florence*. Princeton, NJ: Princeton University Press, 1988.

Flamel, Nicholas. "A Short Tract, or Philosophical Summery" in Waite (ed.) *The Hermetic Museum*. London: James Elliott and Co., 1893. 141–147.

——. *Boken om de Hieroglyfiska Bilderna*. Efterskrift och översättning från latinet av Kjell Lekeby. Stockholm: Vertigo, Philosophiska Förlaget, 1996.

Fontaine, Jean La. *Initiation—Ritual Drama and Secret Knowledge Across the World*. Harmondsworth: Penguin Books, 1985.

Forestier, René Le. *La Franc-Maçonnerie Templière et Occultiste aux XVIIIe et XIXe Siècles*. Paris: Aubier-Montaigne, 1970.

——. *La Franc-Maçonnerie Occultiste au XVIIIe Siècle & L'Ordre des Élus Coens*. Paris: La Table D'Émeraude, 1987.

Fortune, Dion. *The Esoteric Orders and Their Work*. Saint Paul: Llewellyn Publications, 1962.

French, Peter J. *John Dee. The World of an Elizabethan Magus.* London: Routledge & Kegan Paul, 1972.

Frick, Karl R. H. *Licht und Finsternis. Gnostisch-theosophische und freimaurerisch-okkulte Geheimgesellschaften bis an die Wende zum 20. Jahrhudert.* Graz: Akademische Druck-u. Verlagsanstalt, 1975–1978.

———. *Die Erleuchteten. Gnostisch-theosophische und alchemistisch-rosenkreuzerische Geheimgesellschaften bis zum Ende des 18. Jahrhunderts—ein Beitrag zur Geistesgeschichte der Neuzeit.* Graz: Akademische Druck-u. Verlagsanstalt, 1973.

Frisk, Liselotte. "Globalization or Westernization? New Age as a Contemporary Transnational Culture" in Rothstein, Mikael (ed.) *New Age Religion and Globalization.* Aarhus: Aarhus University Press, 2001. 31–41.

Gardner, Gerald. *High Magic's Aid.* London: Michael Houghton, 1949.

———. *The Meaning of Witchcraft.* London: The Aquarian Press, 1959.

Geber. *The Alchemical Works of Geber.* York Beach: Samuel Weiser, 1994.

Gibbons, B. J. *Spirituality and the Occult. From the Renaissance to the Modern Age.* London and New York: Routledge, 2001.

Gilbert, R. A. *The Golden Dawn Companion. A Guide to the History, Structure, and Workings of the Hermetic Order of the Golden Dawn.* Wellingborough: Aquarian Press, 1986.

———. *A. E. Waite. Magician of Many Parts.* Wellingborough, Northamptonshire: Crucible, 1987.

———. "Provenance Unknown: A Tentative Solution to the Riddle of the Cipher Manuscript of the Golden Dawn" in Küntz, Darcy (ed.) *The Complete Golden Dawn Cipher Manuscript.* Edmonds, WA: Holmes Publishing Group, 1996. 17–26.

———. *The Golden Dawn Scrapbook: The Rise and Fall of a Magical Order.* York Beach, Maine: Samuel Weiser, 1997.

———. *A. E. Waite: A Bibliography.* Wellingborough: Aquarian Press, 1983.

———. "Quatuor Coronati Lodge No. 2076, The Premier Lodge of Research" in Bogdan, Henrik (ed.) *Alströmersymposiet 2003.* Göteborg, Frimureriska Forskningsgruppen i Göteborg, 2003. 19–38.

Gilly, Carlos "Between Paracelsus, Pelagus and Ganellus: Hermetism in John Dee" in Gilly, Carlos and van Heertum, Cis (eds.) *Magic, alchemy and science 15th–18th Centuries: The influence of Hermes Trismegistus.* Amsterdam: Centro Di, Biblioteca Nazionale Marciana, Venezia & Bibliotheca Philosophica, 2002. 275–294.

Girard-Augry, Pierre. *Rituels Secrets de la Franc-Maçonnerie Templière et Chevaleresque.* Paris: Éditions Dervy, 1996.

Gist, Noel P. *Secret Societies: A Cultural study of fraternalism in the United States.* University of Missouri Studies. A Quarterly of Research. Vol. XV, No. 4, 1940.

Glass, Justine. *Witchcraft, the Sixth Sense.* No. Hollywood: Wilshire Book Company, 1974.

Gluckman, Max. "Les Rites de passage," in Gluckman (ed.) *Essays on the Ritual of Social Relations.* Manchester: Manchester University Press, 1962. 1–52.

Godwin, Joscelyn. *The Theosophical Enlightenment*. Albany: State University of New York Press, 1994.

Grant, Kenneth. *Manifesto of the British Branch of the Ordo Templi Orientis (O.T.O.)*, [London, 1948].

———. *Vault of the Adepts. The seven-pointed figure of its ceiling and floor with a study of doctrines enshrined in its symbols*. [London: Privately published, 1963.]

———. *The Magical Revival*. London: Muller Ltd, 1972.

———. *Nightside of Eden*. London: Muller Ltd, 1977.

———. *Remembering Aleister Crowley*. London: Skoob Books, 1991.

Grimes, Ronald. *Deeply into the Bone. Re-inventing rites of passage*. Berkeley: University of California Press, 2000.

Håkansson, Håkan. *Seeing the Word. John Dee and Renaissance Occultism*. Lund: Ugglan Minervaserien 2, 2001.

Hakl, Hans T. *Der verborgene Geist von Eranos: Unbekannte Begegnungen von Wissenschaft und Esoterik. Eine alternative Geistesgeschichte des 20. Jahrhunderts*. Bretten: Scientia Nova, 2001.

Hamill, John. *The Craft—A History of English Freemasonry*. Wellingborough, Northamptonshire: Crucible, 1986.

———. (ed.) *The Rosicrucian Seer—Magical Writings of Frederick Hockley*. Wellingborough: Aquarian Press, 1986.

———. "The Seeker of Truth: John Yarker 1833–1913" in *Wege und Abwege. Beiträge zur europäischen Geistgeschichte der Neuzeit. Festschrift für Ellic Howe zum 20. September 1990*. Freiburg (2 Auflage) 1993. 135–142.

Hammer, Olav. *Claiming Knowledge. Strategies of Epistemology from Theosophy to the New Age*. Lund: Ph. D. Dissertation, Department of Theology, 2000.

———. "Same Message from Everywhere: The Sources of Modern Revelation" in Rothstein, Mikael (ed.) *New Age Religion and Globalization*. Aarhus: Aarhus University Press, 2001. 42–57.

Hanegraaff, Wouter J. "The Problem of «Post-Gnostic» Gnosticism" in Bianchi, Ugo (ed.) *The Notion of "Religion" in Comparative Research. Selected Proceedings of the XVIth Congress of the International Association for the History of Religions. Rome, 3rd—8th September, 1990*. Rome: L'Erma di Bretschneider, 1994. 625–632.

———. "Empirical Method in the Study of Esotericism" in *Method & Theory in the Study of Religion*, Vol. 7-2 (1995). 99–129.

———. *New Age Religion and Western Culture. Esotericism in the Mirror of Secular Thought*. Albany: State University of New York Press, 1998.

———. "The Birth of a Discipline" in Faivre and Hanegraaff (eds.) *Western Esotericism and the Science of Religion*. Leuven: Peeters, 1998. vii–xvii.

———. "On the Construction of 'Esoteric Traditions' " in Faivre and Hanegraaff (eds.) *Western Esotericism and the Science of Religion*. Leuven: Peeters, 1998. 11–61.

———. "La fin de l'ésotérisme? Le mouvement du Nouvel Age et la question du symbolisme religieux" in *Symboles et Mythes dans les mouvements initiatiques et ésotériques*. Paris: Aries, 1999. 128–147.

———. "Beyond the Yates Paradigm: The Study of Western Esotericism between Counterculture and New Complexity," *ARIES*, Vol. 1, Issue 1, 2001. 5–37.

———. "Prospects for the Globalization of New Age: Spiritual Imperialism Versus Cultural Diversity" in Rothstein, Mikael (ed.) *New Age Religion and Globalization*. Aarhus: Aarhus University Press, 2001. 15–30.

———. "The Study of Western Esotericism: New Approaches to Christian and Secular Culture" in Antes, Geertz and Warne (eds.) *New Approaches to the Study of Religion, Volume 1: Regional, Critical, and Historical Approaches*. Berlin and New York: Walter de Gruyter, 2004. 489–519.

———. "How Magic Survived the Disenchantment of the World" in *Religion* Vol. 33, No. 4, 2003. 357–380.

——— (edited by) in collaboration with Faivre, van den Broek and Brach *Dictionary of Gnosis & Western Esotericism*. Leiden, Boston: Brill Academic Publishers, 2005.

Hankins, James. "Cosimo de' Medici and the 'Platonic Academy,'" *Journal of the Warburg and Coutauld Institutes*, Vol. 53 (1990). 144–152.

Hannah, Walton. *Darkness Visible—A Revelation & Interpretation of Freemasonry.* London: Augustine Press, 1952.

Harkness, Deborah. *John Dee's Conversations with Angels. Cabala, Alchemy, and the End of Nature.* Cambridge: Cambridge University Press, 1999.

Heckethorn, Charles W. *The Secret Societies of all Ages and Countries.* New York: University Books, 1966.

Heimbrock, Hans-Günther and Boudewijnse (eds.). *Current Studies on Rituals. Perspectives for the Psychology of Religion.* Amsterdam, Atlanta GA: Rudopi, 1990.

Hofmeier, Thomas. "Philology versus imagination: Isaac Casaubon and the myth of Hermes Trismegistus" in Gilly, Carlos and van Heertum, Cis (eds.) *Magic, alchemy and science 15th–18th Centuries: The influence of Hermes Trismegistus*. Centro Di, Biblioteca Nazionale Marciana, Venezia & Bibliotheca Philosophica, Amsterdam 2002. 563–572.

Hornung, Erik. *The Secret Lore of Egypt: Its Impact on the West*. Ithaca and London: Cornell University Press, 2001.

Howe, Ellic. *The Magicians of the Golden Dawn. A Documentary of a Magical Order 1887–1923*. London: Routledge & Kegan Paul, 1972.

Howe and Möller. "Theodor Reuss—Irregular Freemasonry in Germany, 1900–23" in *AQC* Vol. 91, 1979. 28–42.

Huffman, William H. *Robert Fludd and the End of the Renaissance*. London and New York: Routledge, 1988.

Hunter, Michael (ed.). *Robert Boyle Reconsidered*. Cambridge: Cambridge University Press, 1994.

Hutton, Ronald. *The Triumph of the Moon. A History of Modern Pagan Witchcraft*. Oxford: Oxford University Press, 1999.

Idel, Moshe. *Kabbalah. New Perspectives*. New Haven: Yale University Press, 1988.

"In Memoriam" in *The Co-Mason* Vol. V. London, 1913. 65–71.

Introvigne, Massimo. "After the New Age: Is There a Next Age?" in Rothstein, Mikael (ed.) *New Age Religion and Globalization*. Aarhus: Aarhus University Press, 2001. 58–69.

Jackson, A. C. F. *English Masonic Exposures 1760—1769*. London: Lewis Masonic, 1986.

———. *Rose Croix. The History of the Ancient and Accepted Rite for England and Wales*. Addlestone, Surrey: Lewis Masonic, 1993.

Jackson, Keith B. *Beyond the Craft*. London: Lewis Masonic, 1980.

James, Geoffrey. *The Enochian Evocation of Dr. John Dee*. Gillette, New Jersey: Heptangle Books, 1984.

Johns, June. *King of the Witches. The World of Alex Sanders*. New York: Coward-McCann, Inc., 1969.

Jones, Bernard E. *Freemason's Guide and Compendium*. Kent: Dobby, (1950) 1994.

———. *Freemason's Book of the Royal Arch*. London: George G. Harrap & Company, 1957.

Kaczynski, Richard. *Perdurabo. The Life of Aleister Crowley*. Tempe, AZ: New Falcon Publications, 2002.

Kahn, Didier. "The Rosicrucian Hoax in France (1623–24)" in Newman and Grafton (eds.) *Secrets of Nature: Astrology and Alchemy in Early Modern Europe*. Cambridge and London: MIT Press, 2001. 235–344.

Kelly, Aidan A. *Crafting the Art of Magic*. St. Paul, Minnesota: Llewellyn Publications, 1991.

———. "An Update on Neopagan Witchcraft in America" in Lewis & Melton (eds.) *Perspectives on the New Age*. Albany: State University of New York Press, 1992. 136–152.

Kervella and Lestienne. "Un haut-grade templier dans les milieux jacobites en 1750: L'Ordre Sublime des Chevaliers Elus" in *Renaissance Traditionelle* no. 112 (1997). 229–266.

Kieckheffer, Richard. *Forbidden Rites: A Necromancer's Manual of the Fifteenth Century*. Phoenix Mill Thrupp: Sutton Publishing, 1997.

———. *Magic in the Middle Ages*. Cambridge: Cambridge University Press, (1989) 1990.

King, Francis. *Ritual Magic in England 1887 to the present day*. London: Neville Spearman, 1970.

Kinnander, Magnus. *Svenska Frimureriets Historia*. Stockholm: Bokförlaget Natur och Kultur, 1943.

Knight, Stephen. *The Brotherhood: The Secret World of the Freemasons*. London: Granada Publishing, (1983) 1985.

Knoop, Douglas and Jones, G. P. *The Genesis of Freemasonry: An Account of the Rise and Development of Freemasonry in its Operative, Accepted, and Early Speculative Phases*. Manchester: Manchester University Press, 1947.

Knoop, Douglas; Jones, G. P., Hamer, Douglas. *Early Masonic Pamphlets*. Manchester: Manchester University Press, 1945.

————. *The Early Masonic Catechisms.* Manchester: Manchester University Press, 1963.

Köppen & Hymmen. *Crata Repoa. Oder Einweyhungen in der alten geheimen Gesellschaft der Egyptischen Preister,* [Berlin] 1770.

————. "Crata Repoa" (English translation) *The Kneph—Official Journal of the Antient and Primitive Rite of Masonry* Vol. II, No. 15–No. 22 (1882).

Lantoine, Albert. *Histoire de la Franc-Maçonnerie Française.* Paris: Émile Nourry, 1927.

————. *La Franc-Maçonnerie Ecossaise en France.* Paris: Émile Nourry, 1930.

Lenhammar, Harry. *Med murslev och svärd: Svenska frimurarorden under 250 år.* Delsbo: Åsak, 1985.

Lennhoff, Eugen and Posner, Oskar. *Internationales Freimaurerlexikon.* Zürich, Leipzig, Wien: Amalthea-Verlag, 1932.

Lévi, Éliphas. *Transcendental Magic: Its Doctrine and Ritual.* London: George Redway, 1896.

————. *The History of Magic: Including a Clear and Precise Exposition of its Procedure, its Rites and its Mysteries.* London: William Rider & Son, 1913.

Ligou, Daniel. *Dictionnaire de la Franc-Maçonnerie.* Paris: Presses Universitaires de France, (1974) 1987.

Linden, Stanton J. *The Alchemy Reader: From Hermes Trismegistus to Isaac Newton.* Cambridge: Cambridge University Press, 2003.

Luhrmann, T. M. *Persuasions of the Witch's Craft: Ritual Magic and Witchcraft in Present-day England.* Oxford: Basil Blackwell Ltd., 1989.

Mackenzie, Kenneth. *The Royal Masonic Cyclopaedia.* Introduced by John Hamill and R. A. Gilbert. Wellingborough, Northamptonshire: Aquarian Press, 1987.

Maier, Michael. *Laws of the Fraternity of the Rosie Cross (Themis Aurea).* Los Angeles: Philosophical Research Society, 1976.

Manget, Jean-Jacques. *Bibliotheca Chemica Curiosa.* 1702.

Mathers, S. L. MacGregor. *The Kabbalah Unveiled.* London: Routledge & Kegan Paul, 1970.

————. *The Book of the Sacred Magic of Abra-Melin the Mage.* Wellingborough: Aquarian, 1976.

————. *The Key of Solomon the King (Clavicula Salomonis).* York Beach: Samuel Weiser, 1991.

McIntosh, Christopher. *Éliphas Lévi and the French Occult Revival.* London: Rider and Company, 1975.

————. "The Alchemy and the *Gold- und Rosenkreuz,*" in von Martels, Z.R.W.M. (ed.) *Alchemy Revisited. Proceedings of the International Conference on the History of Alchemy at the University of Groningen 17–19 April 1989.* Leiden, New York: E. J. Brill, 1990. 237–244.

————. *The Rosicrucians: The History, Mythology, and Rituals of an Esoteric Order.* York Beach, Maine: Samuel Weiser, Inc., 1997.

————. *The Rose Cross and the Age of Reason. Eighteenth-Century Rosicrucianism in Central Europe and its Relationship to the Enlightenment.* Leiden, New York, Köln: E. J. Brill, 1992.

Mellor, Alec. *Our Separated Brethren the Freemasons.* London: George G. Harrap & Co., 1964.

Mogstad, Sverre Dag. *Frimureri: Mysterier, Felleskap, Personlighetsdannelse.* Oslo: Universitetsforlaget, (1994) 1995.

Molendijk, Arie and Pels, Peter (eds.). *Religion in the Making: The Emergence of the Sciences of Religion.* Leiden: Brill, 1998.

Mollier, Pierre. "Le Chevalier du Soleil: Contribution à l'étude d'un haut-grade maçonnique en France au XVIIIe siècle." Ecole Pratique des Hautes Etudes: Ve Section—Sciences Religieuses. La Sorbonne, Paris 1992.

———. "Des Francs-Maçons aux Templiers: Aperçus sur la constitution d'une légende au Siècle des Lumières," in *Symboles et Mythes dans les mouvements initiatiques et ésotériques.* Paris: Aries, 1999. 93–101.

———. "L'«Ordre Écossais» à Berlin de 1742 à 1751" in *Renaissance Traditionelle* 131–132, 2002. 217–227.

Montgomery, John Warwick. *Cross and Crucible: Johann Valentin Andreae (1586–1654) Phoenix of the Theologians.* The Hague: Nijhoff, 1973.

Moore, Sally F. and Myerhoff, Barbara G. (eds.) *Secular Ritual.* Assen and Amersterdam: Van Gorcum, 1977.

Moran, Bruce T. *Distilling Knowledge. Alchemy, Chemistry, and the Scientific Revolution.* Cambridge, Mass.: Harvard University Press, 2005.

Naudon, Paul. *Histoire, Rituels et Tuileur des Hauts Grades Maçonniques.* Paris: Éditions Dervy, 1993.

Nauert, Charles G. *Agrippa and the crisis of Renaissance thought.* Urbane: University of Illinois Press, 1965.

Noël, Pierre. "De la Stricte Observance au Rite Ecossais Rectifié" in *Acta Macionica* Vol. 5 [1995]. Published for the Regular Grand Lodge of Belgium by the lodge of research Ars Macionica No. 30 in Brussels. 91–126.

Owen, Alex. *The Place of Enchantment. British Occultism and the Culture of the Modern.* Chicago and London: University of Chicago Press, 2004.

Paracelsus. *The Hermetic & Alchemical Writings of Paracelsus the Great.* London: Elliott, 1894.

Pasi, Marco. *Aleister Crowley e la Tentazione della Politica.* Milano: Franco Angeli, 1999.

Patai, Raphael. "Maria the Jewess—Founding Mother of Alchemy" in *Ambix* Vol. 29, Part 3, 1982. 177–197.

Pearson, Jo. " 'Going Native in Reverse': The Insider as Researcher in British Wicca" in Arweck and Stringer (eds.) *Theorizing Faith. The Insider/Outsider Problem in the Study of Ritual.* Birmingham: University of Birmingham Press, 2002. 97–113.

Pernety, Antoine-Joseph. *An Alchemical Treatise on the Great Art.* York Beach: Samuel Weiser, 1995.

Piatigorgsky, Alexander. *Freemasonry. The Study of a Phenomenon.* London: Harville Press, (1997) 1999.

Pike, Albert. *Morals and Dogma of the Ancient and Accepted Scottish Rite of Freemasonry.* Charleston (1871) 1923.

————. and Cummings, William C. "The Spurious Rites of Memphis and Misraim" in *Heredom*, Vol. 9, 2001. 147–197.

Prescott, Andrew. "The Study of Freemasonry as a New Academic Discipline" in *Vrijmetselarij in Nederland*. Den Haag: OVN, 2003. 5–31.

Quinn, William. *The Only Tradition*. Albany: State University of New York Press, 1997.

Randolph, Paschal. *Sexual Magic*. New York: Magickal Childe, 1988.

Regardie, Israel. *The Golden Dawn. An Account of the Teachings, Rites and Ceremonies of the Order of the Golden Dawn*. Chicago: Aries Press, 1937–1940.

————. *The Complete Golden Dawn System of Magic*. Scottsdale: New Falcon Publications, (1984) 1990.

Reuss and Crowley. *O.T.O. Rituals and Sex Magick*. Edited by A. R. Naylor. Essex House, Thame: I-H-O Books, 1999.

Rich, Paul and Merchant, David. "The Egyptian Influence on Nineteenth-Century Freemasonry" in *Heredom*, Vol. 9, 2001. 33–51.

Richardson, A. *Priestess—The Life and Magic of Dion Fortune*. Wellingborough, Northamptonshire: Aquarian Press, 1987.

Riffard, Pierre. *L'Ésotérisme: Qu'est-ce que l'ésotérisme? Anthologie de l'ésotérisme Occidental*. Paris: Editions Robert Laffont, Collection Bouquins, 1990.

————. *Dictionnaire de l'ésotérisme*. Paris: Éditions Payot & Rivages, 1993.

————. "The Esoteric Method" in Faivre and Hanegraaff (eds.) *Western Esotericism and the Science of Religion*. Leuven: Peeters, 1998. 63–74.

Rossi, Paolo. *Logic and the Art of Memory. The Quest for a Universal Language*. London: Athlone Press, 2000.

Rothstein, Mikael (ed.) *New Age Religion and Globalization*. Aarhus: Aarhus University Press, 2001.

Sanders, Alex. *The Alex Sanders Lectures*. New York: Magickal Childe, 1984.

Scanlan, Matthew. "Freemasonry and the Mystery of the Acception, 1630–1723—A Fatal Flaw" in Weisberger, McLeod and Morris (eds.) *Freemasonry on Both Sides of the Atlantic*. New York: Columbia University Press, 2002. 153–192.

Scholem, Gershom. "The Beginnings of the Christian Kabbalah" in Joseph Dan (ed.) *The Christian Kabbalah: Jewish Mystical Books and their Christian interpreters*. Cambridge, Mass.: Harvard College Library, 1997, 17–51.

Schumaker, Wayne. *The Occult Sciences in the Renaissance. A Study in Intellectual Patterns*. Berkeley, Los Angeles, and London: University of California Press, 1972.

Sedgwick, Mark. *Against the Modern World: Traditionalism and the Secret Intellectual History of the Twentieth Century*. Oxford and New York: Oxford University Press, 2004.

Skinner, Stephen and Rankine, David. *Practical Angel Magic of Dr John Dee's Enochian Tables*. London: Golden Hoard Press, 2004.

Smith, James Fairbank. *The Rise of the Ecossais Degrees*. Proceedings of the Chapter of Research of the Grand Chapter of Royal Arch Masons of the State of Ohio. Dayton, Ohio: The Otterbein Press, 1965.

Smith, Jonathan Z. *Map is not territory. Studies in the History of Religions.* Chicago: University of Chicago Press, 1993.

Smith, William Robertson. *Lectures on the Religion of the Semites.* Edinburgh: A. & C. Black, 1889.

Snoek, J.A.M. *Initiations. A Methodological Approach to the Application of Classification and definition Theory in the Study of Rituals.* Pijnacker: Dutch Efficiency Bureau, 1987.

———. "Oral and Written Transmission of the Masonic Tradition" in *Acta Macionica* Vol. 8, 1998. 41–57.

———. "On the Creation of Masonic Degrees: a Method and its Fruits" in Faivre and Hanegraaff (eds.) *Western Esotericism and the Science of Religion*, 1998. 145–190.

———. "The Evolution of the Hiramic Legend from Prichard's *Masonry Dissected* to the *Emulation Ritual*, in England and France" in *Symboles et Mythes dans les mouvements initiatiques et ésotériques (XVIIe–XXe siècles): Filiations et emprunts (ARIES).* Paris: Aries, 1999. 59–92.

———. "The Allusive Method," in *Acta Macionica* Vol. 9, 1999. 47–70.

———. "Swedenborg, Freemasonry, and Swedenborgian Freemasonry: An Overview" in *Acta Macionica* Vol. 11, 2001. 249–281.

———. "A Manuscript Version of Hérault's Ritual" in Caron, Godwin, Hanegraaff and Vieillard-Baron (eds.) *Ésotérisme, Gnoses & Imaginaire Symbolique: Mélanges offerts à Antoine Faivre.* Leuven: Peeters, 2001. 507–521.

———. "Printing Masonic Secrets: Oral and Written Transmission of the Masonic Tradition" in Bogdan, Henrik (ed.) *Alströmersymposiet 2003.* Göteborg: Frimureriska Forskningsgruppen i Göteborg, 2003. 39–56.

Starr, Martin P. *The Unknown God: W.T. Smith and the Thelemites.* Bolingbrook: Teitan Press, Inc., 2003.

———. "Halls of Learning: American Masonic Research in Review" in Bogdan, Henrik (ed.) *Alströmersymposiet 2003.* Göteborg: Frimureriska Forskningsgruppen i Göteborg, 2003. 57–68.

Stevenson, David. *The Origins of Freemasonry. Scotland's century 1590–1710.* Cambridge: University of Cambridge Press, (1988) 2001.

———. "James Anderson: Man & Mason" in *Heredom. The Transactions of the Scottish Rite Research Society.* Vol. 10, 2002. 93–138.

Sutin, Lawrence. *Do What Thou Wilt. A Life of Aleister Crowley.* New York: St. Martin's Press, 2000.

Sullivan, Lawrence. *Hidden Truths. Magic, Alchemy, and the Occult.* New York: Macmillan, (1987) 1989.

Thorndike, Lynn. *History of Magic and Experimental Science.* New York: Columbia University Press, 1923–1958.

Thulstrup, *Anteckningar till Svenska Frimureriets Historia.* Stockholm: Meddelanden från Stora Landslogens arkiv och bibliotek, 1892, 1898.

Tilton, Hereward. *The Quest for the Phoenix: Spiritual Alchemy and Rosicrucianism in the Work of Count Michael Maier (1569–1622).* Berlin and New York: Walter de Gruyter, 2003.

Torrens, R. G. *The Golden Dawn. The Inner Teachings*. New York: Samuel Weiser, 1973.

———. *The Secret Rituals of the Golden Dawn*. Wellingborough: Aquarian Press, 1973.

Turner, Victor. *The Ritual Process. Structure and Anti-structure*. New York: Aldine de Gruyter, 1995.

Urban, Hugh B. *Tantra. Sex, Secrecy, Politics, and Power in the Study of Religion*. Berkeley, Los Angeles, and London: University of California Press, 2003.

Valiente, Doreen. *Witchcraft for tomorrow*. London: Robert Hale, 1987.

Van Gennep, Arnold. *Les Rites de Passage*. Paris: Émile Nourry, 1909.

Vaughan, Thomas. *The Magical Writings*. London: George Redway, 1888.

———. *The Works of Thomas Vaughan*. Edited by Rudrum, Alan. Oxford: Clarendon Press, 1984.

Ventura, Gastone. *Les Rites Maçonniques de Misraïm et Memphis*. Paris: Editions Maisonneuve and Larose, 1986.

Vibert, Lionel. "The Development of the Trigradal System" in Carr, *The Collected "Prestonian Lectures" 1925–1960* (1967). London: The Quatuor Coronati Lodge No. 2076, 1967. 31–45.

———. "The Evolution of the Second Degree" in Carr, *The Collected "Prestonian Lectures" 1925–1960* (1967). London: The Quatuor Coronati Lodge No. 2076, 1967. 47–61.

Voorhis, Harold V. B. *The Story of the Scottish Rite of Freemasonry*. Richmond, Virginia: Macoy Publishing & Masonic Supply Co., Inc. Revised ed. 1980.

Waite, Arthur Edward. *The Secret Tradition in Freemasonry*. London: Rebman Limited, 1911.

———. "The Pontifical Ceremony of the Admission to the Grade of Adeptus Minor." Privately printed 1917.

———. *Emblematic Freemasonry and the Evolution of its Deeper Aspects*. London: William Rider & Son, 1925.

———. *A New Encyclopaedia of Freemasonry*. London: Virtue & Company Limited, 1930.

———. *The Brotherhood of the Rosy Cross*. London: Rider, 1924.

———. *The Templar Orders in Freemasonry*. Edmonds: Sure Fire Press, 1991.

———. (ed.) *The Hermetic Museum*. London: James Elliot and Co., 1893.

Walker, Daniel Pickering. *Spiritual and Demonic Magic from Ficino to Campanella*. London: Studies of the Warburg Institute, 1958.

Wasserstrom, Steve M. *Religion After Religion. Gershom Scholem, Mircea Eliade, and Henry Corbin at Eranos*. Princeton, NJ: Princeton University Press, 1999.

Weckman, George. "Secret Societies" in Eliade (ed.), *Encyclopaedia of Religion*. Vol. 13. New York: Macmillan, 1987. 151–154.

Weeks, Andrew. *Paracelsus—Speculative Theory and the Crisis of the early Reformation*. Albany: State University of New York Press, 1997.

Westcott, William Wynn. *Collectanea Hermetica*. York Beach: Samuel Weiser, 1998.

Whaling, Frank (ed.). *Theory and Method in Religious Studies. Contemporary Approaches to the Study of Religion.* Berlin and New York: Mouton de Gruyter, 1995.

White, Ralph (ed.). *The Rosicrucian Enlightenment Revisited.* Hudson: Lindisfarne, 1999.

Williams, Thomas A. *Eliphas Lévi: Master of the Occult.* Alabama: University of Alabama Press, 1975.

Wilmshurst, W. L. *The Meaning of Masonry.* New York: Bell, (1927) 1980.

Wolfson, Eliot R. (ed.). *Rending the Veil. Concealment and Secrecy in the History of Religions.* New York and London: Seven Bridges Press, 1999.

Yates, Frances A. *The Rosicrucian Enlightenment.* London: Routledge, (1972) 1996.

———. *The Occult Philosophy in the Elizabethan Age.* London: ARK, (1979) 1983.

———. *Giordano Bruno and the Hermetic Tradition.* London: Routledge & Kegan Paul, 1964.

Zambelli, Paola. "Magic and radical reformation in Agrippa of Nettesheim" in *Journal of the Warburg and Coutald Institutes,* Vol. 39 (1976). 69–103.

———. "Cornelius Agrippa, ein kritischer Magus" in Buck (ed.) *Die okkulten Wissenschaften in der Renaissance.* Wiesbaden: Otto Harrassowitch, 1992. 65–89.

Zika, Charles. "Reuchlin's *De verbo mirifico* and the magic debate of the late fifteenth century." *Journal of the Warburg and Coutald Institutes,* Vol. 39 (1976). 104–138.

Index